TEAM OF FIVE

TEAM OF FIVE

THE PRESIDENTS CLUB
IN THE AGE OF TRUMP

KATE ANDERSEN BROWER

HARPER

An Imprint of HarperCollins*Publishers*

HarperCollins books may be purchased for educational, business, or sales promotional use. For information, please email the Special Markets Department at SPsales@harpercollins.com.

FIRST EDITION

Designed by Fritz Metsch

Library of Congress Cataloging-in-Publication Data has been applied for.

ISBN 978-0-06-266897-4

20 21 22 23 24   LSC   10 9 8 7 6 5 4 3 2 1

To my team:
my husband, Brooke,
and our wonderful Graham, Charlotte, and Teddy

The country is far more important than any of us.

—DWIGHT D. EISENHOWER

CONTENTS

THE TEAM OF FIVE
AND THEIR FIRST LADIES

———

JIMMY AND ROSALYNN CARTER, NO. 39
In office 1977–1981
Secret Service code names: Deacon and Dancer

GEORGE H. W. AND BARBARA BUSH, NO. 41
In office 1989–1993
Secret Service code names: Timberwolf and Tranquility

BILL AND HILLARY CLINTON, NO. 42
In office 1993–2001
Secret Service code names: Eagle and Evergreen

GEORGE W. AND LAURA BUSH, NO. 43
In office 2001–2009
Secret Service code names: Trailblazer and Tempo

BARACK AND MICHELLE OBAMA, NO. 44
In office 2009–2017
Secret Service code names: Renegade and Renaissance

TEAM OF FIVE

"I'M A DIFFERENT KIND OF PRESIDENT"

He probably wouldn't invite me. Why should he?

—President Donald Trump, when asked if he would attend
the opening of Barack Obama's presidential library

It was a brilliantly sunny day in the spring of 2019 when I sat across from President Donald Trump in the Oval Office. I was there to find out what he truly thought of the men who came before him. How did he think he would be received in the so-called Presidents Club when the time came for him to leave the White House? Had the years he spent in that awe-inspiring office, both literally and figuratively, given him empathy for what his predecessors went through?

When we spoke Trump sat behind the Resolute desk, which presidents have used in the Oval Office since John F. Kennedy had it installed, including Jimmy Carter, Bill Clinton, George W. Bush, and Barack Obama. (George H. W. Bush decided to use the desk in the Treaty Room, a private study in the residence.) The ornate and iconic desk weighs a thousand pounds and was carved from the oak timbers of a British Arctic exploration ship named the H.M.S. *Resolute.* It was given as a gift to President Rutherford B. Hayes by Queen Victoria in 1880, and it has come to represent the presidency almost as much as the presidential seal or the White House itself. It became world-famous because of a playful photo of Kennedy's son John F. Kennedy Jr. peeking his head out from the desk's built-in panel as his father worked. There is a sense of awe that comes over you when you step into that room, so steeped in history. I could not help but think of the important decisions presidents agonized over there, from the Cuban Missile Crisis to America's response to the terrorist attacks of 9/11. Now a man who has been called a "carnival barker" and a "blowhard" by his predecessors was sitting behind it looking at me intently. I was surprised that the interview had come together at all, especially since he occasionally seemed unsure of what I was writing about. "I guess you're writing about first ladies," he said at one point, referring to a book I had written on the subject. "No," I told him, "this is about the former presidents." He asked me what I was working on more than once.

Trump's then–press secretary, Sarah Huckabee Sanders, scheduled the interview after it had been canceled twice at the last minute. She sat next to me, and his controversial, omnipresent aide Kellyanne Conway perched on one of the sofas behind us. Conway occasionally chimed in during our conversation to back up her boss. Trump was subdued and thoughtful; a glass of Diet Coke on ice was one of the only things on his desk. The room was so bright that it felt like there were television lights shooting down from the ceiling, which would have been appropriate for the first president to have been a reality TV star. There were also three U.S. flags and three presidential ones on display—three times as many as in each of his predecessors' offices.

We spoke shortly after the release of the Mueller Report, and Trump was in a buoyant, almost exuberant mood about its results. "You're here. And it was so calm. It's fake news, it's all fake," he said, gesturing around the room, which was indeed calm, because there were only four of us present. "We had a great exoneration, *no collusion*—if they would have found one little thing, I'm sure they would have loved to have said it." Barack Obama was behind the investigation, he said, referring to emails sent between two FBI officials looking into Russia's interference in the 2016 election. In one exchange, one of the officials wrote, "POTUS wants to know everything we are doing." Trump was indignant. "They weren't talking about me, 'cause I wasn't president yet. There was only one POTUS, and he wanted to know everything." A voice from behind me spoke up and said, "Had you not won the election . . ." It was Kellyanne. Trump peered over my head, flashed her a self-satisfied smile, and said, "If I had not fired Comey, this stuff wouldn't have been found out."

One overlooked casualty of Trump's upturning of presidential norms is the way he has also upended the norms among living former presidents, who have traditionally enthusiastically welcomed one another, regardless of party, into the world's most exclusive club. Surely Trump will not receive a warm welcome. He accused his predecessor of wiretapping his office ahead of the 2016 election and called his most recent Republican predecessor's foreign policy the worst in history. When I asked whether he would go to Obama's presidential library opening, the question sounded preposterous once it was spoken. Presidents have always attended one another's library openings as a sign of respect. "I don't know. He probably wouldn't invite me." Trump mulled it over for a moment and said, as though he had never thought of the far-reaching ramifications of his ostracism from the club, "Why should he?" It was an astonishing reminder of just how much had changed.

Unlike the former presidents, Trump has few people in his inner circle, and he is surprisingly accessible to the press. All I had done to get my interview was send Sarah Sanders an email— getting an interview with a president normally requires months of waiting and maneuvering around a slew of gatekeepers. Our interview was in keeping with his freewheeling, no-holds-barred style, which stands in such stark contrast to those of his most recent predecessors (with the notable exception of Bill Clinton). At one point Trump called out from behind the Resolute desk and asked his then-assistant, Madeleine Westerhout, who sat in what is called the outer Oval, to bring in a three-page, single-spaced document titled "Trump Administration Accomplishments" for me to read. "I would say this: Nobody in the first two years in office has done anything close to what we've done." No other president would feel the need to present a journalist with such a list. It included some specifics, like wage growth, and some vague generalities like "We have begun building the wall and support strong borders and no crime."

In addition to the list, Westerhout accidentally brought in top secret letters from North Korean leader Kim Jong Un. (At least Trump said it was a mistake, even though it was feeding into his narrative that he was handling the relationship with Kim Jong Un better than any president who came before him.) "So . . . this is off the record," Trump told me as he slid the folder across the desk, not the least bit fazed. I was not meant to see this, he said, but I could have a look at the classified messages. "They're very friendly letters, and think of where we were. When I came in, he was testing rockets every week." (The content of the letters was off the record, and when I asked if I could take a photo with my iPhone, Sanders quickly objected.) It was surreal, and it made clear that he wanted to talk about how much better he was at the job than the men who came before him, even if that meant showing a journalist sensitive material.

Trump is proud of his ostracism from the Presidents Club, and his contempt for his predecessors is obvious. The scorched-earth path he's chosen has made it impossible to maintain any friendships, or even civility, with the men who once occupied the

Oval Office. "I'm a different kind of president," he declared. And fractured relationships were to be expected. He said he and Bill Clinton had once been good friends, "until I decided to go into politics." Before he announced his campaign, in 2015, he said, he and Clinton got together "relatively a lot." "We'd play golf together at Westchester—the course I have in Westchester—we'd play in Florida. I got along with him fantastically until I ran for office and then, lo and behold, it was his wife that was running against me, so, you know, that can change your relationship rather quickly."

The two men have more in common than a shared love of golf: Clinton is the only other living president to have been impeached. This is the first time in history when two impeached presidents are alive at the same time (Clinton and Trump join just one other president, Andrew Johnson, who was impeached in 1868). Clinton told Trump, who called his own impeachment proceedings a "witch hunt" again and again, that using impeachment as a reason not to work with Democrats was just an "excuse."

"I would say, 'I've got lawyers and staff people handling this impeachment inquiry and they should just have at it. Meanwhile, I'm going to work for the American people.' That's what I would do." The other former presidents kept low profiles rather than risk doing or saying anything that might tip the scales of history.

Trump has not "asked anybody for advice" and does not care about having subverted the long-standing club. "We all love our country, but we all have different visions and we have different ways of doing things, and in a way we're competing with each other. We shouldn't be—we should be able to do this without competition, because there should be only one goal—but we have different ways and very different philosophies and different end results and different ways of getting there, too, very," he said with a shrug of his shoulders. Unlike most of the men who came before him, who aged prematurely and struggled with insomnia while in office,

I

THE PEACEFUL TRANSFER OF POWER

I feel the same sense of wonder and majesty
about this office today as I did when I first walked in here.

—George H. W. Bush on his last day as president, January 20, 1993

Every president and first lady experience that final day and night in office and the often bewildering first days at home with little to do and few people to help. While in office, presidents cannot drive or go for a walk. They also cannot eat out without the Secret Service doing a so-called sweep of the restaurant to make sure there are no threats. So, in theory, leaving the White House should be liberating, because there are fewer Secret Service agents and fewer restrictions, but it is almost always fraught with regret and angst over what to do next. And what they could have done differently.

Most miss the power of the presidency and its many perks, one of which is flying on Air Force One. "I don't miss being president," George W. Bush said. "But I do miss Air Force One." On board, commanders in chief trade in their suit jacket for a light-weight blue windbreaker with the presidential seal and AIR FORCE ONE on the right chest panel and their name on the left. They read, listen to music, and even exercise in their private compartment. "It was like you had your own little community there," said

Bill Clinton. "The experience took on a life of its own, because we worked there. We played there, we slept there. . . . It became like a floating family." The souped-up plane offers an escape from the White House. Clinton logged the most miles of his term in 1998, at the height of the Monica Lewinsky scandal, when it was easier to be away from the White House than in it. He flew more than 1.4 million miles in all—more than twice the mileage of Ronald Reagan, who had been the most traveled president.

They learn to ignore the Secret Service agents sweeping the runway, looking for anything suspicious, and the armed officers and snipers with rifles scattered throughout the field at Andrews Air Force Base. The fire trucks and ambulances on standby in case of an emergency become so familiar that they barely notice them after a while. But they become used to the luxury and ease of travel, and most miss it dearly. On his last flight on Air Force One, Lyndon Johnson made sure to keep blankets, towels, and anything he could get his hands on bearing the presidential seal. Somehow he absconded with the president's chair, which had been bolted to the floor. When his wife, Lady Bird, returned to Texas—her first time back as a private citizen—she found mountains of luggage piled up, with no one from the enormous White House staff in sight to help. "The chariot had turned into a pumpkin and all the mice have run away," she said with a sigh.

Presidents are haunted by the legacies of their predecessors. Not a day went by when Richard Nixon did not speak of JFK, the man who beat him in 1960. On October 10, 1972, Nixon wrote a note to himself late at night. Unable to sleep (he was plagued with insomnia), Nixon found himself questioning his legacy before Watergate complicated it forever: "Presidents noted for—F.D.R.—Charm. Truman—Gutsy. Ike—Smile, prestige. Kennedy—Charm. LBJ—Vitality. RN—?"

Inside the White House, the staff is acutely aware of all these conflicting emotions—the desperate desire to cling to power and to cement a legacy that will hold up for generations, and the sheer exhaustion that comes with being the most powerful person in the world. The approximately one hundred maids, butlers, chefs, and others who make the White House run every day stay from one administration to the next, and they see it as their job to make the transition between presidents as seamless as possible. But they experience the upheaval when one president and his family leave and another comes in almost as acutely as the presidents do themselves. Their sadness is overwhelming and heartfelt. Alonzo Fields was a White House butler and maître d' in the 1930s, '40s, and '50s, and he described how traumatic it is for the staff when the first family moves out. "The transformation in the household from one Administration to another is as sudden as death," he wrote in his memoir. "By that I mean it leaves you with a mysterious emptiness. In the morning you serve breakfast to a family with whom you have spent years. At noon that family is gone out of your life and here are new faces, new dispositions, and new likes and dislikes."

On that often freezing day in January, Americans' eyes are focused on the public transfer of power from one president to the next as thousands gather on the National Mall to watch the president-elect take the oath of office on the steps of the Capitol. Lady Bird called the carefully choreographed moment "the great quadrennial American pageant." Though it may look like a peaceful ceremony, it is complete havoc behind the scenes back at the White House. There are so many complex logistics involved in moving one family out and another in that residence staffers refer to what goes on inside the White House on Inauguration Day as "controlled chaos." Laura Bush called the "transfer of families" a "choreographic masterpiece, done with exceptional speed." The hum of White House activity starts even earlier than usual on Inauguration Day, with workers coming in before the break of dawn. By the time their day has ended, a new president is in office and a new era has begun.

The White House belongs to the outgoing family until noon, when the new president's term begins. On the morning of the inauguration, the president and the first lady host a small coffee reception for the new first family. Just before the two families depart to ride to the Capitol together, the staff crams into the opulent State Dining Room, where they have served so many state dinners, to say goodbye. They are often overcome by a range of emotions—in the span of just six hours, they are trading in an old boss for someone they do not know at all. "When the Clintons came down and Chelsea came with them, they didn't say a word," Head Housekeeper Christine Limerick recalled about Inauguration Day 2001. "I'll get emotional about this now—[President Clinton] looked at every person dead on in the face and said, 'Thank you.' The whole room just broke up." The departing family is presented with a gift from the residence staff, whom they come to love. It is a tradition to give them the flag that flew over the White House on the day the president was inaugurated—placed in a beautiful hand-carved box designed by White House carpenters. In 2001, Limerick, Chief Florist Nancy Clarke, and Chief Curator Betty Monkman gave Hillary Clinton a large pillow made from swatches of fabrics that she had selected to decorate different rooms in the house.

There is almost no time for reflection. At around eleven o'clock in the morning, the two first families leave the White House for the Capitol. Between then and approximately five in the afternoon—when the new president and his family return to rest and prepare for the inaugural balls—the staff must complete the job of moving one family out and another family in. Professional movers are off-limits, for security reasons, so it is the residence staffers who are solely responsible. In just six hours, everyone pitches in, from maids and butlers to engineers and florists, who become professional movers for a day, lugging furniture and placing picture frames just so. They even place toothbrushes in toothbrush holders on bathroom counters. No detail is too small. It is an incredible sight as the trucks carrying the new family's belongings are allowed in through one set of gates while the departing family's truck sits at the other, ready to take their things to their new home. The departing first family pay for their personal things to be moved out of the White House. The incoming president also pays for bringing belongings into the mansion, either out of the new first family's own coffers or from funds raised for the campaign or transition. It is the job of the incoming family to coordinate with the Secret Service to get their personal effects to the White House the morning of the inauguration.

Because the residence staff get to know the family so well, they are sensitive to the fact that they are being forced to leave. The transfer of the incoming first family's furniture and larger belongings to the White House is done very delicately. After the election of 1960, the Kennedys' social secretary, Letitia Baldrige, told Jackie Kennedy in a memo that she had asked the Eisenhowers' social secretary, Mary Jane McCaffree, "if we couldn't smuggle a lot of stuff over without the [Eisenhowers] knowing and she said yes, the head Usher could store cartons, suitcases, etc., out of sight and then whisk them into sight on the stroke of 12 noon. Isn't that marvelous??? Right out of Alfred Hitchcock." Baldrige recalled pulling up to the White House with Jackie's maid, Providencia Paredes, and Jack Kennedy's valet, George Thomas, in a car with Jackie's inaugural gown and all of the Kennedys' luggage. They arrived while everyone else was gathered at the Capitol for the inauguration ceremony. The snow-covered South Grounds were alight in brilliant sunshine. "We had timed the pilgrimage

to Houston. After rising and circling the Capitol dome, the helicopter flew down Pennsylvania Avenue for one last, sentimental aerial view of the White House. Four years earlier, on Inauguration Day in 1989, the Bushes had walked down the steps of the East Front of the Capitol with the Reagans. They escorted the Reagans across the thirty yards of red carpet leading to the helicopter that would whisk them out of Washington. "I was trying to keep the tears from flooding down my cheeks," Bush recalled. "After eight years of friendship, it's pretty tough."

The pilot had also surprised the Reagans by circling the Capitol, flying past the Washington Monument and the Lincoln Memorial, and then getting lower to hover over the White House. Reagan was still astounded by the executive mansion, even after living there for eight years. "There it was, complete with its sweep of green lawn and sparkling fountains. I said: 'Look, honey, there's our little shack.'"

Bush shared Reagan's sense of reverence for the White House and the presidency. He tried to inject some humor into the day by telling hundreds of people gathered at Ellington Field, in Houston, after their three-hour flight home, "There's a time to stay, and a time to go, a time to fold 'em, and we only wish our new President all the best." In customary fashion, Bush did not want a big crowd, and he was too emotional to thank the pilots and stewards on the plane. When he tried, he teared up. After greeting a few people standing in the receiving line, he said that he was marking "the first minute of our new life."

That Bush was a one-term president made their departure even more gut-wrenching. He felt guilty after his defeat. "Barbara and I sat at our bedroom desk, across from each other, each of us lost in our own thoughts," he said. "We looked at each other, but we didn't speak much. Ours had been a wonderful chance to serve, a wonderful opportunity. I hope history will show I did some things right, but on that flight I kept thinking of where I had let good people down—of how I had lost the presidency three months before." The White House was a mostly happy place during the years George H. W. and Barbara Bush lived there. Bush broke down that final morning when he saw the residence staff gathered before him. The butlers, housekeepers, chefs, and nearly one hundred permanent staff loved the Bushes best. "We were too choked up with emotion to say what we felt, but I think they knew the affection we had for them all," recalled Barbara Bush. Before leaving for the Capitol, she raced through the Red and Blue Rooms to hug all the butlers privately. "From then on it was all downhill. The hard part for me was over."

The Bushes truly appreciated life in the White House. "I'd like to go back and live there and not have the responsibility," Barbara Bush told me in a 2013 interview. President Bush said, "Whenever I see the place, instead of thinking, 'Well, I lived in that museum,' I think, 'I lived in that house for four years.' That part was perfect."

Decades after George and Barbara Bush moved out of the White House, the tradition of a stealth and astonishingly quick move was still in place. The Obama family's advisers started meeting with residence staff soon after the 2008 election, and by the week before the inauguration, much of the Obamas' furniture had already been shipped to the White House, where it was stored in the China Room, on the Ground Floor, so that it could be moved quickly upstairs. The Bushes had told Chief Usher Stephen Rochon that they wanted to make the move as easy as possible for everyone, but Rochon wanted to make sure the Bushes never felt as if they were being pushed out the door. "We want to keep it out of the sight of the existing family. Not that they didn't know it was there, but we didn't want them to feel that we were trying to move them out." The former presidents share the experience of suddenly having their lives change forever, first moving into the world's most famous private home and then being shown the door and told to leave. "You guys are going to be on the ride of a lifetime. Your whole life is changing today," Head Butler George Hannie told the Obamas when they moved in. "You don't have to wait for no more airplanes, you don't have to do anything but just show up. Everything is right there ready for you." But Michelle Obama wanted to cling to a sense of normalcy. When she met with Admiral Stephen Rochon, who, as the chief usher of the White House, was in charge of running the private side of the home, Michelle told him, "Please, call me Michelle." He replied, "I can't do that, Mrs. Obama."

Gerald Rafshoon, who was a close friend and adviser to Jimmy Carter, told me the same thing happened when Carter, who was a longshot candidate, became president. When Rafshoon walked into the Oval Office and saw Carter sitting there for the first time, he said, "Congratulations, Mr. President."

Carter replied, "Please, call me Jimmy."

"I can't do that, Mr. President. We both worked too hard to get you here," Rafshoon told him apologetically.

After Barack Obama was sworn in on the steps of the Capitol, George W. Bush and Laura Bush walked down the Capitol steps to the waiting helicopter that would take them to Andrews Air Force Base and on to their home in West Texas. It was all tradition and part of the carefully choreographed event. George and Barbara Bush, or "Bar and Gampy," as Laura Bush called them, were waiting for them on Marine One. They knew all too well the range of emotions the younger Bushes were feeling. A thousand members of their staff were gathered at Andrews to say goodbye. "As the helicopter rose over the Capitol, George took my hand," Laura Bush recalled. "We looked at the city below and out into the vibrant blue January sky, toward home." When they landed in Crawford, Texas, late that night, Bush carried his best friend Don Evans's suitcases up to the room he stayed in at the ranch. They were happy to have houseguests that evening; they were a welcome distraction. The next morning the Bushes were up at dawn—finding it difficult to break the habit of getting up with the sun—and struggling with the new reality of going "from a hundred miles an hour to about ten." Retirement would take some adjusting to. Bush said he had to learn to "force myself to relax."

PRIVATE LETTERS

There are sacred traditions embedded in the presidency. One thing is the Secret Service code names that follow presidents and first ladies throughout their lives. They have to choose from a list of names beginning with a certain letter. During a Republican primary debate, Donald Trump said he would pick the name "Humble," which was an unlikely choice for the billionaire businessman. But when he was actually given Secret Service protection, names beginning with H were not an option. When he was presented with a list of names beginning with M, Trump picked Mogul, a much more fitting moniker. Melania Trump chose Muse. Jimmy Carter's code name is Deacon, and Rosalynn's is Dancer. Bush 41's was Timberwolf, and Barbara Bush's was Tranquility. Bill and Hillary Clinton are Eagle and Evergreen, respectively. Bush 43's is Trailblazer, and Laura Bush's is Tempo. Barack Obama is Renegade, while Michelle Obama is Renaissance. (Our forty-first president became known as Bush 41 in 2001, to distinguish him from his son, Bush 43, once the younger George became the forty-third president.)

The tradition of the departing president leaving behind a note for his successor is relatively new, and keeping these correspondences private has helped forge important relationships.

Ronald Reagan started the tradition, and, as one would expect, his note had an ebullient touch, in part because the man who followed him into the White House was his trusted vice president, George H. W. Bush, but also because anything less affable was not in Reagan's nature. "Don't let the turkeys get you down" was the note's heading. Every page had a cartoon at the top showing a crowd of turkeys trying to pull down an elephant, the symbol of the Republican Party. "Dear George, You'll have moments when you want to use this particular stationery. Well, go for it. George, I treasure the memories we share and wish you all the very best. You'll be in my prayers. God bless you and Barbara. I'll miss our Thursday lunches.—Ron." Reagan wrote the note the morning he left office and stuck it in the top drawer of the Resolute desk. It was the beginning of a wonderful tradition. (Bush made the unusual decision to make the note public the next day.)

Bush's 1993 letter to Clinton was similarly lighthearted and encouraging: "I wish you great happiness here. I never felt the loneliness some Presidents have described. There will be very tough times, made even more difficult by criticism you may not think is fair. I'm not a very good one to give advice; but just don't let the critics discourage you or push you off course. . . . Your success is our country's success. I am rooting hard for you." Bush wrote in his diary as he sat alone in the Oval Office on his final day as president. "I feel the same sense of wonder and majesty about this office today as I did when I first walked in here. I've tried to serve here with no taint or dishonor; no conflict of interest; nothing to sully this beautiful place and this job I've been privileged to hold."

These are heartfelt letters between one man exiting the most stressful and important job in the country and another about to enter into it. Bill Clinton's letter to George W. Bush was made public only on January 19, 2017, years after both men had left office. In it Clinton wrote, "The burdens you now shoulder are great but often exaggerated. The sheer joy of doing what you believe is right is inexpressible." Trump did something that most of these presidents chose not to do and, just eight months into his presidency, leaked the handwritten note Obama had left for him. Obama was particularly annoyed that his note had been made public so soon. Traditionally these presidential messages are meant to serve as private buoying words of support, to be reached for during difficult moments and kept private until the end of the new president's term. Obama had not told even his closest aides what was in the letter. But Trump showed it to White House visitors in the Oval Office as a point of personal pride. A week after becoming president, he talked about the letter and called it "long" and "complex." "It was thoughtful. And it took time to do it, and I appreciated it," he said.

"Obama was not happy," an aide who worked in Obama's post-presidential Washington, D.C., office told me. "He thought it was just cheesy."

Obama had left the note in the top drawer of the Resolute desk, and it was decidedly less cheerful than others had been. In it, he warned Trump to "sustain the international order." And he asked Trump to be kind, a request found in no other letters between presidents. "We've both been blessed, in different ways, with great good fortune," Obama wrote. "Not everyone is so lucky. It's up to us to do everything we can [to] build more ladders of success for every child and family that's willing to work hard." He ended the letter by wishing Trump and his wife, Melania, good luck and offering "to help in any ways which we can."

Trump called to thank Obama for the note right after reading it on the day of his inauguration, but Obama was traveling to Palm Springs for a vacation with his wife and missed the call. By the time Obama had one of his aides call Trump back, it was several days later and the new president had signed an executive order banning entry to citizens from seven mostly Muslim countries for ninety days. Obama wrestled with whether he should personally release a statement condemning the ban, which would destroy the norm that former presidents traditionally refrain from criticizing their successors, at least for a couple of months. After much intense discussion with his staff, Obama settled on a statement from his spokesman that said Obama "fundamentally disagrees" with the ban. The time for any hint of camaraderie between the two men had clearly passed. The Trump staffer told the Obama aide trying to arrange the call, "President Trump just wanted to thank President Obama for the letter, no need to disturb them now."

The letter George W. Bush left for Obama was made public by Bush on the very last day of Obama's presidency. "There will be trying moments," Bush wrote. "The critics will rage. Your 'friends' will disappoint you. But, you will have an Almighty God to comfort you, a family who loves you, and a country that is pulling for you, including me." Speaking at the dedication of the George W. Bush Library, in 2013, Obama recalled having first read Bush's letter. "He knew that I would come to learn what he had learned—that being President, above all, is a humbling job. There are moments where you make mistakes. There are times where you wish you could turn back the clock." He ended sounding hopeful that whoever would take over the presidency from him would feel the same: "What I know is true about President Bush, and I hope my successor will say about me, is that we love this country and we do our best." That was not going to be the case.

II

THE UNWRITTEN RULES OF THE CLUB

There has never been a single man who filled that office
who did not respect it when he left.

—Harry Truman

With great power comes great responsibility, and the former presidents, unlike leaders of most other countries, who disappear from the public eye, never lose their luster or fade into obscurity. When German chancellor Angela Merkel leaves office, she is unlikely to be a force in German politics. Former British prime minister Tony Blair and former French president François Hollande have largely faded into the background of political discourse. In Europe and the United Kingdom, there is generally a sense that when politicians are out of office, they should recede politely and quietly into their private lives. But American presidents are larger-than-life and often polarizing personalities who are unknowable in part because of the enormous power they wield. So when they leave office, the shine never wears off completely. And if they are being completely honest, none of them want it to.

In the club, which has its own set of rules and its own unique set of personalities, power is never completely relinquished—the four living former presidents will always be called "Mr. President," and that is how they want it. The late George H. W. Bush, a role model to the four still living, was more than happy to be invited to the White House and serve as a kind of moral beacon for his successors. The former presidents may never disappear from the American psyche, but very few people understand how this group of men and women—including the former first ladies, who operate in an equally rarefied atmosphere filled with unspoken rules, personality clashes, and intrigue—actually live their lives once they are no longer in power. There may be no clubhouse for the men who were once the most powerful people in the world, but there is a very strict understanding among them.

It is easiest for the sitting president when his predecessors are no longer engaged in public life, because their voices can be so powerful. During a visit to Japan early in his administration, George W. Bush was shocked when Japanese prime minister Junichiro Koizumi told him that most former prime ministers go on to become legislators. A stunned Bush said, "No wonder you can't get anything done because you have all these formers undermining you."

There have been points in history when there were no living ex-presidents to weigh in, good or bad. When Lyndon Johnson died, in 1973, Richard Nixon became only the sixth living president to have no former presidents to ask for advice (including George Washington, who obviously had no predecessors). There have been only four periods when five former presidents were alive: from March 1862 to January 1862, when Abraham Lincoln was in office and Martin Van Buren, John Tyler, Franklin Pierce, Millard Fillmore, and James Buchanan still lived; from January 1993 to April 1994, when Nixon, Ford, Carter, Reagan, and Bush were alive during Clinton's first term; from January 2001 to June 2004, a three-and-a-half-year stretch in the Bush 43 administration when Ford, Carter, Reagan, Clinton, and the president's own father were alive; and from January 2017 to November 2018, during the Trump era, when both Bushes, Carter, Clinton, and

Obama were all members of the Presidents Club, until the elder Bush's death.

The presidency is about much more than the person who has the job. Harry Truman once told a journalist, "When you get to be president, there are all those things, the honors, the twenty-one-gun salutes, all those things, you have to remember it isn't for you." There are shared, inescapable experiences that bind every president to the men who came before him, both in how they governed and in what they accomplished afterward. The moment a president leaves office, he faces the existential questions everyone confronts when they retire: *What am I going to do with my life? What legacy will I leave behind when I'm gone?* Sometimes, retirement can offer unexpected fulfillment.

The ways in which the former presidents have lived out their post-presidential lives reflect how they approached the presidency: Jimmy Carter could not help but think he was right all the time, both as president and after; George H. W. Bush never had to try too hard to be respected, because of his patrician pedigree, and he had a quiet confidence both in office and afterward; Bill Clinton approached the post-presidency with the same voracious need for acceptance and relevance as he had during his presidency; George W. Bush never hungered for the presidency in the same way his predecessors did, and he has been content to recede from the spotlight; and Barack Obama is a hybrid of the Bushes, Clinton, and Carter. He has sought privacy—the Obamas' spokeswoman, Katie Hill, insists that they "are private citizens now"—all while banking on his stature as a former president to make enormous amounts of money.

Former presidents may find it liberating to escape the presidency, but, even years after leaving office, it proves impossible. As a so-called private citizen, Nixon would take daily walks through the streets of New York City at 5:30 a.m. to avoid being recognized. Former presidents all know what it is like to live with the constraints of the presidency, including the reality of being whisked in and out of buildings, often through the kitchen. "When I was president, I didn't see a lobby for years," George H. W. Bush recalled. After they leave the confines of the White House, they can breathe a sigh of relief when the phone does not ring in the middle of the night, for those calls almost always foreshadow bad news. They know what it is like to be disliked, even hated, by some voters. Once they leave office, the decisions they made are often seen in a new and flattering light. Another bonus that comes with retirement: they can go to a baseball game, as the elder Bush joked, and not worry about getting booed by their critics. "Hell," he said after attending a Texas Rangers game, "if I had done this when I was president, no way."

Despite their different political trajectories, all the members of the team of five have lived their post-presidential years fully understanding what is expected of them. Some are more engaged than others, but there are unspoken rules that they all adhere to—with the exception of Jimmy Carter, who has paid for his disobedience with occasional suspensions from the club. There have been times throughout history when other former presidents have shirked these rules, but doing so has come at a steep price— their all-important legacies are forever tarnished.

RULE NO. 1:
HONOR A SHARED HISTORY

I always loved Jefferson, and still love him.

—John Adams

There are only five men alive today (including President Trump) who know the loneliness and isolation of the presidency. It is extraordinary that Trump has not talked to his predecessors at any length and that his predecessors have not reached out to him in a meaningful way. Even the worst, most strained relationships of the previous presidents were not quite like this. There have always been rivalries, but usually a sense of mutual respect and a grudging admiration have brought former adversaries together. Three presidents have even written books about their predecessors: Herbert Hoover wrote one about Woodrow Wilson; Wilson wrote one about George Washington; and George W. Bush wrote a book about his father.

John Adams, the second president, sought reelection in 1800 and lost to Thomas Jefferson. He was so bitter that he did not even attend his successor's inauguration. The Massachusetts native Adams and the Virginian Jefferson fought for the same cause during the American Revolution, but they had grown apart because of conflicting views on the role of the federal government. The only message Adams left behind for Jefferson was a terse note alerting him to the fact that there were seven horses and two carriages he was leaving behind in the White House stables. Remarkably, after twelve years of silence, the two rivals developed a close friendship. Their mutual friend Benjamin Rush heard that Adams had declared, "I always loved Jefferson, and still love him." When Rush told Jefferson what he had heard, Jefferson wrote, "This is enough for me." Adams and Jefferson recognized how important their shared history was and reconciled. They developed a warm friendship preserved in fourteen years' worth of letters sent between Jefferson's Monticello estate, in Virginia, and Adams's home, in Quincy, Massachusetts. "We too must go," Jefferson wrote in one letter, "and that ere long. I believe we are under half a dozen at present; I mean the signers of the Declaration [of Independence]." They wrote each other regularly up until their deaths, just hours apart, on

July 4, 1826, the fiftieth anniversary of the Declaration's signing. Jefferson was the first to pass away, at eighty-three, and Adams died five hours later, at ninety. About a year before he died, Adams wrote Jefferson, "Every line from you exhilarates my spirits and gives me a glow of pleasure."

In his final letter to Adams, Jefferson told him that his grandson, Thomas Jefferson Randolph, would be in Boston and wanted to visit with him. "Like other young people, he wishes to be able, in the winter nights of old age, to recount to those around him what he has heard and learnt of the Heroic Age preceding his birth, and which of the Argonauts particularly he was in time to have seen." Both men also had direct influence on their successors: Jefferson was a mentor to fellow Virginians James Madison and James Monroe, and Adams lived to see his son John Quincy Adams become the sixth president.

When I asked Trump if he could see himself becoming friendly with a former president after leaving office or rekindling a friendship with Bill Clinton, as Adams and Jefferson had done, he said, "It's possible. Anything's possible."

RULE NO. 2:
RESPECT THE OFFICE AND ONE ANOTHER

There's a reverence there for that office that is independent of you,
and if you don't feel that you shouldn't be there.

—Barack Obama

Margaret Truman said that her father vowed never to voice his opinions about the men who followed him. He said that "more time must pass before anyone, even an ex-president, can evaluate the performance of a man in the White House." But they are, of course, fascinated by one another. Richard Nixon roamed the halls of the White House late at night and into the early-morning hours, examining presidential portraits. "You cannot walk in those old rooms without feeling or hearing the footsteps of those who have gone before you," he said. Bill Clinton's study is full of books on former presidents, from Lincoln to Truman to Kennedy. The former presidents share a unique understanding of the incredible responsibility that comes with the highest office in the country and the weight each president bears when making decisions that affect people on a global scale. When Kennedy was flying home from a summit with Soviet leader Nikita Khrushchev in 1961, with the tension of the Cold War building, his secretary found a note he had written to himself. It was a quote from Abraham Lincoln that had fallen to the floor. It read, "I know there is a God—and I see a storm coming. If He has a place for me, I believe I am ready." The awesome responsibility that comes with the presidency binds all these men together long after they leave the White House.

Alexander Hamilton worried that ex-presidents, after those all-consuming and exciting years in office, would spend their remaining days "wandering among the people like discontented ghosts." Indeed, only two men had post–White House careers that rivaled their time as president: John Quincy Adams, the son of John and Abigail Adams, and William Howard Taft, the twenty-seventh president. John Quincy had not looked forward to those years after the White House, declaring shortly before leaving office, "There is nothing more pathetic in life than a former president." When he left, he moved into a mansion in Washington, D.C., and wrote, "It was my intention to bury myself in complete retirement as much as any nun taking the veil."

Nothing he could do, he thought, would come close to having been president. But, remarkably, Adams was recruited to run for Congress, even though his wife and son were unimpressed by the prospect. It was an odd idea—a former president becoming a congressman. Charles Francis Adams Sr., the Adamses' youngest son, told his father that accepting the job "diminished the man." But Adams was intrigued at the opportunity to step back into public life. On December 5, 1831, he attended the first session of the Twenty-second Congress and became the first—and last—former president to do so. Adams considered his new job a major demotion at first, and he predicted that it would lead to "slights, mortifications—insults—loss of reputation—and perhaps, exposure of myself by infirmities of temper unsuited to the trials." But by the end of his nine terms in Congress he had built a reputation as a leader in the fight against slavery and was known as "Old Man Eloquent." He led a full life after the presidency. He died in 1848 in the Speaker's chamber and murmured, "This is the last of Earth: I am content." His post-presidency was inspirational to the presidents who followed him, including Bill Clinton, who has read voraciously about John Quincy Adams and his years after the White House.

In 1912, after he lost his bid for reelection, William Howard Taft joked about what the country should do with its ex-presidents. "A dose of chloroform," he said, to protect the country "from the troublesome fear that the occupant could ever come back." (The memory of Grover Cleveland's two nonconsecutive terms in the late nineteenth century was still fresh.) But, like Adams, Taft had a satisfying life after the presidency. Unlike any other former president, he very much wanted to hold another high office, but his aspirations were toward another branch of the government. He fulfilled his lifelong ambition when he became Supreme Court chief justice in June 1921, a post he held until his retirement, in 1930, a month before his death. Taft and Adams are rare exceptions of former presidents who stepped into official roles that, although prestigious, were less august than the presidency.

Former presidents traditionally look out for one another.

Herbert Hoover wrote to Harry Truman, a fellow member of the Presidents Club, and said, "I think we need an agreement that we will not allow promoters of causes to trap us into joint actions for their schemes without our having prior consultations." Anyone in the role understands the weight of it. Whenever people gossiped about FDR while he was in office, Hoover always stopped them, even though there was no love lost between the two men. Hoover came to FDR's defense because he believed that criticism was disrespectful of the presidency, not just the man himself.

Unlike John Quincy Adams and William Howard Taft, Herbert Hoover was a frustrated former president. Franklin Delano Roosevelt would not give Hoover, who was a critic of his New Deal, the chance to help during World War II. Hoover had played an important role as a humanitarian and helped feed starving civilians in Europe during World War I, and he wanted to be of service again. After Pearl Harbor, he conveyed that to FDR, but he was never called upon. "My activities in the Second World War were limited to frequent requests from Congressional committees," he lamented. When Roosevelt's advisers suggested he seek Hoover's help aiding war-torn Europe, Roosevelt replied, "I'm not Jesus Christ. I'm not waking him from the dead."

Roosevelt's successor, Harry Truman, was sympathetic to Hoover, who he thought had been mistreated and whom he admired for his work during World War I. When Truman invited Hoover to the White House thirteen years after he'd left office, Hoover's eyes flooded with tears and he had to excuse himself for a moment. Truman understood. "I knew what was the matter with him," Truman said. "It was the first time in thirteen years that anybody had paid attention to him." Franklin Roosevelt had gone so far as to have the Hoover Dam renamed the Boulder Dam, but through an act of Congress, encouraged by Truman in 1947, it was to be called the Hoover Dam once again. Truman put Hoover to work on relief efforts and had him oversee a reorganization of federal executive departments.

It is entirely natural for there to be tension between the outgoing president and his successor, especially if they are from different parties, as they often are, and if the new occupant's victory was in part a rebuke of the sitting president. But conflicts are largely kept private, and there is an underlying respect among anyone who has held the job. Truman and his successor, Dwight D. Eisenhower, did not get along, but they did respect each other on a very fundamental level. Much of their animosity was rooted in Truman's astonishment that Eisenhower, who was once a friend, would run as a Republican in 1952, and in Eisenhower's sense of betrayal when Truman made cutting remarks about him during the campaign. As the two men rode in the armored Lincoln on their way to Eisenhower's inauguration, Eisenhower, a five-star general, said, "I did not attend your inauguration in 1948 out of consideration for you, because if I had been present I would have drawn attention away from you." Truman replied coolly, "You were not here in 1948 because I did not send for you. But if I *had* sent for you, you would have come." Eisenhower never sought Truman's counsel during his two terms in office.

At the end of Truman's *Years of Trial and Hope*, the second installment of his memoir, he outright criticized his successor. He said that during the transition he had been "troubled" by Eisenhower's "frozen grimness." "He may have been awestruck by the long array of problems the President had to face," he wrote at the tail end of the book. "But it may have been something else. He may have failed to grasp the true picture of what the administration had been doing because in the heat of partisan politics, he had gotten a badly distorted version of the true facts. Whatever it was, I kept thinking about it."

Even though Truman did much to bring Hoover back into public life, Hoover did not enjoy his post-presidency. At the 1957 opening of the Truman Presidential Library, in Independence, Missouri, he was asked about life as a former president and said modestly, "Madam, we spend our days taking pills and dedicating libraries." In the 230 years since George Washington became president, forty-four men have taken the oath of office (counting Cleveland just once), and thirty-five have gone on to lead post-presidential lives. Now they are living longer than ever. Before Truman, presidents lived an average of eleven years after leaving the White House; from Truman to Clinton, their longevity jumped to fifteen years. They are doing far more than "taking pills and dedicating libraries," and they largely keep their disagreements private.

RULE NO. 3:
AVOID CRITICIZING THE SITTING PRESIDENT
AT ALL COSTS

Stay the hell out of Dodge.

—George H. W. Bush

Despite the gentlemen's agreement among former presents to not hit back, there have been times when this rule has been broken. Theodore Roosevelt, born and bred in New York City, served as New York City police commissioner, ran for mayor, became governor of New York, and, like Donald Trump, had a larger-than-life personality. Trump tweeted a quote from Roosevelt in

January 2014, seeking to compare his own take-no-prisoners approach to politics to Roosevelt's. "The unforgivable crime is soft hitting," Trump tweeted, quoting Roosevelt. "Do not hit at all if it can be avoided; but never hit softly." There are so many differences between Trump and Roosevelt, but they share a belief in head-on confrontations with their predecessors, which binds them. In modern times, this kind of public animosity was far more muted—until Donald Trump.

Theodore Roosevelt was William McKinley's vice president, and he the youngest person ever to become president. Roosevelt was just forty-two when he ascended to the presidency after McKinley was assassinated. When he left office he was only fifty. Roosevelt picked his successor, his secretary of war, William Howard Taft, in the hope that he would win the Republican nomination and the presidency in 1908 and continue his policies. Taft defeated William Jennings Bryan in the general election. But Roosevelt did not adhere to the gentlemen's agreement among former presidents. He grew so disenchanted with Taft and his move to more conservative policies that Roosevelt ran against him as a third-party candidate in 1912. It was a remarkable and brazen decision for Roosevelt to challenge his chosen successor. Taft, in turn, called Roosevelt "a flatterer of the people," "a dangerous egotist," and "a demagogue." Roosevelt called Taft, who weighed 340 pounds, a "fathead" and a "puzzle wit." Roosevelt and Taft ran against each other as well as Democratic challenger Woodrow Wilson, the New Jersey governor. Roosevelt came in second, winning 27 percent of the popular vote to Wilson's 42 percent—still the highest percentage won by any third-party candidate. The rivalry between Roosevelt and Taft, however, contributed to Wilson's victory.

Even though he lost, Roosevelt never left the spotlight. A full-time reporter was even stationed outside Oyster Bay, his Long Island home, long after his defeat. In a 1918 op-ed, Roosevelt defended the press against an edict from President Wilson's administration demanding that the president not be criticized. The decision that "we are to stand by the president, right or wrong, is not only unpatriotic and servile but is morally treasonable to the American people," Roosevelt said.

Wilson did not attend Roosevelt's funeral; he was off negotiating the Treaty of Versailles, which ended World War I. Taft was there and was seated with the Roosevelt family servants. When Roosevelt's son Archie saw Taft, he said, "You're a dear personal friend and you must come up farther." Taft was moved up and placed behind the vice president, who was seated where President Wilson would have been. The seating did not seem accidental.

Modern presidents have learned from Roosevelt's mistake. While he is considered a great president, his decision to attack Taft and then to challenge him led to Woodrow Wilson's election.

RULE NO. 4:
DON'T BE TOO PROUD TO ASK FOR HELP

No one knows how rough this job is until after
he has been in it a few months.

—John F. Kennedy

Sitting presidents, presidential hopefuls, and presidents-elect have come together for the greater good of the country—even if it has meant occasionally swallowing their pride. Joseph Kennedy was constantly manipulating situations to help his son John secure the presidency. He wanted Nixon to meet with JFK after Kennedy narrowly defeated him in the 1960 election. (Kennedy kept a slip of paper in his pocket with the number of votes he won by—118,574—so that he would never forget how close the election was.) As calls for a recount mounted, the elder Kennedy thought it was important for the two men to display a united front and appear together publicly, so he called his old friend Herbert Hoover and asked for help. Kennedy asked Hoover to call Nixon, who was mourning his loss at his vacation home in Key Biscayne, Florida. The Nixons were at a restaurant having dinner with friends when a waiter came to their table and told Nixon (who was still the vice president) that Hoover was trying to reach him. Nixon picked up the restaurant phone. "Hello, Chief," Hoover said. "The Ambassador [Joseph Kennedy had been U.S. ambassador to Great Britain] has just called me and suggested that it would be a good idea for you and the president-elect to get together for a visit." Nixon was not enthusiastic about being used by Kennedy for a photo-op. "Some indications of national unity are not only desirable, but essential," Hoover reminded him. Before he agreed, Nixon wanted to clear it with his boss, President Dwight D. Eisenhower, who was at his Gettysburg farm that evening. "You will look like a sorehead if you didn't," Eisenhower told him. Finally, a few minutes after he got off the phone with Eisenhower, John F. Kennedy himself called Nixon to make the arrangements.

That no recount was called—which could have upended the country and its faith in the democratic process—was thanks in part to this incredible series of phone calls, and the power of the Presidents Club. Nixon was amused by the calls. "As I hung up and walked slowly back to our table," Nixon recalled, "it dawned on me that I had just participated in a probably unprecedented series of conversations. In the space of less than ten minutes, I had talked to a former president of the United States, the present president and the president-elect!"

Once in office, Kennedy sought advice from his predecessors during the most trying moments of his presidency, because he understood the value of these relationships. During those thousand days, Kennedy worked to cultivate ties with the trio of former presidents who were still alive: Truman (the only Democrat), Hoover, and Eisenhower. Truman was the first visitor to the Kennedy White House—it was his first time back since he had left, in 1953. He had been spending his post–White House years relishing his freedom in his small hometown of Independence, where he could be found every day walking at a brisk 120 steps per minute around his neighborhood. And with no Secret Service protection—that would not come until 1965, when Congress authorized the Secret Service to protect a former president and his spouse during his lifetime—he became used to eager strangers running up to him to say hello. JFK's relationship with Eisenhower, who had been supreme commander of the Allied forces in Western Europe during World War II, was especially important. Kennedy pushed for legislation to restore Eisenhower's five-star military rank so that, following Eisenhower's wishes, he would be referred to as "General" and not "Mr. President" after he left office. (Shortly before announcing his candidacy, Eisenhower had resigned from the military.) Once it was approved, Kennedy wrote to Eisenhower: "The legislation constitutes a reaffirmation of the affection and regard of our nation for you." He enclosed a copy of the bill in his letter.

The challenges of the presidency would spur Kennedy to once again reach out to the man he had defeated, and to Eisenhower. He knew he could not afford to be too proud to ask for help. On April 17, 1961, when Kennedy had been in office less than a hundred days, a U.S.-supported group of exiles tried to overthrow Fidel Castro, the Communist leader of Cuba, at the Bay of Pigs. It was a complete disaster that led to the deaths of hundreds of Cubans. Four days later, having been completely humiliated, Kennedy invited Nixon to the White House. (Nixon's daughter

Tricia said, "I knew it! It wouldn't be long before he would get into trouble and have to call on you for help.") Kennedy told Nixon that the bungled invasion was "the worst experience of my life" and asked him for advice on how to handle the fallout. Nixon left feeling sorry for Kennedy, who had the job he so desperately wanted. "I felt empathy for a man who had to face up to a bitter tragedy that was not entirely his fault but was nonetheless his inescapable responsibility." (Eisenhower had approved the invasion in March 1960.)

Eisenhower's public support would be critical for the young and inexperienced president. Two days after his visit with Nixon, Kennedy invited Eisenhower to Camp David for lunch. The two met at the secluded presidential retreat, nestled in Maryland's Catoctin Mountains, about sixty miles north of the White House. Eisenhower had named Camp David after his grandson, and it was Kennedy's first trip there. The two men walked along the meandering pathways of the 125-acre refuge. Kennedy made sure photographers captured their meeting as a show of national unity. Publicly, Eisenhower played by the rules of the Presidents Club and warned against any "witch hunting" on the Bay of Pigs. Privately, however, he chastised Kennedy for not having met with his entire national security staff before he approved the plan.

"No one knows how rough this job is until after he has been in it a few months," Kennedy said.

"Mr. President, if you will forgive me, I think I mentioned that to you three months ago," Eisenhower replied.

But Eisenhower stood by Kennedy when it mattered most— in public comments. "I am still in favor of the United States supporting the man who has to carry the responsibility for our foreign affairs," he said. Kennedy could have changed Camp

David's name, but three days after his visit with Eisenhower, the White House made an announcement: Camp David would remain Camp David as long as Kennedy was president. It was a small show of gratitude for Eisenhower's priceless public support.

The next year, Kennedy was confronted with the Cuban Missile Crisis, when the United States and the Soviet Union teetered on the brink of nuclear war. Once again he relied on the advice of the men who came before him. During the agonizing thirteen-day standoff between the two countries over Soviet nuclear missiles being built in Cuba, Kennedy called all three of his predecessors to ask for their help. Nelson Pierce, a White House usher for twenty-six years, said it was the most frightened he had ever been in his life. "You knew that those missiles were aimed right at us," he recalled, trembling at the memory of walking through the White House's Northwest Gates on Pennsylvania Avenue, knowing he was walking into a bull's-eye. "You knew that if you heard that something [a missile] was on the way, you had to get the first family out, or to a safe place, and you were there re-gardless. You'd be the last one to leave," he paused, "if you left at all."

Kennedy was desperate to find a way to avoid nuclear war. He asked Eisenhower, who had vast military experience, if he thought the Soviet Union would fire nuclear missiles if the United States attacked Cuba. "You would take that risk?"

"What can you do?" Eisenhower replied. "Something may make these people shoot them off, I just don't believe this will. In any event, I'll say this, I'd want to keep my own people very alert."

"We'll hang on tight," Kennedy replied, laughing nervously.

During the Vietnam War, Lyndon Johnson also relied on Eisenhower—even though he was a Republican—so much so that he routinely sent an aide to visit "the General" in Gettysburg and brief him on developments. Johnson also greatly admired

Harry Truman and traveled to Independence to hand-deliver Medicare cards to Truman and his wife, Bess. They were the first and second card ever issued. "This is to show you we haven't forgotten who is the real Daddy of Medicare. Because of the fight you started nineteen years ago, nineteen million Americans will benefit on July 1 and . . . will have another cause to bless Harry S. Truman."

But it was Eisenhower who was especially revered as a former president. In Ike's final weeks, every member of Richard Nixon's cabinet went to visit him in Ward Eight at Walter Reed Army Medical Center, where he was hospitalized as his health declined. The Eisenhowers and the Nixons would be united by marriage when Nixon's younger daughter, Julie, married Eisenhower's grandson, David, shortly after the 1968 election. After becoming president, Nixon went to visit Eisenhower, who had lost twenty pounds during his illness, and told him, "You can always take great pride in the fact that no man in our history has done more to make America and the world a better and safer place in which to live."

"Mr. President," Eisenhower replied, raising his hand weakly to salute Nixon, "you do me great honor in what you have just said." He passed away two days later.

Eisenhower was an avid golfer who often wore his golf cleats in the Oval Office so that he could sneak out to play on the South Lawn when he had a free moment. Kennedy refused to repair the marked-up floor, out of respect, and Johnson followed suit. It was Nixon who, in 1969, shortly after his inauguration, decided it was time to replace the floor. He saved some of the scarred pieces of the old floor and had them cut into two-inch squares, which he had placed on small plaques and sent out to Eisenhower's close friends. The general's memory was considered sacred among his successors.

RULE NO. 5:

UNITE IN TRAGEDY

To paraphrase Mr. Jefferson: We are all Democrats, we are all Republicans, because we are all Americans.

—Ronald Reagan

The former presidents were united in tragedy when, on November 22, 1963, they got word that Kennedy had been assassinated, just as his idol Lincoln had been. It was the first time a president had been killed since William McKinley, in 1901. The day after Kennedy's murder, Eisenhower, who was seventy-three at the time, drove from his Gettysburg farm to the White House. He had grown fond of the young president, whom he had once derided as "the boy," and he was devastated by his loss. All the living presidents had assassination threats, and the anguish of Kennedy's death reminded him of his own mortality. (Before he was in the White House, Eisenhower was president of Columbia University and had a concealed-weapons permit so that he would feel safe walking around New York City.) He met with Lyndon Johnson, who had suddenly been thrust into the presidency, and handed him one piece of yellow legal-size paper. At the top of it he wrote, "Confidential Notes for the President," by hand. In his notes he suggested that Johnson call a joint session of Congress and make a short speech, not more than twelve minutes long, to make it clear that no major change in policy "is intended or will occur" and that the "noble objectives" of Kennedy would be upheld. A month after taking office, Johnson told reporters that he was planning to "keep the ex-presidents informed." Harry Truman, who had left office a decade earlier, and who had also come to like and respect Kennedy, was too overcome with emotion to immediately make a statement or even to leave his house, though he spoke with Johnson on the phone. Truman's daughter,

Margaret, recalled, "Dad was terribly shaken by it. For the first time in his life, he was unable to face reporters."

Every important world leader traveled to Washington, D.C., for Kennedy's grand and somber state funeral. Eisenhower and Truman were the only former presidents to attend; Herbert Hoover was alive but too ill to make the trip. Though Eisenhower and Truman did not get along, the tragedy brought them together. The Trumans stayed at Blair House, and the Eisenhowers were at a nearby hotel. Eisenhower placed a call to Truman asking if they could pick them up so that they would arrive at Kennedy's memorial service together. "Certainly," Truman said, and he invited Eisenhower and his wife, Mamie, to stop by Blair House for coffee afterward. The two couples spent an hour talking; they buried the hatchet and were united in their shared sorrow. Their tense ride to Eisenhower's 1953 inauguration seemed petty now, under the circumstances.

RULE NO. 6:
COME TOGETHER FOR CELEBRATIONS

Though we hail from different backgrounds and ideologies, we're singularly unique, even eternally bound, by our common devotion and service to this wonderful country.

—George H. W. Bush

Other than funerals, former presidents most often come together at the openings of presidential libraries. In 1991, four former presidents and five former first ladies (Lady Bird Johnson was there without her husband, who had died in 1973) gathered together for the dedication of the Ronald Reagan Presidential Library, in Simi Valley, California. Along with George H. W. Bush, who was in office at the time, all the living former presidents attended: Richard Nixon, Gerald Ford, Jimmy Carter, and

Reagan. Nixon's 1994 funeral brought Ford, Carter, Reagan, Bush 41, and Clinton together; Reagan's 2004 funeral was attended by Ford, Carter, both Bushes, and Clinton; and five presidents were together again on April 25, 2013, for the dedication of the George W. Bush Presidential Library and Museum, in Dallas: Carter, both Bushes, Clinton, and Obama.

On January 7, 2009, three former presidents joined George W. Bush, a soon-to-be former, and Barack Obama, who was days away from taking office, in the Oval Office for a historic photo of all the former living presidents together. Bush invited Obama and the former presidents to the White House to give Obama some insight into what it is like to live there. Bush decided on lunch instead of dinner, as was originally suggested, because he antici-pated how late Clinton, a famous night owl, would keep them all up talking. George H. W. Bush, George W. Bush, and Clinton were secretly hoping that Carter, who was on a foreign trip and who annoyed them all by weighing in on their policies, would not change his plans to come home. One former Clinton aide and one former aide to George W. Bush told me they had specifically scheduled the meeting then with Carter's absence in mind. "The one thing that bonded them together was their dislike of Car-ter," said the Clinton aide. "There are such deep-seated issues with each other." But Carter did come home, and photos from their meeting show him standing awkwardly off to the side of the group.

The meeting was the first time in a generation that all the living presidents had been in the White House together. Though they all had different political philosophies and very different ap-proaches to the presidency, every one of the former presidents and former first ladies sought out the butlers who had served them when they were in office. Jenny Botero, the White House's head of housekeeping at the time, said fondly, "It was surprising to see how the individual husbands and wives wanted to see staff members who had worked for them in the residence, like butlers James Ramsey and George Hannie." Originally, the event was supposed to be in the Rose Garden, but the weather took a bad turn, so they had to move it to the Oval Office, which dramatically limited the number of staff present. George W. Bush's aide Pete Seat was there and remembered people huddling in areas of the West Wing trying to catch a glimpse of the presidents and watching them walk down the colonnade before they turned into the Oval Office. After Bush spoke, the press was told to leave the room. Suddenly Seat realized that Obama wanted to speak. "We realized this and shoved everyone back into position, got the lights turned back on, and he made his comments. We were all conditioned so well to telling the media the event was over when President Bush said 'Thanks' that we just moved forward and forgot about Obama." After they posed for photographs, Obama, the Bushes, Clinton, and Carter vowed to sign just 250 copies, so that each president would receive fifty copies signed by all five men, making them all the more valuable.

"All the gentlemen here understand both the pressures and possibilities of this office, and for me to have the opportunity to get advice, good counsel and fellowship with these individuals is extraordinary and I'm very grateful to all of them," Obama said. "The tone was set by 43 [George W. Bush]," Seat recalled. "It was very clear how he wanted us to conduct ourselves: however you felt about Jimmy Carter, Bill Clinton, or Barack Obama, you knew that Bush wanted you to treat them with respect." After the photo-op they gathered in the small private dining room off the Oval Office and had lunch together. They talked about what they had done to make the White House feel like a home, their experiences sending their children to school in Washington, D.C., and what it was like having almost one hundred people working on the residence staff catering to their every whim. They also talked about the near-constant presence of the Secret Service.

But the relationship between George W. Bush and Barack Obama was murky, and though the two men respected each other and shared a common sense of decency, their policy differences were stark. Obama had run against the Bush administration's Iraq War; his opposition to the 2003 invasion was key to his 2008 primary defeat of Hillary Clinton, who had voted in the Senate to give Bush the authority to go to war with Iraq. Obama blamed Bush for the economic crisis that he would have to deal with: "When Bill Clinton left office, we had a record surplus. We hadn't had a surplus since World War II. And suddenly by the time I took office, we had a $1.3 trillion deficit," Obama said in 2010, sounding as though he were still campaigning. But he also praised Bush for the PEPFAR program, which had invested billions of dollars into HIV/AIDS treatment and prevention, and for his recognition that the immigration system needed fixing. In a 2010 *Today* show interview, Obama said with a laugh, "I think that, having sat in the Oval Office as president, I am much more sympathetic to all presidents."

According to Ben Rhodes, a foreign policy adviser to Obama, Obama invited a group of historians to the White House, including Doris Kearns Goodwin, David McCullough, and Douglas Brinkley, to help give him perspective on the presidency. "It's interesting: They made the point that the most important thing a president can do on foreign policy is avoid a costly error," Obama said. He listed the presidents who'd had their legacies defined by such mistakes: Johnson in Vietnam, Carter with the failed rescue attempt during the Iran hostage crisis, and Bush in Iraq. The takeaway, Obama thought, was "Don't do stupid shit." It was hardly a perspective that Bush or his aides found flattering.

But their relationship is complex. Bush and Obama had little choice but to work together. The months between Obama's election and his inauguration were marked by the chaotic financial crisis, which became all-consuming for Obama and his aides. It was the first presidential transition to take place after 9/11, and there was a genuine imperative for the two men to work together in the interest of the safety and security of the country. During the 2008 campaign, Bush's director of national intelligence, John Michael McConnell, had arranged for Obama and his Republican rival, Senator John McCain, to get a report with the thirteen most important national security issues at hand. Once, during the last two months of the 2008 campaign, Obama and McCain found themselves sitting at the same table in the Roosevelt Room, with Bush sitting between them, as they discussed the $700 billion authorization by Congress to save the sickeningly sinking market. One top intelligence aide told *New York Times* reporter David E. Sanger, in the summer of 2008, "Bush wrote a lot of checks that the next president is going to have to cash."

Even while recognizing that the financial crisis was worse than they had first thought, there was a mutual respect and a level of trust between Bush and Obama that was apparent at the May 2012 unveiling of George W. and Laura Bush's official portraits at the White House. "President Bush understood that rescuing our economy was not just a Democratic or a Republican issue, it was an American priority. I'll always be grateful for that," Obama said. In a 2013 weekly radio address, Obama praised a speech Bush had given on immigration reform, in support of a bipartisan comprehensive bill. "If Democrats and Republicans, including President Bush and I, can agree on something, that's a pretty good place to start." At the 2013 opening of the George W. Bush library, in Dallas, Obama left out any mention of the Iraq War and instead cited Bush's "compassion" and "resolve" and praised him for his leadership after 9/11.

"No one can be completely ready for this office. But America needs leaders who are willing to face the storm head-on, even as they pray for God's strength and wisdom so that they can do what they believe is right," Obama said, flanked by every living former president: Carter, the two Bushes, and Clinton. "And that's what the leaders with whom I share this stage have all done. That's what President George W. Bush chose to do. That's why I'm honored to be part of today's celebration." An Obama aide watching the scene that day described it as a "searing, interesting moment," because it was the only time all of them had been together since the 2009 inauguration. To see them in such close proximity—there was a clear sense of genuine warmth, familiarity, and levity. In a 2016 interview before leaving office, Obama said, "There hasn't been a radical change between what I did and what George Bush did and what Bill Clinton did and what the first George Bush did" on domestic policy. And at their core both men are decent human beings who respect the people who work in the White House. Peggy Suntum was a White House stenographer for more than three decades; her job was to transcribe every word the president said. Before she passed away in August 2019 she got calls from both George W. Bush and Barack Obama seeking to boost her spirits.

George W. Bush cares about making it clear that some issues are not partisan at all. On March 7, 2015, he and his wife, Laura, were among the only prominent Republicans to show up at the fiftieth anniversary of the Selma march. The event marked the anniversary of "Bloody Sunday," when peaceful protesters march- ing for voting rights for African Americans were teargassed and beaten as they walked across the Edmund Pettus Bridge, in Selma, Alabama, on their way to Montgomery. Bush listened in rapt at- tention as Obama spoke.

RULE NO. 7:
TREASURE "THE MOST PERFECT HOUSE
IN THE UNITED STATES"

You cannot walk in those old rooms without feeling or hearing the footsteps of those who have gone before you.

—Richard Nixon

When Jacqueline Kennedy embarked on her famous restoration of the White House, which had very few historical pieces of furniture on display when she moved in in 1961, she said she wanted to make it "the most perfect house in the United States." And she was successful. All the presidents and first ladies I've spoken with, including the Bushes and the Carters, say that living in the White House was an honor, not only because of its physical beauty but because of its unmatched place in American history.

But it was reported that Donald Trump called the White House "a real dump" the summer after he moved in, around the time Melania and their son, Barron, moved to Washington, five months after the inauguration. Bob Scanlan, a White House florist who worked at the mansion from 1998 to 2010, told me that he had to catch his breath when he read the story. "It's hurtful," he sighed. Another called it "a terrible slap in the face!" The one hundred or so men and women who work as butlers, maids, chefs, florists, and plumbers in the White House serve the institution of the presidency, and not just the president himself. This tradition is a wonderful and rare aspect of our democracy that many people are completely unaware of. Residence staffers have always been private, since discretion is part of their job description, but they are especially worried about talking to reporters now, because, as several of them told me, they feel "like everyone is being watched."

Former first daughter Chelsea Clinton took to Twitter after the story broke, saying, "Thank you to all the White House ushers, butlers, maids, chefs, florists, gardeners, plumbers, engineers & curators for all you do every day." The White House is no dump. It has six floors, with two small mezzanine levels; the entire complex is an astounding 200,000 or so square feet, sitting on eighteen acres in downtown Washington. Its grounds are cared for by the National Park Service. The 55,000-square-foot executive mansion is the main building, divided into public and private rooms, with its Ground Floor and State Floor (also known as the first floor) open to the public for guided tours. The family's private lives are lived on the second and third floors, which tourists never visit. One main corridor links the sixteen rooms and six bathrooms on the second floor. Another twenty rooms and nine bathrooms are joined by a main corridor on the third floor. Maids, valets, and presidential children all have had rooms there.

The signs of age in the home are important to our history, such as the worn marble steps on the Grand Staircase from the Ground Floor to the State Floor, used by presidents and leaders from around the world. "There is no way that the supervisors of all the different departments that keep the house running would cause a problem or issue to sit there without taking care of it," Scanlan said. "Between housekeeping, the painters . . ." Maybe, he reasoned, Trump said what he said because he had not yet decorated the second floor of the residence completely. It can take years to complete the effort, especially since the first family mostly bring in their own furniture instead of pulling from the White House collection. The Obamas' private bedroom was almost completely personal property.

Even Nancy Reagan, who was famously hard to please, compared living in the White House to life in a five-star hotel. (The guest rooms do not have numbers on their doors, but they are known among the residence staff by their room numbers, just like at a hotel.) Trump may have been referring to some parts of the West Wing that need updating. No president wants to vacate the Oval Office during his presidency, so having it renovated is almost impossible. The last major overhaul of the White House took place between 1948 and 1952, during Harry Truman's presidency. The Trumans relocated to Blair House, the president's guest house across Pennsylvania Avenue, for those four years. In his 2006 book *The Audacity of Hope*, Barack Obama described being less than impressed when he first visited the White House as a senator. "The inside of the White House doesn't have the luminous quality that you might expect from TV or film; it seems well kept but worn, a big old house that one imagines might be a bit drafty on cold winter nights."

But Obama understood the incredible history that comes with the home. "Still, as I stood in the foyer and let my eyes wander down the corridors, it was impossible to forget the history that had been made there—John and Bobby Kennedy huddling over the Cuban missile crisis; FDR making last-minute changes to a radio address; Lincoln alone, pacing the halls and shouldering the weight of a nation." One cannot sit in the Oval Office and not feel the magnitude of problems that must be addressed by every president. Obama has called the presidency a "humbling job" and one where "you know that there are going to be times where you wish you could roll back the clock."

RULE NO. 8:

GIVE BACK

With each decision throughout life we shape our own character and destiny by making the basic choice: "This is the kind of person I want to be."

—Jimmy Carter

On October 21, 2017, the five living former presidents came together to raise money for relief efforts after Hurricanes Harvey,

Irma, and Maria—among the most expensive hurricanes in history—for a concert they called "Deep from the Heart: The One America Appeal." Tens of millions of dollars were raised in the charity drive. An event had already been planned that fall marking the twentieth anniversary of the opening of President George H. W. Bush's Presidential Library and Museum, at Texas A&M University, and library friends and donors were already invited. When the catastrophic hurricanes hit Texas, Louisiana, Florida, the Virgin Islands, and Puerto Rico, the celebration turned into a fund-raiser. George H. W. Bush's chief of staff, Jean Becker, got on the phone with George W. Bush's chief of staff, and they got Carter's, Obama's, and Clinton's top aides on the phone with a request that they do a video. The Presidents Club was being mobilized. The hurricane had struck the Bushes' home state, and they wanted to do something to help. Once all the former presidents were on board, they moved the venue from "[Texas country musician] Larry Gatlin in a tent with BBQ" to "Reed Arena with Lady Gaga." (Lady Gaga's mother had called Obama's office to say that her daughter wanted to be a part of it.) The five former presidents playfully interacted onstage and on Twitter. George H. W. Bush tweeted, "Not sure abt 39, @BillClinton, 43 and @BarackObama, but I would have sung w @ladygaga if asked. Thanks to all for supporting @AmericaAppeal." Obama retweeted and added, "I'll let you and @ladygaga handle the singing, and we'll handle the donations."

At the concert, which raised $41 million from more than 110,000 donors, Becker was put in charge of making sure that the former presidents got onstage in time for the televised event. "Jean, we need to go lights down and curtain up now," Bush aide Jim McGrath told her. Of course, Clinton, who is famously bad with time, was late. Becker found Clinton and said, "Mr. President, you need to get onstage. Now." George W. Bush's vice president,

Dick Cheney, was there and remembered that the Bushes wanted to get a photo with Clinton and all their grandchildren before a private dinner with the former presidents. Bill Clinton was the last one to show up, Cheney recalled gruffly. "He was twenty minutes late and we couldn't eat before he got there."

RULE NO. 9:
FAMILY COMES FIRST

Nothing can ever be written that will drive a wedge between us—nothing at all.

—George H. W. Bush, in a 1998 letter to his sons George W. and Jeb

Having children has provided common ground for all the living former presidents. In his memoir, *My Life,* Bill Clinton recalled visiting the Bushes at their six-acre oceanfront estate in Kennebunkport, Maine, in the summer of 1983, when George H. W. Bush was Ronald Reagan's vice president. Clinton was governor of Arkansas at the time, and he brought Hillary and their three-year-old daughter, Chelsea, to the barbecue. Chelsea, Clinton wrote, "marched up to the vice president and said she needed to go to the bathroom. He took her by the hand and led her there. Chelsea appreciated it, and Hillary and I were impressed by George Bush's kindness. It wouldn't be the last time." At a dinner when Bush was president and Clinton was governor, Hillary Clinton sat next to the president. Bill Clinton recalled the two of them getting into a heated discussion about America's infant mortality rate. Bush was shocked when she said eighteen countries do better than the United States in helping babies survive until they're two years old. The indefatigable Hillary was relentless. "When she offered to get him the evidence, he said he would find it himself," Clinton recalled. "He did, and the next day he gave me a note for Hillary saying she was right. It was a gracious gesture that reminded me of the day in Kennebunkport six years earlier when he had personally escorted three-year-old Chelsea to the bathroom."

The shared experience of raising children strengthened the bonds between the former presidents. Clinton's grandchildren call him "Pop-Pop," and George W. Bush is known to his grandchildren as "Jefe," which is Spanish for "boss." At a 2017 summit, Bush and Clinton, two of the fourteen presidents in American history who have served two consecutive terms, were asked what their greatest accomplishment was over their respective eight years in office. Bush said his was that both of his daughters love him. When asked if it was intimidating for young men to meet him, Bush joked, "Well, I certainly hope so." Clinton recalled a remarkably relatable problem he had with one of Chelsea's boyfriends. "She had one boyfriend in high school [whom] I really liked, but he wouldn't take his baseball cap off inside. Finally, he sat down at dinner one night and I said, 'I really like you, you know that, don't you?' And he said, 'Yes sir, I do.' 'You can't wear that cap at dinner. I'm an old-fashioned guy. Take that cap off.'"

At a campaign rally in Portsmouth, New Hampshire, when he was running for reelection in 2012, Obama said, to laughter, "Malia and Sasha love New Hampshire not only because this is where they go to camp, but it's also where they first campaigned with us. And I think the first day of campaigning, they got ice cream four times in a row. So they turned to Michelle and me, and they said, we love this campaigning thing."

Partisan politics has nothing to do with parenting or with being a kid in the glare of incredibly famous parents. Chelsea Clinton has repeatedly come to Barron Trump's defense. Barron was only ten years old when his father took office, and Clinton has again and again supported him. When a reporter suggested that Barron should dress less casually, she tweeted, "It's high time the media

& everyone leave Barron Trump alone & let him have the private childhood he deserves." "Barron Trump deserves the chance every child does—to be a kid. Standing up for every kid also means opposing @POTUS policies that hurt kids," Chelsea wrote after Trump was sworn in. Chelsea knows better than anyone what it is like to grow up in the spotlight as the child of incredibly famous and highly controversial parents.

Before the Senate voted to acquit her husband on charges of perjury and obstruction of justice in the case involving his relationship with White House intern Monica Lewinsky in February 1999, Hillary Clinton was upset to learn that *People* magazine was planning to run a cover story on Chelsea. She pleaded with them not to publish it, no matter how kind it was. Bill Clinton lamented, "We hate to have her so exposed." But Chelsea would always be overexposed because of her parents. The cover story ran. When she was born, her father was the governor of Arkansas. Years later, in 2012, Chelsea gave a rare interview to *Time* magazine. "I don't remember a time in my life where people haven't recognized me or come over and talked to me about something they've loved that my parents have done or something that they've hated that my parents have done," she said. Sometimes people approach her in New York when she is grocery shopping and thank her for her parents' work. And sometimes they are "vitriolic," she said, confronting her with questions like "What would have happened if your parents had aborted you?" It can feel like a high price for presidential children to pay, and presidents have been unified by their shared desire to protect their children. Because they agreed with Jackie Kennedy, who famously said, "If you bungle raising your children, I don't think whatever else you do well matters very much."

III

UNEXPECTED FRIENDSHIPS

His friendship has been one of the great gifts of my life.
—Bill Clinton on George H. W. Bush

There was a time, not long ago, when a candidate running for president referred to his or her challenger as a "distinguished opponent." No matter how bitter or close the election, there was always room for reconciliation and genuine personal friendships to develop. Candidates understood that, despite petty differences and opposing political philosophies, leading the country is about something much bigger than individual success and that so much good could be done if they could look past their differences and work together.

In 2004, both Presidents Bush attended the opening of Bill Clinton's library in Arkansas—this was just a couple weeks after Clinton had campaigned against the younger Bush on behalf of his Democratic rival, John Kerry, and a month before Clinton and George H. W. Bush began their work together in the aftermath of the tsunami in Asia. The Bushes and Jimmy Carter came together to celebrate Clinton for his accomplishments and to welcome him into the Presidents Club. "[After you leave the White House] one of the great blessings is the way one-time political adversaries have the tendency to become friends, and I feel such is certainly the case between President Clinton and me," George H. W. Bush said. "There's an inescapable bond that binds together all who have lived in the White House. Though we hail from different backgrounds and ideologies, we're singularly unique, even eternally bound, by our common devotion and service to this wonderful country. And that certainly goes for the 42nd president of the United States."

George W. Bush was president at the time, and he walked onto the outdoor stage near the two-story glass-and-steel library, next to the Arkansas River, to tens of thousands of cheering people. He said of his father's onetime rival, "Visitors to this place will be reminded of the great promise of our country and the dreams that came true in the life of our 42nd president." Undeterred by the pouring rain, he added, "The William J. Clinton Presidential Library is a gift to the future by a man who always believed in the future, and today we thank him for loving and serving America."

Former presidents end up feeling a sense of empathy for one another, and they privately rally around one another in times of need, regardless of political party. When a newly elected president seeks the advice of a former president, it is not unlike a new hire in any profession talking to a veteran of the job. It is about asking questions as much as it is about showing respect. It is a kind of sacred visit and a key part of the to-do list of any member of the club, and it is something Donald Trump has deemed a waste of time. The newly elected Bill Clinton, then forty-six, made a pilgrimage to pay his respects to Ronald Reagan, who was eighty-one, at his Century City office in southern California shortly after his election. In the thirty-fourth-floor office, with soaring views of both the Pacific Ocean and Beverly Hills, the two men, despite being separated by decades in age, and by just as big a gap in personal politics, spent more than an hour together.

Reagan, the Great Communicator, had plenty of sage advice. He told Clinton to get out of Washington as often as possible and to take advantage of Camp David, where presidents can go to get fresh air and have a semblance of privacy. He also told Clinton that he should work on his salute. It was Reagan who had begun the tradition of presidents saluting the men and women who stand at the bottoms of the stairways exiting Marine One and Air Force One. Before Reagan, uniformed personnel had to salute presidents, but presidents rarely saluted them back. Reagan had been an Army cavalry officer, and he thought returning the salute was the only appropriate thing for a sitting president to do. He noticed that Clinton, who had never served in the military and who had spent time during the campaign defending his draft evasion, did not know how to do it properly. So Reagan gave him an impromptu lesson: move the hand slowly up to the temple and flick it down fast. At the end of their meeting, after Clinton had perfected his salute, Reagan gave him a jar of the signature red, white, and blue jelly beans he kept in his White House office his entire two terms.

Barack Obama has publicly praised George H. W. Bush and Bill Clinton for decisions they made to raise taxes and balance the budget. At the dedication ceremony for George W. Bush's presidential library, Obama said, "America needs leaders who are willing to face the storm head-on, even as they pray for God's strength and wisdom so that they can do what they believe is right. And that's what the leaders with whom I share this stage have all done. That's what President George W. Bush chose to do. That's why I'm honored to be part of today's celebration."

At another event a day earlier, Obama said, "President Bush loves this country and loves its people and shared that same concern and was concerned about all people in America, not just some, not just those who voted Republican. I think that's true about him, and I think that's true about most of us."

GERALD FORD AND JIMMY CARTER:
"I WAS GRIEVED, BUT HONORED TO FULFILL
MY PROMISE"

Gerald Ford and Jimmy Carter became friends only after they were both former presidents. The 1976 election was close, and when Gerald Ford finally went to bed at 2 a.m., he still had not conceded. A few hours later, however, it was clear that he had been defeated by Carter, the former governor of Georgia, who ran as a Washington outsider. Ford had been president for only two years, and he was devastated. He was so exhausted and emotional that when it came time to concede, he had lost his voice. Ford's wife, Betty, read his concession speech to the press, surrounded by their four children. Afterward, Ford and his chief of staff, Dick Cheney, walked into the Oval Office and called Carter. All Ford could muster was a whispered introduction of the two men, and then Cheney read Ford's concession statement to Carter. "That was the low point of my political career," Cheney told me.

When Carter was elected, in 1976, Ford and Nixon were the only two living former presidents, and Carter assigned a member of his staff—in keeping with his outside-the-Beltway reputation, it was his cousin Hugh—to be their point of contact. Carter's national security adviser, Zbigniew Brzezinski, and other top aides briefed Ford and Nixon so regularly that Nixon eventually asked that the updates be scaled back. Ronald Reagan, Carter said, did not return the courtesy when he was president. "After I left the White House I rarely had any such briefings, except under George H. W. Bush," Carter lamented. "When I told Reagan that I planned to inform the media that neither he nor his staff had kept their obligation to brief me, he sent his national security adviser to Plains, but the briefing was pointless. All he gave me were a few items of information that had already been published in the news media."

Carter's relationship with his immediate predecessor was not much better. He said at the beginning of his term that he and Ford were like "oil and water." Ford was equally blunt about his feelings. During the campaign, he said, Carter seemed "cold and arrogant, even egotistical." The warmest words he could muster for Carter were apathetic ones; after the campaign he said, "I do not remember ever saying anything bad about Jimmy Carter, and I do not remember Jimmy Carter ever saying anything bad about me." In October 1981, President Reagan asked Nixon, Ford, and Carter to represent him at the funeral of Egyptian president Anwar Sadat in Cairo. Sadat had been gunned down while reviewing a military parade. The Secret Service told Reagan, who, just sixty-nine days into his presidency, had himself been shot and almost died, that it was too dangerous for him or his vice president, George H. W. Bush, to attend the funeral. Secretary of State Alexander Haig came up with the idea of sending the former presidents in their place. He cleverly referred to it as "the presidential hat trick."

Ford had survived two assassination attempts, and his family was concerned for his safety, but he felt obligated to go. The scene at Andrews Air Force Base was dramatic. Two days after Sadat's murder, three Air Force jets landed there, each one carrying a former president. When the three men, each of whom had once been the most powerful person in the world, walked to the helicopter that would bring them to the White House to meet with Reagan before the trip, they encountered a vexing question: Which former president should board the helicopter first? Nixon said the man to most recently hold the presidency should be the first to walk up the steps, so Carter was the first on board. But they barely spoke on the helicopter ride to the South Lawn of the White House. "Look," Ford said, breaking the ice, "for the trip, at least, why don't we make it just Dick, Jimmy, and Jerry?" No one objected.

Rosalynn Carter, who had been a remarkably active first lady, accompanied her husband because she had developed a close friendship with Sadat and his wife, Jehan, while they were working on the Camp David peace treaty. Hundreds of staffers gathered on the South Lawn and watched as the former presidents and the former first lady stepped off the helicopter and walked across the sweeping White House grounds to meet with the Reagans. What no one could see was the look on Barbara Bush's face as she peered through heavy silk drapes from a window in the White House, taking in the scene on the lawn with a wry smile. "It all rather amused me," she said. "I don't really think they liked each other very much." The visit was brief. At the White House, Reagan posed for photos with his three predecessors and declared, chummy as always, "Ordinarily, I would wish you happy landings, but seeing as you're all navy men, I wish you bon voyage."

Once on board, they were clearly made to feel like *ex*-presidents. Alexander Haig relegated them to staffers' seats as he took up the entire forward cabin on the plane, which was called Special Air Mission 26000 and served as a backup for Air Force One. Carter said Haig treated them "like children." It was a remarkable sight as the former presidents settled in next to one another as though they were sitting in a restaurant booth: Nixon, in a cardigan sweater, and Ford, in shirtsleeves, sat across from Henry Kissinger, who had been secretary of state in both of their administrations. Reagan's secretary of defense, Caspar

Weinberger, sat next to Kissinger. The Carters sat across the aisle facing the Egyptian ambassador to the United States, Ashraf Ghorbal, and his wife. The star power—and brainpower—on board were formidable.

At first the trip was awkward for the former presidents. Ford had lost in 1976 in part because of his pardon of Nixon, who had never offered a full apology for Watergate, even after accepting the pardon. And Carter had won the election in 1976 by campaigning against Ford's policies and Nixon's legacy. Nixon was mostly quiet on the plane. After the funeral, he stayed behind in the Middle East and did not fly back to the United States with Carter and Ford.

Those two men, once rivals, chatted on the flight to Egypt, commiserating about the stress of raising money for their presidential libraries. But it was on the eighteen-hour flight home that the once-bitter adversaries became friends. They had seemingly nothing in common—Ford was a staunch midwestern Republican who had spent decades in Congress, and Carter was a southern Democrat who had been a governor and had never served in Congress. But aside from when the flight attendants came in to serve them meals and snacks and when they got the occasional call from Haig checking in on them, they spoke almost nonstop the entire flight home. Any bad blood from the 1976 election faded away as they began to relate to each other on a very human level. They had more in common than they thought: both could understand the devastation of losing a presidential election and forever being one-term presidents. Ford confided that he needed to work hard on the lecture circuit and on corporate boards to earn money for his family. He had never accumulated a fortune, he explained, during his many years as a Republican congressman from Michigan and during his brief time as vice president and president. Carter, unlike the wealthy Bush and Reagan, also needed to keep on earning money.

They consoled each other and talked about how they could help each other. Ford agreed to co-chair initiatives at the Carter Center, and Carter agreed to participate in a conference at the Ford Library. In 1989, Ford even went with Carter to monitor elections in Panama. They teamed up on important policy issues, too. In 1994, Carter and Ford joined forces with an unlikely ally, Ronald Reagan, in a plea to Congress to pass Bill Clinton's assault weapons ban. "This is a matter of vital importance to the public safety," the bipartisan trio wrote in a letter to the House of Representatives. Reagan, who had loosened gun restrictions as president, changed at least two members' votes, and the ban narrowly passed.

Four years later, Carter and Ford argued for Bill Clinton, another member of the Presidents Club, to be censured instead of impeached during the Monica Lewinsky scandal. Clinton had sought Ford's advice early on. "Bill, you have to be straightforward on this crisis," Ford told him. "You'd better be honest because it's not going to go away." The two former presidents wanted to avoid a Senate trial, because they worried that it would tear the nation apart. They teamed up for an op-ed in the *New York Times* titled "A Time to Heal Our Nation." In it, they referred to Ford's pardon of Nixon after Watergate and Carter's decision to grant amnesty to men who had avoided the draft in Vietnam: the ability and desire to forgive bound them. The bipartisan resolution they sought, however, would require Clinton to acknowledge that "he did not tell the truth under oath." He refused to do it. Clinton called Ford a few days after reading the op-ed and said he still believed he had not lied under oath and that Congress could not grant him immunity even if he did admit to lying. Ford was disappointed in Clinton. "History will be the judge of President Clinton," he said years later. "And you can't spin history." He and his wife, Betty, who was addicted to pain medication and alcohol while in the White House and whose Betty Ford Center treats addiction, agreed that Clinton had a problem. "Betty and I have talked about this a lot," Ford told his biographer Thomas DeFrank in 1998. "He's sick—he's got an addiction. He needs treatment." Betty added, "There's treatment for that kind of addiction. . . . But he won't do it, because he's in denial." Hillary Clinton agreed with the Fords. In a 1999 interview published in *Talk* magazine, she did not object when the reporter called her husband's cheating "an addiction." "That's your word," she said. "I would say 'weakness.' Whatever it is, it is only part of a complex whole."

Carter and Ford seemed just as surprised by their friendship as everyone else. In November 2000, the two men attended the two hundredth anniversary of the White House. "Certainly few observers in January 1977 would have predicted that Jimmy and I would become the closest of friends," Ford told historians and family members gathered at the elegant dinner. "Yet we have, bonded by our years in this office, and in this house." Carter said, "I challenge any historian here tonight to find any former presidents who, after leaving the White House, have formed a closer and more intimate relationship than Gerald Ford and I. I am grateful for that."

They grew so close, Carter said, that when they went to events together they rode in the same car, and "we kind of hate to get there," because they enjoyed talking so much. They talked regularly on the phone, and in 2006, shortly before he passed away, Ford called Carter and said he had an important favor to ask his friend and fellow president: "Would you deliver the eulogy at my funeral?" Carter's answer, of course, was yes, but only if he would do the same at his funeral. "A few months later," Carter said, "I was grieved but honored to fulfill my promise." Carter blushed at the memory and called their friendship "intimate and pure."

At Ford's 2007 funeral, in Grand Rapids, Michigan, Carter had to collect himself because he was near tears during his eulogy. Ford had put it in his funeral plans that his former chief of staff Dick Cheney would accompany his body to his museum in Grand Rapids. He arranged for the Carters and Cheney to have to kill a lot of time together in Grand Rapids, recalled Cheney, who always believed that Ford had done that on purpose. "I'm convinced the president knew exactly what he was doing when he sent me up to see Jimmy Carter," he said, laughing. Cheney and Carter have very little in common, except for a shared love of fly-fishing—and Gerald Ford. But Ford wanted the two of them, a staunch Democrat and a dyed-in-the-wool Republican, to talk, and maybe then they would better understand each other. Who knows, Ford must have thought, they might even become friends.

RICHARD NIXON AND BILL CLINTON:
EMPATHY AND FORGIVENESS

Like most presidents, Richard Nixon was addicted to the power of the office. Unlike every other president, though, that addiction, fueled by paranoia, led to his resignation. He particularly wanted to have a connection to his successors because of his humiliating departure just ahead of impeachment in 1974. By speaking with them and sharing his perspective, he could make himself feel more relevant—and, of course, he genuinely believed he had valuable advice to share. In the days after leaving Washington, Nixon, the one and only president ever to resign, sank into a deep depression. "One after another," he said, "the blows rained down." He lived in self-imposed exile at his twenty-nine-acre, Spanish-style estate known as La Casa Pacifica, in San Clemente, California, with breathtaking views of the Pacific Ocean. The gorgeous estate had once been referred to as the Western White House, but to

Nixon it felt like a prison. The stain of Watergate would never be erased. When his former vice president and successor, Gerald Ford, granted him an unconditional pardon shortly after taking office, Ford's approval ratings plummeted, falling from 71 percent to 49 percent. But Nixon was determined to rehabilitate his image, and he kept a rigid schedule, complete with briefings from his aides on things as mundane as the season's football schedule. In exile, he rose at 6 a.m. and dressed in full suits to go to work in his private office, stubbornly clinging to a sense of routine. Nixon felt unending guilt for what he had put his wife, Pat, through. Pat spent most of her days obsessively tending to her garden at La Casa Pacifica and taking on the hardest jobs, including climbing up on the roof to remove palm fronds—anything to avoid reporters and the gaze of the public.

In order to rehabilitate his image and to make use of his restless energy, Nixon wanted to become a sounding board and adviser to presidents. In 1992, George H. W. Bush sent his commerce secretary, Barbara Franklin, to China to restart the economic relationship that had been almost destroyed by the tragedy at Tiananmen Square in 1989. Not long after the *New York Times* ran a front-page story about the trip, Nixon called Franklin, who had worked in his administration. He had famously normalized relations with China, and he had some advice for her: "Don't slobber all over them," he told her. Decades later Franklin mused, "My interpretation of what he meant: Being overly effusive at this moment will not play well back home." She took his advice, and the trip was considered a success.

Nixon privately called Bush's successor, Bill Clinton, "a phony and a fraud." "If he is elected," Nixon told an aide, "I'll know this country has finally gone to hell." But after Clinton's election, Nixon desperately wanted to be of use to him. He thought that by becoming an informal adviser he could become relevant again. He had been deeply disappointed that he did not get to be of more use to Ronald Reagan and George H. W. Bush, the China trip being an exception, and he was determined for that to change. And Nixon was not above using threats to secure a meeting. He told then–Clinton adviser Dick Morris that Clinton could "buy a one-year moratorium" on criticism of his administration if Clinton would meet with him to discuss foreign policy. In 1993, two months after being sworn in, Clinton called him. A White House operator placed the call to Nixon and asked him to stand by for the president, who kept him waiting for more than ten minutes. "I'll wait," Nixon said. "He's a helluva lot busier than I am." After they talked for more than half an hour, Clinton invited Nixon to visit him in the White House a week later. Clinton wanted to know logistical things, including the best ways to organize the day. Nixon, who outlined his thoughts on Russia and Somalia, said it was "probably the best [visit] I've had to Washington since I left the presidency."

An unlikely friendship formed between baby boomer Bill Clinton and Richard Nixon, then eighty. Clinton wanted Nixon's advice on global diplomacy, but Nixon knew that the best way to warm up to the Clintons was through their daughter, Chelsea. The relationship was particularly complicated because First Lady Hillary Clinton had worked on the House Judiciary staff in charge of making the case for Nixon's impeachment nearly two decades earlier. When the second-floor elevator opened to the White House residence and Hillary was there to greet him, he was understandably nervous. Some of Clinton's most senior advisers did not want him to invite Nixon. But when Nixon told Hillary that he was a Quaker, a fact she surely knew, and that his daughters, Julie and Tricia, had gone to the Quaker school Sidwell Friends, where

Chelsea was going at the time, she lit up. Nixon made sure to leak the meeting to his friend Bill Safire at the *New York Times*, who promptly wrote about it in a column.

The Nixons moved to New York City in 1980 to be closer to their daughters, after five and a half years in California. Not long after that, they bought a home in Saddle River, in northern New Jersey, where Nixon penned his memoirs and where they spent time with their grandchildren. In 1991, when Pat's health was in decline, they moved to a smaller house with an elevator, in a gated development in nearby Park Ridge. Pat was eighty-one when she died of lung cancer, in 1993. Nixon "exploded," according to an aide, when neither Clinton showed up to her funeral. Ronald and Nancy Reagan and Gerald and Betty Ford were there. Nixon's youngest brother, Ed, remembered how difficult her funeral was. She had stood by her husband's side during his darkest days. "I had never seen Dick so torn up, he was really out of it," Ed remembered. "After the ceremony out on the lawn he came inside and spoke to those who were still there—he got front and center like a cheerleader saying, 'We have to go on now. We'll never forget this lady and what she meant to all of us.'" That the Clintons had not attended felt like a slap in the face.

Life inside the Clinton White House was chaotic. As the Whitewater investigation and the death of her close friend and White House lawyer Vince Foster consumed her husband's administration, Hillary held a press conference in the State Dining Room and took questions from dozens of reporters. It was the first time a first lady had ever done a full press conference, and networks interrupted their afternoon programming to air it live. It happened to coincide with Nixon's hospitalization after he suffered a stroke at eighty-one. The press conference went on and on; the thirty-fourth reporter Hillary called on asked a striking question of the first lady. "Considering what you've been through, do you have any greater appreciation of what Richard Nixon might have been going through?" Hillary gave a surprisingly emotional response, given her work to impeach Nixon. "From my perspective," she said as her eyes began to fill with tears, "you know, it was a year ago April that my father died at the age of 81, and so, you know, I'm just mostly thinking about his daughters right now." Nixon died a few hours later, at 9:08 p.m. In a Rose Garden statement that night, President Clinton answered the question the reporter had asked his wife. He said that, yes, he could empathize with Nixon more now, after sitting in the Oval Office. "It's impossible to be in this job without feeling a special bond with the people who have gone before," he said.

Clinton's critics were comparing Whitewater to Watergate, and when he met with his staff in the Oval Office to go over remarks he was to make later that week at Nixon's funeral, one line in particular worried his aides. It read, "The day of judging Richard Nixon based on one part of his life alone has finally come to a close." It was a not-so-veiled statement about how Clinton wanted his own legacy to be viewed beyond the scandals that were engulfing his White House. "We just can't say that," said Clinton's adviser George Stephanopoulos.

The Clintons both attended Nixon's funeral, held at his library and birthplace, in California, on April 27, 1994. Clinton agreed to tweak the sentence in dispute by making it Clinton's wish, not a statement of fact. "May the day of judging President Nixon on anything less than his entire life and career come to a close," he said.

GEORGE H. W. BUSH AND BILL CLINTON:
"THE A-TEAM"

George W. Bush called the relationship between his dad and Bill Clinton "one of the most unique" friendships in U.S. political history. And that is not hyperbole. "Bill Clinton was a person who refused to lord his victory over Dad. In other words, he was humble in victory, which is very important in dealing with other people," Bush said. "And I think Dad was willing to rise above the political contest . . . it starts with the individual's character." Bush joked that Clinton "hangs out in Maine [where the Bush family compound is located] more than I do." Longtime Bush aide and family friend Chase Untermeyer explained the relationship to me in less glowing terms: Bush 41 and Barbara, he said, "have always loved celebrities—and Bill Clinton was a celebrity."

There has always been intense partisanship in politics, but before Donald Trump, there was also a chance for real connection and empathy. Bush and Clinton, though, first had to move past the 1992 campaign, which made Bush a one-term president and ended a twelve-year Republican hold on the presidency. These are political creatures with strong convictions, and even the best of them are competitive and jealous. During the campaign, Bush said that, if elected, Clinton would use "Elvis economics" and America would end up back at the "Heartbreak Hotel." He used his stature as a World War II veteran to ridicule Clinton's opposition to Vietnam. "While I bit the bullet, he bit his nails," Bush said on the trail. He even joked that his dog Millie knew more about foreign policy "than those two bozos," referring to Clinton and his running mate, Al Gore. Clinton said that Bush had given himself "over to the right-wing extremists" in the Republican Party and that he had no vision for the country. Bush was humiliated after his defeat, and both he and Barbara Bush were personally insulted that the country had chosen a man they considered immoral. A year after the Clintons moved into the White House and scandal continued to swirl around them, Bush, who had known Clinton's chief of staff, Mack McLarty, for years, generously warned him: *Be careful about Whitewater.*

Untermeyer and his wife went to the Bush family compound in Kennebunkport in June 1993, a few months after the Bushes left Washington, while Bush was "still in the dumps" after having lost to Clinton. But Clinton knew he needed Bush's support. When Israeli prime minister Yitzhak Rabin and Palestinian leader Yasser Arafat came to meet for the first time at the White House in 1993, McLarty called Bush and invited him to be part of the historic event. It would mean returning to the White House less than a year after they were forced out of it. The Clintons invited the Bushes to stay overnight, but the former president declined. He said that his wife, Barbara, would not want to go back. Finally, McLarty called Bush's best friend, former secretary of state James Baker III, who convinced Bush to accept the invitation. McLarty said he would have the plane ready for him. Bush replied, with an edge to his voice, "Just a tiny little plane for me."

The two families seemed to always be on a collision course as they both vied for the highest office in the land, which makes their friendship all the more remarkable. The Bushes and the Clintons clashed forcefully in 1992 and then again in 2000, when George W. Bush ran against Clinton's vice president, Al Gore. In his campaign, W. brought up Clinton often, trying to seize on a message of morality that would stand in stark contrast to Clinton. "There is no question the president embarrassed the nation," Bush said. "You're either part of an administration, or you're not part of an administration." If Gore had differences with Clinton, he said, "he ought to say loud and clear what they are." Meanwhile, Clinton considered a Gore victory a crucial way to cement his own legacy.

The elder Bushes were particularly upset by the Monica Lewinsky story. But George H. W. Bush was much more reticent than his son about criticizing Clinton. In a 1998 interview on NBC's *Today* show, Bush would not answer questions about Lewinsky, insisting that Clinton had "enough critics out there now." Eventually he said that he thought the presidency had been "diminished" by the scandal, but that the office was "bigger than any one person." Privately, he was aghast. In 1999, he wrote to his friend Hugh Sidey, a longtime reporter at *Time*. He said how surprised he was that on a recent visit to meet with French president Jacques Chirac, Chirac had not shared his outrage about Lewinsky. Americans, Chirac said, were overreacting. "Oddly," Bush wrote, "no one I talked to in France focused in on 'lack of respect for the office' [to] say nothing of lying under oath or obstruction of justice." At a November 9, 2000, dinner hosted by the Clintons in honor of the two hundredth anniversary of the White House, the Bushes flew to Washington as the disputed election between their son and Al Gore was unfolding. After Bill Clinton quoted John Adams's prayer, "May none but honest and wise men ever rule under this roof," Barbara Bush, who was incapable of hiding how she felt, rolled her eyes. She was appalled. "What absolute nerve," she wrote in her diary. "He was impeached because he lied to the American public and special prosecutor. I have come to the conclusion that he really does not know right from wrong."

Still, Bush refused to publicly criticize Clinton. On January 27, 1998, as the Lewinsky scandal was becoming public, journalist Bob Woodward sent Bush a letter requesting an interview for his book *Shadow*, about how Watergate had affected the presidencies of the five presidents living at the time. Three weeks later he got a letter from Bush declining the invitation and adding, "I do not want to try to direct history. I am not writing a memoir . . . Barbara's memoir gave our family history and did it well. That's enough for now. Oh there may be a handful of additional interviews, but if they relive ancient history and reopen old wounds I'm sorry but I want no part of it." Journalists, he said, invoking one of his favorite phrases, "are free to do their thing; and I am free to do mine.

Mine is to stay the hell out of Dodge." After several years, the wounds from the 1992 campaign began to heal. At the 2004 dedication of Bill Clinton's presidential library, George H. W. Bush called his onetime rival "one of the most gifted American political figures in modern times. Trust me, I learned this the hard way." He added, to laughter from the crowd, that Clinton "was a natural, and he made it look too easy, and oh, how I hated him for that."

But it took time for their rivalry to give way to genuine friendship. It all started with George W. Bush's idea that his father and Clinton would make a good team. In 2005 he sent them on a trip around the world on a humanitarian mission after the tsunami that devastated the coasts of Indonesia, Sri Lanka, India, and Thailand and killed nearly a quarter million people on the day after Christmas 2004. The devastation was mind-boggling; some waves reached one hundred feet high and wiped out entire villages. Before they set out on their trip to Southeast Asia, Bush called his good friend Alan Simpson, who, as a Republican senator, had worked with President Clinton, and asked him what Clinton was really like. He wanted to know what he was getting into, and Simpson predicted that they would get along just fine. Clinton was also wary of embarking on such a big trip with the man he had defeated. Simpson sang Bush's praises. "Bill," Simpson said, "he's a good egg. This is an amazing guy. You're going to like him."

"I don't know, I don't know him that well," Clinton replied.

"He loves a good story, and so do you," Simpson said, a fact that Clinton appreciated. Clinton was the last president to grow up without a television at home; he was ten years old when his family got one, and he says that is a reason for his loquaciousness. "My family couldn't afford to take vacations, so every meal was a feast of the imagination. You had to learn to entertain yourselves and before you could tell a story you had to learn to listen to one and recount it."

Bush and Clinton did not get along before that trip, according to McLarty. But Simpson was right: though they were separated by decades, backgrounds, and political parties, they became friends once they got to know each other. Clinton aide Justin Cooper said Clinton was happy to accept the offer to work with Bush: "These are people who want to be called upon to serve." Also, Clinton liked to be where the action was. His deference to Bush was heartwarming. On their travels, he would wait at the stairs for Bush as the two disembarked the plane. "It's called manners," Simpson told me wryly. "It doesn't exist anymore. 'Manners' is a word that people think is a house on top of the hill."

On their first international trip, Bush flew from Houston to meet Clinton in Los Angeles, and from there they crossed the Pacific. There was only one stateroom on the plane and only one bed. Clinton, who was twenty-two years younger than the eighty-year-old Bush, insisted that Bush take it. Bush would agree only if he could bring a portable mattress on board for Clinton. They were an unusual pair. Clinton was always running late—when he was president he occasionally left reporters who had traveled with him, and who were eager to return home, waiting on the tarmac at Andrews Air Force Base until 1 or 2 a.m. while he finished a game of hearts. "Clinton standard time" became a commonly understood phrase in Washington during his tenure. Bush, on the other hand, was always on time or early.

During their trip, Clinton was the star of the duo, Bush knew, and he seemed all right with it. Once, at a dinner hosted by Sri Lanka's president, Bush tried to no avail to get Clinton to stop talking to guests so they could leave on time. After Clinton finally finished, he told Bush in the car, "George, you owe me big time for getting us out of there a lot earlier than we expected." Bush sighed and simply thanked him. "You cannot get mad at the guy," he recalled later. Clinton, in turn, admired his friend's vast capacity for empathy. After Bush's death, Clinton wrote an op-ed in the *Washington Post* remembering their journey to the devastated region. "When we met with children who lost their parents in the tsunami, he [Bush] was moved almost to tears when they gave us drawings they'd made to capture their pain and slow recovery in grief counseling."

The work of the two former presidents helped raise an estimated $100 million, and an additional $12 million in donations was sent to them directly so they could determine how to use it. The two became near-constant companions, doing interviews together and even traveling with the president as part of the American delegation when Pope John Paul II passed away in 2005. "Come on," Bush said. "It will be better with you along." Nicknamed "the A-team" in the press, they became like father and son. After Hurricane Katrina hit New Orleans and killed nearly two thousand people, Bush asked his father and Clinton to team up again. They raised more than $136 million for disaster relief in that region. *Time* made them "Partners of the Year" in its 2005 "Person of the Year" issue and put both former presidents on the cover. After seeing how powerful the Clinton/Bush team was, then-president Obama dispatched George W. Bush and Clinton to Haiti to raise awareness and funds after the devastating 2010 earthquake. In the two years following the earthquake, the Clinton Bush Haiti Fund gave $54.4 million to the devastated region.

At the Bushes' home on the Maine coast, Clinton could occasionally be found riding around in the elder Bush's beloved Mercury-powered Fountain speedboat, *Fidelity V*, which Clinton said Bush "drove like a bat out of hell." The experience, Clinton recalled, was not "for the faint of heart." (Bush emailed his grandchildren when he was seventy-nine to tell them he had reached sixty miles per hour on his boat. "I felt about 19 years old," he said.) Barbara Bush took to calling her husband and Clinton the "odd couple."

In March 2011, Carter, Clinton, and George W. Bush went to the Kennedy Center to honor Bush, who was then eighty-six years old. The event raised money for his Points of Light initiative encouraging volunteerism. "I literally came to love this man," Clinton said unabashedly from the podium. Backstage, Laura Bush asked twenty-seven members of the Bush family to gather together and pose for a photograph. "Bill, Bill! Brother from another mother! Get in here!" hollered Neil Bush, one of George and Barbara's sons. Clinton smiled and got in the family portrait. "The family's black sheep," Clinton said. "Every family's got one." Clinton's father had died three months before he was born, and he had a difficult relationship with his alcoholic stepfather. "Maybe I'm the father he never had," Bush said. Clinton joked that Barbara Bush accepted him as an adopted son because she wanted to brag about having a third president in the family.

George H.W. Bush respected Clinton's intellect. "I thought I knew him; but until this trip I did not really know him," Bush wrote to Hugh Sidey after their first foreign trip together. "Bill did have an opinion on everything and asked questions on a lot of things. When the questions were answered he would then opine based on some experience of his own, somewhere, sometime ago," Bush wrote. "In grade school they had a place on our report cards 'Claims more than his fair share of time and attention in the class room.' Bill would have gotten a bad mark there." But Bush appreciated that Clinton could step in and take over any conversation, and he was charmed by him. "I did not mind this a bit. . . . If we got in a bind for things to say or answers to be given to questions it was reassuring to know that 'he was de man!'" When Clinton had a chest operation in 2005, George W. Bush said, he "woke up surrounded by his loved ones: Hillary, Chelsea . . . and my dad."

"President Clinton beat me like a drum back in 1992 and then we became friends," Bush said in a 2009 speech, adding that many of his friends still did not understand how they could be in the same room together. "Just because you run against someone does not mean you have to be enemies. Politics does not have to be mean and ugly." Bush was no political novice, and in a 2006 letter to Bill Clinton he foresaw how, if Hillary decided to run for president in 2008, that would affect their friendship, because she would have to attack George W. Bush and his presidency. "The politics between now and two years from now might put pressure on our friendship," Bush wrote, "but it is my view that it will survive."

Clinton went to the Bush family compound in Kennebunkport for lunch the summer before Bush passed away. He brought only his chief of staff along with him, and they stayed for a couple of hours. Before he left to go see Bush, he told an old friend, sadly, "This is the last time I'll be with him. We're going to lose him."

Not since Gerald Ford and Jimmy Carter have two presidents been so close.

The friendship between Clinton and Bush 41 has warmed Clinton's relationship with Bush 43, who always appreciated how he treated his father. When he left office, Clinton told Bush, "I'll never embarrass you in public." Unlike other presidents, who stiffly refer to each other as "Mr. President," George W. Bush's nickname for Clinton is the familiar "Bubba." "I think President Clinton was pleased when we started calling him '42,'" George H. W. Bush's chief of staff, Jean Becker, told me, laughing. Bush 43 and Clinton certainly have more in common—both are baby boomers and former southern governors who lost their first runs for Congress. Bush is forty-four days older than Clinton, and on Bush's birthday Clinton called him to say, "I'm calling you on bended knee because this begins my forty-four days of respect for my elders."

But the relationship between George W. Bush and Bill Clinton was not always easy, just as Clinton's relationship with Bush's father took time to evolve. They began to talk more once they were both in the Presidents Club, said former Bush press secretary Ari Fleischer. "Trust," he said, "has to be established." There was plenty of bad blood between them. His father, Bush said, at the opening of Bush 41's presidential library, had "left office with his integrity intact." A not-so-subtle swipe at Clinton. The younger Bush, Clinton said to his friend the historian Taylor Branch, was like his mother, who was known to hold grudges. "Of course, he's never forgiven me for beating his father, but that's about as deep as his political conviction gets." In 2000, Bush brought up Clinton's personal flaws and used them against Al Gore, as often as he could. A month before the election, Bush was asked about Clinton's affair and said, "I'm not running against President Clinton. That's a chapter . . . most of us would rather forget." The Lewinsky scandal was never far from the 2000 election, which Bush narrowly won against Gore after the Supreme Court ordered the recount to be stopped.

But the tide turned quickly; in fact, the two men spent ninety minutes having lunch in the residence after Bush was declared the winner. Clinton was well aware of the incoming president's familiarity with the executive mansion and its staff, and he joked that Bush did not need much of a tour, since he knew where to find the light switches, having stayed there so often during his father's tenure. Bush and his family brought only one chest of drawers and some family photos, because, Laura Bush told me, "part of the fun" of living at the White House is going to the warehouse in Maryland and picking out pieces from the White House collection to furnish the house. "I think George and I had a huge advantage moving into the White House," she said, "having stayed there so many times with his parents and having seen them as president and first lady." Clinton had reason to be kind to Bush: now was the time to make the plea for the continuation of his most beloved programs. Eight years before, George H. W. Bush had asked Clinton to preserve his Points of Light initiative. Now Clinton asked Bush to keep his AmeriCorps program going—which he did. Then Bush allowed himself to be vulnerable—something presidents rarely do—and asked Clinton for public speaking advice. Clinton had not always been such a gifted speaker; how had he become so skilled at capturing—and holding—an audience's attention? Clinton told Bush it was all in the timing.

Once he was in office, Bush called Clinton "every now and then," Clinton said. "We would talk. I just made it a project. I wanted to figure him out and get to know him." They did not agree much on policy, but they respected each other. "I like him personally. I think he did what he thought was right," Clinton said. And Clinton really wanted to be wanted. When Bush's chief of staff, Andy Card, would put a call in to Hillary Clinton, who was a New York senator at the time, Bill Clinton sometimes picked up the phone. "He would talk to me and ask what was going on and we would sort of trade information," Card remembered. Occasionally, Card and Clinton would talk for so long that both men forgot the reason for the call, and Card would have to call back to remind Clinton that it was his wife he was looking for.

Bush and Clinton had post-presidencies complicated by relationships with family members who still had presidential ambitions; for Clinton, that was Hillary, and for Bush it was his brother Jeb. They had to be especially careful not to say anything that would harm them, even though they did not always succeed. "The Internet is a brutal place these days for political figures, because there's a high degree of anonymity, there's no personal responsibility whatsoever, people can say whatever they want to say and it becomes currency," Bush said during the 2016 campaign. "I know Jeb and I'm confident Secretary Hillary will elevate the discourse." Neither one could have predicted the outcome of the 2016 election, though Clinton repeatedly told his wife's aides that he thought she was not reaching out enough to blue-collar voters.

Now the two men really are a team of sorts, working together to protect policies they put in place when they were in the Oval Office. At the 2018 International AIDS Conference, Clinton recalled his reaction to Trump's victory: "One of the first things I did after what was for me a heartbreaking election in 2016, within 48 hours I called President George W. Bush. And I told him, 'The best thing you did was PEPFAR (the President's Emergency Plan for AIDS Relief) and they will come after it. You can save it if you get the commitments now before anybody's thinking about it.'" And he did. In April 2017, three months after Trump's inauguration, Bush wrote an op-ed in the *Washington Post* all but begging Trump not to dismantle PEPFAR, a program he started in 2003: "PEPFAR saved millions of lives in Africa. Keep it fully funded." He appealed to Trump's national security concerns when he wrote, "This lifesaving work also has a practical purpose for Americans. Societies mired in disease breed hopelessness and despair, leaving people ripe for recruitment by extremists. When we confront suffering—when we save lives—we breathe hope into devastated populations, strengthen and stabilize society, and make our country and the world safer."

Clinton grieved with George W. when his father died in 2018. "His friendship," Clinton wrote of Bush, "has been one of the great gifts of my life."

BUSH 41 AND BUSH 43:
"WHAT I WANT TO DO IS SUPPORT [HIM]. PERIOD."

George H. W. Bush and Barbara Bush were the second president and first lady to have a son become president. Abigail Adams died before her son John Quincy Adams became the nation's sixth president, in 1825, and John Adams died a year later, in 1826, so neither of them were able to bear witness to their son's successes and failures in office. In tribute to that earlier presidential son, Bush occasionally called his son "Quincy." But unlike John and Abigail Adams, the Bushes lived a decade beyond the end of their son's two terms. "What people can't possibly imagine is what it's like to have two presidents who have a relationship as father and son," George W. Bush said. "They envision us sitting around the table endlessly analyzing the different issues and strategies and tactics. It's much simpler than that and more profound."

The Bush presidency was defined by the events of 9/11, the deadliest attack on American soil since Pearl Harbor. It was a terrible event in American history but also a particularly poignant moment in the relationship between the elder Bushes and their son. On 9/11, Bush called from Air Force One to check on his parents, who had stayed at the White House the night of September 10. Phone lines were clogged all over the country and even the president was having trouble making calls from Air Force One. At 2:30, Bush finally reached his mother. His parents had been traveling to Minneapolis, but the Secret Service had moved them to a motel in Wisconsin.

"Where are you?" he asked her.

"At a motel in Brookfield, Wisconsin," she told him.

"What in the world are you doing there?" he asked her.

"Son," she said, "you grounded our plane."

Three days after September 11, Bush led a moving memorial service at the National Cathedral as the nation was reeling from the shocking events. Former presidents Ford, Carter, Bush, and Clinton were there, providing moral support to the sitting president. "War has been waged against us by stealth and deceit and murder," Bush said to the dignitaries in the audience, many of whom had red-rimmed eyes from crying. "This nation is peaceful, but fierce when stirred to anger. This conflict was begun on the timing and terms of others. It will end in a way, and at an hour, of our choosing." The presidents and first ladies were seated, according to protocol, in chronological order, but George H. W. Bush asked the Clintons if they would switch seats so that he and Barbara could sit next to George and Laura. The elder Bush, who had to send soldiers into harm's way but who had never faced a challenge as daunting as what his son suddenly confronted, reached across his daughter-in-law Laura to grip his son's hand. "It was just a beautiful gesture," the younger Bush recalled of that moment.

Bush relied on his father more than ever, usually calling him early in the morning and circumventing the usual system of presidents first calling White House operators and asking them to place their calls. His parents were happy to answer. "What I want to do is support [him]. Period," George H. W. Bush said. "And because of that [I don't] get into the depths of these issues as I might otherwise be inclined." Even before 9/11, Bush had been in a routine of calling his parents in the early morning, when they were still in bed reading the newspaper and drinking coffee at one of their homes, either in Texas or Maine. The Bushes would put their son on speakerphone. Barbara recalled, "The rules are: no repeating what he tells you and no giving unsolicited advice and no passing on things that people ask you to give the President . . . gifts or advice or ideas or wanting jobs. . . . We were there. We know what it's like." George W. said the most surprising moment during the early days of his presidency came directly after the inaugural parade, when it sank in that he was indeed president. "I decided to go into the Oval Office to see what it felt like," he recalled. "Unbeknownst to me [chief of staff] Andy Card had called upstairs in the residence and asked Dad to come in so I was sitting in the Oval Office at the desk there kind of just taking it all in, and in walks my dad, and I said, 'Welcome, Mr. President,' and he said, 'Thank you, Mr. President.'" Barbara Bush was decidedly less sentimental. "Get your feet off the Jeffersonian table," she told him.

George H. W. Bush and his force-of-nature wife, Barbara, had long been used to balancing family and politics. Bush's father, Prescott, had been a Connecticut senator, and George had seemed destined for the presidency from a young age. Two of their six children, Jeb and George W., wanted to follow in their father's footsteps and get into politics. The Bushes stayed in Houston on Election Night when Jeb lost his first run for governor of Florida, in 1994, the same night that his brother George W. won the governorship in Texas. Jeb was always the one who seemed more likely to succeed. A stunned President Bush told the press at the time, "The joy is in Texas, but our hearts are in Florida." Jeb asked his mother after his defeat, "How long is it going to hurt?" She recalled that that conversation "killed me." Barbara and George H. W. Bush were at Jeb's side when he ran again in 1998 and won— Bush, always worried about his sons, took a Tylenol PM the night before, and still he could not fall asleep. He was proud of his sons, but he knew the baggage they carried because of his political career. His critics, he feared, would be their critics. In an August 1, 1998, letter addressed to George and Jeb, Bush 41 told them, "At some point both of you may want to say, 'Well, I don't agree with my Dad on that point' or 'Frankly I think Dad was wrong on that.'

Do it. Chart your own course, not just on the issues but on defining yourselves. No one will ever question your love of family— your devotion to your parents. We have all lived long enough and lived in a way that demonstrates our closeness; so do not worry when the comparisons might be hurtful to your Dad for nothing can ever be written that will drive a wedge between us—nothing at all."

When George W. Bush announced in June 1999 that he would be seeking the presidency, his father tried to keep his distance. "He doesn't need a voice from the past." This would be his son's campaign and, if he won, his son's presidency. One request Bush did make of his son: If he were to win, would he please restore the horseshoe pit, which he had loved so much and where he'd had countless games and tournaments with White House residence staff? Bush told his father that he was thinking of building a small T-ball field instead—he wanted to do things his own way.

Bush won after a protracted fight that went to the Supreme Court, and he had far fewer votes than his father. In 1988, George H. W. Bush had won with 426 electoral votes, as compared with his son's 271 electoral votes in 2000, only one above the number required to win. But, of course, his parents were incredibly proud. In a letter to a friend after George W. won the election, Barbara Bush wrote, "What a lovely son we were given. I keep reading all sorts of things about our wanting revenge or a dynasty, etc. Baloney! We feel exactly as you would feel if one of your chicks became President. It is an awesome feeling."

The 2003 U.S. invasion of Iraq complicated their relationship as members of George H. W. Bush's administration spoke out against it, including Brent Scowcroft, who had been his father's national security adviser. But the Bushes remained a close-knit family, and as they came together for Christmas in 2002, George W.

Bush remembered trying to avoid the issue. "For the most part, I didn't seek Dad's advice on major issues. He and I both understood that I had access to more and better information than he did." Laura Bush, who was always deferential, even made a suggestion to her father-in-law, who was very concerned about the looming war. *Stop watching television,* she told him.

The day Bush approved the war, he walked out of the Situation Room and went up to the second-floor residence, where he sat down in the Treaty Room, which he used as a private office, and wrote a letter to his father in Texas. "Dear Dad," he wrote. "In spite of the fact that I had decided a few months ago to use force if need be, to liberate Iraq and rid the country of WMD [weapons of mass destruction], the decision was an emotional one. . . . I know I have to take the right action and do pray few will lose life. Iraq will be free, the world will be safer. The emotion of the moment has passed and now I wait word on the covert action that is taking place. I know what you went through," a reference to his father's decision to launch the Gulf War in 1991. Not long after he faxed the letter, he got a note back from his father, who used a sweet phrase that was a favorite of the Bushes' daughter Robin, who passed away from leukemia when she was a toddler:

Your handwritten note, just received, touched my heart. . . .
It is right to worry about the loss of innocent life be it Iraqi
or American. But you have done that which you had to do.
Maybe it helps a little bit as you face the toughest bunch of
problems any president since Lincoln has faced. You carry
the burden with strength and grace. . . . Remember Robin's
words: I love you more than tongue can tell.

Well, I do.
Devotedly, Dad

In 2004, Bush ran against Democrat John Kerry and won reelection. Bush's father was happy, but at the same time he'd been
resigned to the idea that his son might lose. "I am not trying to
build a legacy, I will leave that to the historians," the elder
Bush said. "If I get a good shake, then fine. If I don't, I'll be in
heaven." There was a stark difference in their leadership styles:
George H. W. Bush was always more moderate than his son,
but the two had similar approaches to the presidency, with
Bush 41 calling for a "kinder and gentler nation" and Bush 43's
"compassionate conservatism." But hurt feelings and intense anx-
iety over criticism and decisions made in the Oval Office were
impossible to avoid. Bush senior was furious about the rampant
criticism surrounding his son's handling of Hurricane Katrina. In
a letter to a friend, he wrote, "The critics do not know what is in
43's heart, how deeply he feels about the hurt, the anguish, the
losses affecting so many people, most of them poor."

Years earlier, George W. Bush had been furious about a
Newsweek cover that labeled his dad a "wimp"—an incredibly
unfair characterization, especially since he had been shot down
by the Japanese during World War II, when he served as the
youngest aviator in the Navy. "God, I was mad. I was really, really
hot. . . . 1992 was the worst year of my life, to watch my dad lose."
It was hard on both men to watch the other get attacked, but it
was the price of the presidency. Bush said he would call his father,
and his mother would answer the phone and say, "Your father . . .
I can't believe he's listening to all this stuff, George, you need
to talk to your dad." His father would get on the phone, enraged
about something he had read. After 9/11, George W. Bush, in a
bulletproof vest, threw a perfect strike at a Yankees game. When
some publications wrote that "it appeared to be a perfect strike,"
the elder Bush was angry. It did not *appear* to be a perfect strike,
the elder Bush said; it *was* a perfect strike. "Forty-One was livid

about that," said his spokesman, Jim McGrath. "They couldn't even give him that."

George H. W. Bush was always careful not to say anything that could hurt his son while he was in office. After a November 2006 speech in Abu Dhabi, Bush 41 was questioned by a woman who was incensed about the ramped-up violence in Iraq. "We do not respect your son," she said. He replied, "This son is not going to back away. He's not going to change his view because some poll says this or some poll says that. . . . I have strong opinions on a lot of these things. But the reason I can't voice them is, that would then be flashed all over the world. If it happened to deviate one iota, one little inch, from what the president's doing or thinks he ought to be doing, it would be terrible." Bush would always keep his promise to his son, and he would extend it to every president who followed him—for the rest of his life he did not publicly attack them or take issue with their policies. He often quoted an old Mandarin adage—he was content to, as the saying goes, "stand on sidelines hands in sleeves."

BUSH 43 AND BARACK OBAMA

On the evening of Tuesday, November 4, 2008, George W. Bush sat in the Treaty Room, a cozy office in the residence with a large Victorian chandelier and nearly floor-to-ceiling windows. The room got its name because of the consequential decisions made there, including President Kennedy's signing of the Partial Nuclear Test Ban Treaty, in 1963, which banned atmospheric nuclear weapons tests. On a normal evening at home in the White House, the Bushes would leave these windows cracked open so the president could have a cigar and First Lady Laura Bush could smoke a cigarette at the end of a long day. ("He smoked more than people think!" an aide told me.) On this particular night, Bush was smoking his usual cigar and sitting with just one aide, watching the election results. Barack Obama had been elected the next president, beating longtime Republican senator John McCain, after running in part against Bush's wars in Iraq and Afghanistan. Bush watched as more than a hundred thousand people crammed into Chicago's Grant Park to see the forty-seven-year-old senator, who was the son of a father born in Kenya and a mother born in Kansas, give his victory speech as the country's first African American president. "People were crying in Grant Park," a Bush aide who was there with him recalled. "And Bush, of course, had very sensitive feelings about how African Americans felt about this country."

"People never thought this would happen in their lifetime and look at them now," Bush mused, with tears welling up in his eyes. He was happy for the country, for having achieved this milestone. Even though he largely disagreed with Obama's politics, he understood how incredible it was that he was going to be succeeded by the first black president. He did not know Obama, but he offered him some unsolicited advice. On Inauguration Day, following tradition, Bush rode with his successor to the Capitol in the presidential limousine. At the time, he was caught in a tense standoff with Vice President Dick Cheney, who wanted Bush to pardon his longtime right-hand man Scooter Libby. Bush had refused, and the decision would forever fray their relationship. During their short ride, Bush advised Obama to come up with a pardon policy early on in his administration and to stick to it, no matter what.

But it is not always easy to move past political differences. Obama criticized Bush, both on the campaign trail and in office, for the war in Iraq, for his slow and mishandled response to Hurricane Katrina, and for the financial crisis. At a 2009 fundraiser for then–Connecticut senator Christopher Dodd, Obama said, "We don't mind cleaning up the mess that was left for us. We're busy; we got our mops; we're, you know, mopping the floor here." Bush did not respond publicly, but privately he was stewing. Cheney told me that, while Bush followed his father's lead of not attacking his successors, "privately there are strong feelings." A current Bush aide told me, "Obama ran on not being George W. Bush. There are hurt feelings—Obama is forgiven, but it's not forgotten. As Obama has become a former president, there's been a warming; the two of them can relate better to each other now."

Just once during Obama's two terms as president was Bush almost pushed to the brink, and briefly considered speaking out against him. A close aide said that when President Obama decided to release Bush administration memos used to justify torture, "that almost pushed Bush into saying something." To former Bush staffers, this was a betrayal of the men and women in the CIA who used waterboarding as part of their interrogation techniques. Cheney, who relished a fight, came out in a media blitz, calling on Obama to release secret memos showing that valuable intelligence had been gained using enhanced interrogation techniques, including waterboarding. Bush was privately satisfied with Cheney's approach, but publicly he distanced himself from his VP's criticism of Obama. On Obama's fifty-fourth birthday, Cheney did a television interview that questioned Obama's understanding of national security. "He is making some choices that, in my mind, will, in fact, raise the risk to the American people of another attack." Two days later, at an event in Canada where Bush was speaking to a group of two thousand people, he was asked about Cheney's remarks. "He [Obama] deserves my silence," Bush said of the man who had followed him in office. "I love my country a lot more than I love politics. I think it is essential that he be helped in office."

Bush was sensitive to the fact that he'd been followed by a man who symbolized so much for African Americans, and in 2008 he asked conservative radio hosts to "go easy on the new guy." In October 2009, less than a year after Obama's election, Bush had breakfast with his onetime aide Ron Christie. Christie told Bush he was working on a book. "What's the title?" Bush asked.

"Acting White: The Birth and Death of a Racial Slur," replied Christie, who is African American.

"Really?"

"Yes, Mr. President," Christie replied. (The title was later tweaked to *Acting White: The Curious History of a Racial Slur.*)

"Well, that sounds pretty controversial. Tell me about it."

Christie went on to explain the book, and Bush gave him a warning: "Careful. This sounds like you could be attacking Obama. Don't do that. Your book sounds intellectual and historical. The minute you attack him, this will become a black guy attacking the first black president and they'll have your number that way."

Bush's respect and admiration for Obama was returned. Obama did not call his fellow Democrat Bill Clinton often when he was president; so much had changed in the world since Clinton was in the Oval Office. He spoke more often with Bush. The terrorist attacks of 9/11 had changed the presidency, and it was Bush and now Obama who had to deal with the fallout.

Presidents face the excruciating decision of whether to send soldiers into battle. When he flew to the Middle East to visit troops for Thanksgiving in November 1990, George H. W. Bush, who had deployed hundreds of thousands of U.S. troops in the Persian Gulf area to prepare for the war against Iraq, read Scripture and wrote a note to himself on a yellow legal pad: "This will not be another Vietnam." He kept that legal pad in his desk drawer as a reminder for the rest of his presidency. Bush and Obama each had the experience of visiting wounded warriors at Walter Reed

National Military Medical Center. Bush's White House press secretary, Dana Perino, remembered one 2005 visit when Bush stopped in to see a young Marine whose Humvee had been hit by a roadside bomb. The president was there to present him with a Purple Heart. His wife, parents, and five-year-old son were in the room when Bush walked in. The military aide solemnly presented the award, but as soon as he stopped speaking, the soldier's medical team noticed the injured man's eyes fluttering open. "Read it again," Bush told the military aide, then cupped the Marine's face in his hands, tears streaming down his face. The soldier died six days later during surgery.

Obama knew the agony of sending soldiers to war, and he was adamant about keeping Bush informed. On February 27, 2009, he called Bush from Air Force One, on his way to Camp Lejeune, where he was announcing his timeline for withdrawing U.S. troops from Iraq. During their ten-minute phone call, Obama briefed Bush on his decision to bring troops home in 2011. "They had a few exchanges, and it was all very professional despite the obvious sharp political and policy differences," said Ben Rhodes, a foreign policy adviser to Obama. In May 2011, Obama called Bush first to share the incredible news that al-Qaeda leader Osama bin Laden had been killed. In 2012, at the unveiling of Bush's official White House portrait, he elaborated. "My first call, once American forces were safely out of harm's way, was to President Bush. Because protecting our country is neither the work of one person nor the task of one period of time. It's an ongoing obligation that we all share."

That night, Bush was with his wife and two friends at a restaurant in Dallas when he was told that Obama wanted to speak with him. He went home to take the call. Obama said simply, "Osama bin Laden is dead." He went on to describe the successful Navy SEAL raid that he had approved that led to the death of the mastermind of 9/11, who was tracked down in a house in the Pakistani town of Abbottabad. Bush replied, "Good call." Later that night, Obama hugged his wife, Michelle, in the hallway of the residence and said, "We got him, and no one got hurt." Bin Laden's death was a remarkable victory for all Americans, not just the Obama administration.

Four months later, the tenth anniversary of 9/11 brought the Obamas and the Bushes together. Bush's presidency was forever changed because of that day, and so was Obama's. The two couples met at Ground Zero and walked to the 9/11 Memorial north pool, where the north tower of the World Trade Center had once stood. Obama walked up to where the names of those who were killed are written and gently touched some of them, closing his eyes and tilting his head up to the sky. Bush stood next to him, shaken by his own grief. "President and Mrs. Bush knew every one of those survivors and family members by name," Obama aide Bobby Shmuck told me. "Ten years had passed since 9/11, but the Bush family wasn't just there out of some lingering sense of protocol; it was clear they attended because they continue to mourn." Bush was still overwhelmed by the loss of life that day and read from a letter Abraham Lincoln had written to a widow who lost five sons in the Civil War: "I feel how weak and fruitless must be any words of mine which should attempt to beguile you from the grief of a loss so overwhelming, but I cannot refrain from tendering to you the consolation that can be found in the thanks of a republic which they died to save."

The two men would forever be unified by the proximity of their presidencies to that traumatic event. At a press conference during a 2015 trip to Turkey, Obama said, "I had a lot of disagreements with George W. Bush on policy, but I was very proud after 9/11 when he was adamant and clear about the fact that this is not a war on Islam . . . that's not who we are."

BARACK OBAMA AND THE CLINTONS

The Obamas are not as close to the Clintons as they are to the Bushes, and one reason for that is that they always felt that Clinton permanently damaged the Democratic Party with the Monica Lewinsky scandal. "I never saw a close relationship between Bill Clinton and Barack Obama," Leon Panetta, who was Obama's defense secretary and Clinton's chief of staff, told me. "But there was a close working relationship between Secretary Clinton and Obama." Obama is by nature an introvert, and he did not reach out to Clinton as much as Clinton would have liked and expected. "Bill Clinton is the type who doesn't call to impose his views unless someone really wants him to," Panetta continued. "He's not going to go out of his way to impose his views. That's one of the unwritten rules of past presidents—you don't usually call a successor. The sitting president calls you."

Obama's antipathy toward the man who was the most recent Democratic president had more to do with style than substance. "He occupies a lot of oxygen," said a former senior Clinton aide of his boss. "Presidents are used to being the bride at every wedding—they don't want to share the spotlight or listen to someone going on and on." Clinton seemed resigned to the fact that Obama did not want his advice. "I try to stay out of their way," he said. "I've got plenty to do. I've got a full life." But a much bigger reason for their tepid relationship had nothing to do with Monica Lewinsky or with Clinton's chattiness. It had its roots in the rancorous 2008 campaign for the Democratic nomination that pitted Obama against Hillary Clinton.

During the 2008 primary, Bill Clinton called Obama's argument that he had always opposed the Iraq War "the biggest fairy tale I've ever seen," and during the final days of the South Carolina primary he compared Obama's campaign to Jesse Jackson's in the 1980s. There was an uproar over his remarks, which some people thought were racist. The rift grew when Obama left Clinton off a list of transformational presidents. He said, "I think Ronald Reagan changed the trajectory of America in a way that, you know, Richard Nixon did not and in a way that Bill Clinton did not." And during one Democratic primary debate, Obama accused Hillary Clinton of using her husband to attack him. "I can't tell who I'm running against sometimes," he said. An Obama presidency could be a do-over, a chance to accomplish an overhaul of the health-care system and other Democratic priorities that Obama and his staff thought Clinton had squandered. Hillary wanted to keep Bill at a distance, and he always felt like her campaign did not include him enough. Instead of projecting the image of the charming political operator, he let flashes of anger and frustration show that were not helpful to his legacy, or to his wife's future. Shortly after that bitter South Carolina primary, George W. Bush called Clinton and told him he knew Clinton was no racist. "Hey, buddy," Bush said, "I know you're coming under attack; you just gotta keep your chin up."

It was surprising, then, that Obama would pick Hillary Clinton to be in his cabinet. He recognized her strengths and knew she would be a strong secretary of state. When he first asked her, she declined. But he insisted: "I need you," he told her. Clinton had to untangle herself from her husband's complicated post-presidency and separate the well-financed Clinton Foundation from the charitable work the Clinton Global Initiative (CGI) was doing. (As one journalist put it, Bill Clinton's post-presidency was about wrangling "rich people's money for poor people's problems.") Once she became secretary of state, Obama made it clear that the foundation would have to disclose its donors, and its annual conference could no longer be held outside the United States. She vowed not to participate in international CGI meetings, and she would not take overseas contributions while she was in office. Bill Clinton agreed to run speeches by Obama aides and, in turn, Hillary was able to bring with her some of her longtime aides, such as Capricia Marshall as chief of protocol.

Obama's relationship with Bill Clinton was more complicated. In the summer of 2009, Bill Clinton went to Pyongyang, the capital of North Korea, to negotiate the release of imprisoned American journalists Laura Ling and Euna Lee. North Korea's leaders wanted a former president to do the deal to lend them legitimacy. Not even former vice president Al Gore, who was a co-founder of the media outlet the women were working for, would do. The trip would be strictly humanitarian, Clinton said, and he would need assurances that if he went he would win their release. He met with then–North Korean president Kim Jong Il for over three hours and came back triumphantly with the journalists. Obama did not call Clinton to thank him until their welcoming ceremony was over. "It's no secret Obama didn't love Clinton," said one Clinton aide who was on the trip. "They wanted to be at arm's length in case something went wrong. They were so skittish about it, they were scared of their own shadow."

But, on a personal level, Obama appreciated Clinton's story and his meteoric rise, which was not unlike his own. Like Clinton, Obama was raised by a single mother who did not have much money. "He still remembers as a child waving goodbye to his mom—tears in her eyes—as she went off to nursing school so she could provide for her family," Obama said at a 2013 event honoring Clinton. "And I think lifting up families like his own became the story of Bill Clinton's life. He remembered what his mom had to do on behalf of him and he wanted to make sure that he made life better and easier for so many people all across the country that were struggling in those same ways and had those same hopes and dreams."

Clinton became useful to Obama when his wife was not running. During the 2012 campaign, Obama dispatched Bill Clinton across the country, and it became a running joke that Clinton was able to convey Obama's policies in simpler and more digestible terms than Obama himself could. "He has been breaking it down so well that people tell me I should ask him to be 'Secretary of Explainin' Stuff,'" Obama said in a 2012 speech in New Hampshire. In the fall of 2012, days before the election, Bill Clinton flew to Orlando for a campaign rally with Obama the next morning at the University of Central Florida. He flew out early so that he would beat Hurricane Sandy, which was about to hit the Eastern Seaboard. Justin Cooper was a top Clinton aide who was on the trip, and he said that Clinton would not miss the trip for anything, including the weather. "He wanted to support the president," Cooper recalled. He also wanted to be back in the game.

When he arrived in Florida, Clinton went to meet Obama, who was debating whether to suspend his campaign and go back to Washington or stay for the rally the next morning. The weather was getting so bad that the Air Force One pilots had advised Obama's aides that if he intended to get back to Washington, he would have to leave early the next morning to beat the storm. That meant he would miss the campaign event. Clinton had once been in Obama's position as an incumbent president seeking reelection, and he gave Obama this simple advice: "Don't mess around with this, you should go and be president." George W. Bush had mishandled the response to Hurricane Katrina in 2005, and Obama knew the political costs of continuing his campaign during a national emergency. He decided to miss the rally and cancel the next few days of his campaign swing. He flew back to Washington in the early morning and gave a nationally televised midday address from the White House. Clinton headlined the Florida event and went on to fill in for Obama at several campaign stops. "That's what you do for each other," Cooper said.

IV

THE HANGOVER

---

*I've had a couple of my predecessors tell me you feel lost when
you walk in a room the first four or five months and nobody
plays the song ["Hail to the Chief"] anymore.*

—Bill Clinton

"What are you going to do first?" a reporter asked Harry Truman
in 1953 as he returned to his family's fourteen-room home at 219
North Delaware Street in Independence, Missouri. "Take the
grips up to the attic," Truman replied, nodding at the suitcases in
his hand. The transition back to civilian life is difficult, no matter
how much presidents and first ladies say they crave a return to
relative privacy.

"He was utterly lost," said a longtime friend of Truman's of his
first few months out of office. "After all those years in the White
House with somebody around to do everything for him, he did
not know how to order a meal in a restaurant. He did not know
when to tip. He didn't even know how to call a cab and pay for it."

When he left Washington, Eisenhower, a former president, five-
star general, and supreme commander of Allied forces in Western
Europe during World War II, retired to his quiet farm in Gettysburg, Pennsylvania, with his devoted wife, Mamie. His son, John,
moved to a house a mile away and worked with his father as an

editor on his memoirs. Two weeks after the Eisenhowers moved out of the White House, John noticed a change in his father that at first rattled him. "His movements were slower, his tone less sharp, and he even [had time] for casual conversation," he said. He worried about the change, until he realized that his father had "simply relaxed."

Eisenhower, more than many presidents because of his high rank in the military, was used to being surrounded by aides who did everything for him, down to making simple phone calls. On his first night out of office, he decided to experiment and call his son John. He had grown accustomed to picking up the phone and having a White House operator answer and quickly connect him to anyone, anywhere in the world. When he picked up the phone and heard a dial tone, he was livid. When an aide showed him how the phone worked, he exclaimed, "Oh, so that's how you do it!" He never did get the hang of driving and kept an Army sergeant on staff to drive him around town.

Modern presidents have not had any easier a time adjusting. They spend their years in office living in a home where they are catered to by chefs, butlers, and gardeners. They do not often pay for anything, and on the rare occasions when they do try to pick up the tab, they might have their credit cards rejected, as Barack Obama did at a restaurant in New York when he was there for the UN General Assembly. "It turned out I guess I don't use it enough," he said. "They thought there was some fraud going on. Fortunately, Michelle had hers." When a Latin American reporter asked George W. Bush what he carried in his pockets during a 2005 interview, Bush stood up theatrically, rooted around in his pants pockets, and pulled his hands out holding nothing but a plain white handkerchief, which he waved in the air. "Es todo," he said. That's it. "No dinero." No money. "No mas." Nothing else. "No wallet," he told the Spanish-speaking reporter. Going back into the real world was going to be a challenge.

Bush did not carry a phone, and he gave up on email. On January 17, 2001, three days before he was sworn in as president, he sent out a group email to forty-two of his closest friends and relatives. The note was sent from his old email address, G94B@aol.com. "My lawyers tell me that all correspondence by e-mail is subject to open record requests," Bush wrote to the group, which included his mother. "Since I do not want my private conversations looked at by those out to embarrass, the only course of action is not to correspond in cyberspace. This saddens me. I have enjoyed conversing with each of you." Messages presidents send by email are considered part of the federal presidential record and must be archived. Email is one of their last ties to the outside world. "I will miss your ideas and encouragement," Bush said in the message. "So perhaps we will talk by phone." He had often asked friends and relatives for advice when he was on the campaign trail. "Sadly I sign off," he wrote. Obama famously refused to give up his beloved BlackBerry when he became president. He was allowed to keep it with certain caveats, including that it be a special BlackBerry approved by national security officials and that he would correspond only with a very small group of people who all had to be briefed by the White House counsel's office.

When they first come to the White House, presidents may not immediately take to being waited on, but they get used to it. The residence is served by around six permanent butlers and dozens of part-time butlers who come in on a regular basis to help with state dinners and receptions. Of the six full-time butlers, one is designated as the head butler, or the maître d'. The task of tending to the president's more personal needs is handled by valets, who are always close at hand. There are typically two valets working in shifts. They are military personnel who take care of the president's clothes, run errands, shine shoes, and work with the housekeep-ers. When the president goes to the Oval Office in the morning, a valet stands close by in case he needs anything, whether it is a cup of coffee, breakfast, or just a cough drop. When the president travels, a valet packs for him and often rides in a backup vehicle in the motorcade, carrying a spare shirt or tie in case he spills something and needs a quick change of clothes. On the very first day after his inauguration, George W. Bush was shocked when he met his valets. Laura Bush described the scene to me: "These two men come and introduce themselves to George and say, 'We're your valets.' So George went in and talked to his dad and said, 'These two men just introduced themselves and said they were my valets, and I don't *need* a valet. I don't *want* a valet.' And President Bush said, 'You'll get used to it.'" And he did. That kind of luxury, however, makes the transition to anything resembling real life much more difficult.

When the Reagans said their goodbyes to the residence staff in the State Dining Room, the president joked, "You know the only problem about leaving the White House: When I will wake up tomorrow morning, how am I going to turn the electricity on? I haven't done it in eight years." Nancy Reagan said her hus-band loved the luxury of the residence, and so did she. "Every evening, while I took a bath, one of the maids would come by and remove my clothes for laundering or dry cleaning. The bed would always be turned down. Five minutes after Ronnie came home and hung up his suit, it would disappear from the closet to be pressed, cleaned, or brushed." Even though the Reagans, and the presidents and first ladies who followed them, could afford as much household help as they desired, once they moved out of the most famous house in the country things would never be the same again.

"IF YOU HURT HIM, I WILL KILL YOU"

Members of the first family are spared domestic drudgery during their years in the White House, with cooks, maids, and butlers devoted to making their lives easier. The Bushes had spent decades in public service and were famously not accustomed to buying groceries. During his 1992 reelection campaign, George H. W. Bush was ridiculed after he marveled at a supermarket scanner. His spokesman, Jim McGrath, told me it was a new type of scanner he was trying for the first time. The *New York Times* ran the story, which made Bush look completely out of touch. Bush wrote to the paper's publisher, Arthur Sulzberger, and asked for a retraction, which he never got.

But not long after leaving office, Barbara Bush said, her husband took his first trip to Sam's Club and "bought the world's biggest jar of spaghetti sauce and some spaghetti" for dinner. While he sat down to watch the evening news, the former first lady started to cook. She accidentally knocked the enormous jar of sauce off the counter, sending it crashing onto the kitchen floor. Their dinner plans ruined, they scrambled for an alternative. "That was the night George and I made an amazing discovery: You can call out for pizza!"

Bush, who was sixty-eight years old when he left the White House but still had the energy of a thirty-year-old, never wanted to slow down. Not long after leaving office, the Bushes attempted to relax by going on a commercial cruise on one of the ships featured in *The Love Boat*. Everywhere they went, people approached them. Once, when Bush was leaving the sauna, naked, a fellow passenger asked him, "Do you mind if I take a photo?" He did mind. In addition to hair-raisingly fast rides on his boat, Bush famously took up skydiving in his seventies. Colin Powell called Bush and asked if he was really going to do it. "It's the talk of the Pentagon," he told him. Powell then asked him a series of questions: *How are your ankles? What about your knees?* The U.S. military was worried about this highly unusual hobby for a former president. As he plummeted toward the ground at more than a hundred miles per hour, after jumping from ten thousand feet in the sky, Bush thought, *All is right with the world.* The first time he jumped—not counting when his plane was shot down during the war—was in 1997. As he got older he jumped strapped to a retired member of the Army's elite parachute unit, the Golden Knights. He jumped to celebrate his birthday when he turned seventy-five, eighty (this was his final solo jump), eighty-five, and even ninety.

Retired sergeant first class Mike Elliott, of the Golden Knights Parachute Team, recalled being Bush's tandem skydiving partner. Before they boarded the plane he met the matriarch of the Bush family. "If you hurt him," Barbara Bush told him, "I will kill you." He laughed at the memory. "I think I was more nervous about her than anyone else." As the years went on and Bush became more frail, the jumps became more difficult. "His mind was made up," Elliott said. "He wanted to jump on his 90th birthday, and that's what he did."

At a private dinner at Walker's Point, the family compound in Kennebunkport, Bush, who was always a perfectionist, told Elliott he felt that "he didn't do it right the first time he had to exit an aircraft." During World War II, when Bush was a twenty-year-old pilot, his Grumman TBF Avenger had been shot down over the Pacific. He miraculously survived after parachuting into the sea, but his two crew members did not make it. George W. said their loss had haunted him forever. "What he really wanted was closure," Bush wrote in a book about his father, "to repeat the experience of jumping from a plane on his own terms." Bush's final tandem jump came in 2014, when he turned ninety years old. He was mostly confined to a wheelchair by this point, due to Parkinson's disease, but he did not let it stop him. The final time he skydived, appropriately, was over his beloved Walker's Point.

In those first few years after leaving Washington, Barbara Bush tried to get used to life in Houston, but she could not leave the residence staff behind. She decided that she needed help from White House usher Chris Emery, to whom she had always turned with computer-related questions when she was first lady. She was working on her memoir when she lost a chapter, so she called on Emery for help. "Chris taught me how to use a computer," she told me. Emery was happy to oblige—but the favor fueled the Clintons' suspicion that the staff was too attached to the Bush family. When the Clintons saw the usher's call logs, Emery said, they "came to the conclusion that I was sharing deep, dark secrets with the Bushes in Houston. Which I wasn't." Bush admitted that there was some "risk" in keeping up with the residence staff after they moved out. A short time later, Chief Usher Gary Walters called Emery into his office.

"Mrs. Clinton is not comfortable with you," Walters told him. Emery was stunned. "What does that mean?" he asked. "It means tomorrow is your last day." Barbara Bush admitted that her phone calls to Emery had "caused trouble." After he was fired from the White House, in 1994, the first call he got that night was from Barbara Bush's assistant, saying that the Bushes had heard the news and wanted to help however they could. All these years later, Emery told me sadly, he understands why he was fired. "She was facing so many pressures," he says of Mrs. Clinton, "and unfortunately I was a victim." Barbara Bush might have been miles away from Washington, but her actions directly affected the people who had served them in the White House.

PURGATORY IN CHAPPAQUA

On the flight the Clintons took to New York after George W. Bush's inauguration, someone smashed a champagne glass and shards fell into the farewell cake, making it unsafe to eat. Maybe it was a sign of just how difficult those next few months would be for Bill Clinton, who was just fifty-four years old when he left office and not someone who took to domestic tranquility and rest. "When you leave the White House," he said, "you wonder if you'll ever draw a crowd again." One former senior aide told me recently that both Clintons still worry about becoming "irrelevant," and "that's a very, very hard place for them to be." Clinton was so tired from staying up until the early-morning hours that final day in the White House that he fell asleep for most of the short flight. By the time he had begun settling into their renovated farmhouse in Chappaqua, about an hour outside of New York, controversy over the pardons he had granted on his last day was making headlines, as were allegations about stealing White House furniture and vandalizing keyboards by stripping off the W's.

He could never escape controversy. As is the case with other former presidents, parts of the Clintons' home resembled the White House. The historian Taylor Branch, who is close with Clinton, said the open layout of the eleven-room white Dutch colonial house at the end of Old House Lane, which cost $1.7 million, reminded him of the Aspen Lodge at Camp David, the presidential retreat. And there is even a hallway with photos lining the walls, like the hallway leading to the Solarium on the third floor of the White House. The yellow floral wallpaper the Clintons selected for the master bedroom matched the wallpaper in their bedroom in the White House. Memories from his presidency are everywhere: On the walls are photographs of Nelson

Mandela and Helmut Kohl. There is even a sculpture made with pieces of the plane that his secretary of commerce, Ron Brown, was flying in when it crashed into a Croatian mountainside, killing him instantly. Clinton spent a lot of time alone in his house on a dead-end street in the sleepy town while Hillary stayed in Washington, in another $2.85 million home they owned off Embassy Row. Hillary was embarking on her own career as a U.S. senator, and Chelsea was away at Stanford. "My biggest problem now is I hate to go to sleep at night," Clinton said in a 2000 interview before he left the White House. "I go to bed and I sit there and I read for hours." But he did not wallow for long.

The week after Bush was sworn in, Clinton signed with a lecture agency and set to work on securing a huge advance for his memoir. He would use his time to build the Clinton Global Initiative and work on his book and his library. And he was setting the stage for what was at the time the most lucrative post-presidency in modern history—in no time, he was making more money in a month than he ever had in a year. By 2013 Clinton had lived longer than any man in his family, going back as far as his maternal great-grandfather. He had many health scares, and in 2004, while promoting his memoir, *My Life*, he had tightness in his chest and went to the doctor. "I was a heart attack waiting to happen," he said later. Four arteries were blocked, two of them more than 90 percent.

He recalled the eeriness of his quadruple-bypass heart operation: "At first I saw a series of dark faces like death masks, flying toward me and being crushed. Then I saw circles of light with the faces of Hillary, Chelsea, and others I cared about flying toward me, then away into a bright, sun-like source." After the surgery, he started a low-fat diet and lost twenty pounds. "I was always in a frantic hurry to do whatever I had to do, because I never knew how much time I had," he said in a 2013 CNBC interview. "Whatever he did," he told his friend Taylor Branch, "he would do it intensely because the men in his family were not long-lived." Clinton said, "We're all on borrowed time; we just don't know for sure how much." Six months later, he needed another operation because of unusual complications from the surgery. Some friends say that he has not been the same since and is more easily tired and prone to flashes of anger.

It must be strangely reassuring for Clinton to still be followed by Secret Service agents in his post-presidential years. Just to go out to dinner in Chappaqua, Clinton has a two-car convoy, though it is much less than he had as president. He has a driver's license he barely uses, and he cannot take the train to his Harlem office because there are security concerns. Strange things can happen when former presidents venture out. Branch described sitting with Clinton at a small French bistro in town when a woman came over to their table and welcomed Branch to Chappaqua, without saying a word to Clinton. When she walked away, the president said that she had approached the entire family and had sent them a strange note encouraging them to try family massage. He gave the letter to the Secret Service.

When he was president, Clinton played lots of golf to relax, but now he reads more—he is often reading a dozen books at a time—and golfs less. He has stayed in the limelight more than any other modern president. He says it is because he wants to do good, but a very close friend of the Clintons told me it is also because he cannot stand to be away from the center of power. "I miss the work," Clinton insisted in an interview shortly after leaving office. "I loved the work."

THE AFTERLIFE

The Bushes refer to their years since leaving Washington as "the afterlife in the promised land in Texas." George W. did not want to be like Bill Clinton, constantly chasing the spotlight, he told friends. Instead he wanted to be at peace at home in Texas. Bush feels as though the weight of the world has been lifted from his shoulders, and friends describe the couple as the happiest retired people they know. Bush believes that he did his best while in office and the rest is in God's hands. He has modeled his post-presidency after his father and not Bill Clinton, who never let go of his interest in global affairs and who still thrives on meeting new people and feeling connected to what is happening in the world. Bush said he watched his father "carefully and how he moved on with his life. He didn't linger. He didn't have a sense of needing to hang on to the presidency. I learned from him that when it's over, it's over. . . . Once you're off the stage, you're off the stage." For Bush, politics is "a chapter" in his life, not his whole life. In stark contrast to Clinton, Bush does not want to be recognized. "I realize I will never regain my anonymity, but I can certainly give it a try. And it's a lot of fun to give it a try."

The Bushes take long walks on the grounds of Prairie Chapel Ranch, their sixteen-hundred-acre home in Crawford, Texas, which became the "Western White House" when Bush was in office. Bush goes bass fishing, rides his mountain bike, and watches sports, especially the Texas Rangers, a team he once owned, and the Little League World Series. Bush's best friend, Don Evans, describes his life after Washington as "Baseball, Apple Pie, and America." Their three-bedroom house and two-suite guesthouse are built into a small hill, and when the weather allows, they open all the windows to create an indoor-outdoor living environment that they jokingly refer to as "motel-style." It is all very peaceful and very unlike Washington, D.C. When they are at their other home, in Dallas, Bush is known to surprise school groups as they visit the replica of the Oval Office in his presidential library, on the campus of Southern Methodist University. But even though

Bush comes across as an affable, easygoing Texan, even his best friends still call him "Mr. President." The days of being a completely private citizen are long over.

It makes sense that George and Laura Bush have relished their years as "formers." As the wars in Iraq and Afghanistan raged on and the financial crisis rocked the country, Bush left the White House with a dismal 22 percent approval rating, according to a CBS News/*New York Times* poll, making him one of the least popular departing presidents in history. And although there were few protesters at Obama's inauguration, which set a record for attendance, there were scattered boos when Bush and Vice President Dick Cheney were introduced onstage. As the Bushes took off in the helicopter, headed for retirement, some people in the crowd on the Mall could be heard chanting, "Na na na na, hey hey, goodbye." Still, more than four thousand people waited to greet them at the airport in Waco.

Laura Bush always knew that they would never lead a completely normal life again. How could they? "At the airport with my mother, well-wishers ask for pictures and I stop to smile underneath the dangling Hertz Car Rental sign," she wrote. "At times I wonder when this curiosity will fade . . . I wonder too about the passions that seem to be so permanently entrenched in all sides of American politics, where elected officials become near instantaneous celebrities and crowds are expected to swoon as teenagers once did for the Beatles almost half a century ago. Celebrity is a particularly poor model for politics." At home at their ranch, she said, she could appreciate the privacy and freedom she never had in the White House. She no longer had to be looking over her shoulder, worried about the next crisis that would consume their lives. "I could at last exhale; I could simply be."

Her husband also felt free. "One thing you had to learn" after the presidency, Bush said, "was that you no longer had the sense of responsibility that became ingrained in your system—so when I read the newspapers, the *Dallas Morning News* and the Waco newspaper, I saw the headlines (and I can't remember what they were, of course) and there was a 'what are we going to do about this?' And then I realized, it wasn't me. It was my successor." Bush tries not to spend too much time worrying about Donald Trump. A close friend of Bush's told me, "He's not happy with it—it's not in the long-term interest of the country. Will we get past this? Yes, we will. This country has been through the Civil War."

When asked during a joint interview with Bill Clinton what the biggest difference was between being a former president and a sitting president, Bush said he woke up in Crawford the day after he left the White House "expecting someone to bring the coffee. Laura didn't bring the coffee." As president, Bush said, you're dealing with "incoming fire" every day; afterward, you no longer have that "clutter." But it is more difficult to get things done in the post-presidency, which is an unwelcome reality for these men who used to be all-powerful. The construction of the building for the Presidential Leadership Scholars program, a leadership training project led by Clinton and Bush in conjunction with the presidential libraries of George H. W. Bush and LBJ, was a challenge. "There's no appropriations bill," Bush said, acknowledging the ways presidents can push through legislation to get what they want. Former presidents have to work harder.

Bush is not interested in dwelling on the past. When former presidents get together at library dedications and funerals, his first thought is *When is this program going to start and when is it going to end?* Clinton said Bush will often make a friendly suggestion to him to "give shorter answers." Becoming history does not bother Bush; it has liberated him. "There's no need to defend myself," he said in a 2013 interview. "I did what I did and ultimately history will judge."

THE MOST GLAMOROUS POST-PRESIDENCY
IN HISTORY

Leaving is harder when the person who replaced you has vowed to dismantle the work you have done. After watching Donald Trump's grim inaugural address, the Obamas were seen off by a few hundred aides in an airplane hangar at Andrews Air Force Base. They left for a long-awaited vacation to Palm Springs. "A transition is exactly that—a passage to something new," Michelle Obama wrote in her memoir. "A hand goes on a Bible; an oath gets repeated. One president's furniture gets carried out while another's comes in." Deputy national security adviser Ben Rhodes was one of about ten staffers who joined the Obamas on the flight to California. "George W. Bush's team had recommended we do this to make the flight less lonely for them after eight years when they were surrounded by dozens of people," he recalled.

On board the plane, Michelle Obama sat down on a couch and her husband put his arms around her and whispered in her ear. It was the end of a grueling eight years. Later, Michelle said, getting on the plane leaving Washington "was a release of eight years of trying to have to show up." (She had long been ready to leave. At the 2016 White House Correspondents' Dinner, President Obama had joked about someone jumping the White House fence the week before. "I have to give the Secret Service credit. They found Michelle and brought her back. She's safe back at home now. It's only nine more months, baby. Settle down.") The Obama girls were on board the flight out of Washington; they had been just seven and ten when their father became president, and now they towered over many of his aides. Rhodes wrote in his memoir that during the flight, Obama told him, "I came to see the presidency like a game of Pac-Man," and he mimicked holding a joystick. "Sometimes I felt like I was just outrunning people, trying to avoid getting tripped up before I got to the end of the board." There was nothing more he could do. When Rhodes asked him what he would do the next morning, he replied simply, "Sleep in."

The plane circled Palm Springs for about an hour because of bad weather, and eventually it had to land in dense cloud cover at March Air Reserve Base, in Riverside, California, about an hour from Palm Springs. Rhodes recalled that sitting on the tarmac felt "eerily like all the stops we'd made to refuel Air Force One at U.S. military bases over the years—in Anchorage and Guam, in the Azores and in Germany—short breaks in the middle of long-haul trips around the globe. There was no arrival party, no red carpet." After the Obamas deplaned to drive off to Palm Springs, Rhodes and the others got back on the plane to head back to Washington, with no fanfare.

The Obamas immediately took to life after the White House. "It was great. I did not miss the trappings of the office," the president said in an interview with David Letterman. "I sort of enjoyed puttering around the house, trying to figure out how does the coffee maker work and fighting with Michelle for closet space." A few days after leaving the White House, he and Michelle spent ten days on Virgin CEO Richard Branson's private Necker Island, in the British Virgin Islands. (It costs more than $40,000 to rent the whole island for a night and more than $25,000 to stay in a villa for a week.) When Michelle got off the plane she declared, "We're free!" Photos showed Obama and the British entrepreneur kitesurfing—Obama won the competition—and revealed a relaxed and rested former president. Shortly after the Obamas' trip with Branson, a former aide saw him and told me he was in good spirits despite Trump's taking office. "He was sanguine. He knew exactly what was going on—there was no delusion about this administration. He had spent the better part of two years warning about it in the United States and overseas. His attitude seemed to be that folks have to get engaged and this could be a catalyst for that." In 2019, the Obamas spent time with George and Amal Clooney at their home in northern Italy during a European summer vacation that included a stop in France, where they had lunch with U2's Bono and the Edge.

It was a continuation of the most star-studded, glamorous post-presidency in history. The Obamas spent the rest of their first spring out of the White House traveling to a luxury resort in French Polynesia and a villa in Tuscany, whitewater-rafting in Bali, and visiting Java to see where Obama's mother had once lived. Obama picked Anita Decker Breckenridge to be his chief of staff and to manage his life after the presidency. Breckenridge first began working for him in 2003 when he was an Illinois state senator. "The beauty, maybe for lack of a better word, of becoming a former president is he's going to take some time to figure out" what his priorities are, Breckenridge said. "He can't do it all, right?" The Obamas' close friend Valerie Jarrett said he does not yearn for the spotlight: "Of course he'll miss being in the thick of things. But I think he's also really grounded and pragmatic. So he won't indulge the emotion of saying, 'Oh gosh, I wish it wasn't over.' It's over."

Like Hillary Clinton, who showed up everywhere after she was defeated in 2016—from hiking trails in suburban New York to Broadway shows—Obama began making unannounced stops at very public events after he left office. Seeing former presidents in unexpected places creates a sort of "Where's Waldo?" effect as viral videos show bystanders shocked. Jimmy Carter understands the strangeness of these interactions. "I think when folks get to know me they can talk to me easily," he said, "and relate to me as a human being. But at the beginning, when I [would] go into a crowd or meet a stranger—you know, obviously they look at me as kind of a unique creature."

Even though he spent much of his time in highbrow environments, with celebrities in exotic locations, Obama also spent time watching his favorite sport, basketball. In February 2019, he attended the game between the University of North Carolina Tar Heels and the Duke Blue Devils in Durham, North Carolina. He was there when Duke star Zion Williamson's Nike shoe ripped apart less than a minute into the game. "His shoe broke," Obama said, pointing at the drama on the court as he sat next to Reggie Love, himself a former Duke player who went on to become a close White House aide. Obama was wearing a custom designer black bomber jacket with "44" embroidered on the sleeve. Back in Washington, he needed to find a place to golf. After some members of the predominantly Jewish Woodmont Country Club outside of D.C. tried to block him from joining because they said he was not supportive enough of the Jewish state, he joined the Columbia Country Club in Chevy Chase instead, where he can frequently be found playing golf. He caused much consternation there, though, because he was bringing three guests when the limit is one guest per member—and even former presidents have to play by the rules. (Once he was told, he complied.) He even got himself a temporary officiant license through the District of Columbia so that he could preside over weddings. In January 2018, he led the service at the wedding of Dana Remus, the general counsel for the Obama Foundation and for his personal office, and Brett Holmgren, who'd also worked for Obama in the White House. He signed their marriage certificate, and once the reception began, he left so that he would not detract from their day. "It was a very, very exciting moment," said the groom's mother. "Everybody who was there was just flabbergasted and amazed at just what a nice person he is."

The Obamas have largely been under the radar in Washington and are rarely spotted out in public. When they do go out, they are usually tucked away in a VIP room with longtime friends from their tight-knit inner circle. They still own their home in Chicago's Hyde Park. In Washington they have privacy in their relatively secluded and very upscale part of town. The street in front of their house is blocked by a police car and a security detail. "We don't have the anonymity that allows you to be in the world with normalcy," Michelle Obama said. "I go to restaurants, I still work out and travel, but I can't sit at a sidewalk cafe and just watch other people without it becoming a scene."

And when Barack Obama is home, he is often restless. "I think there was a sense that I had run the race, I had completed it. I was proud of the work we had done," he said. "I was ready for the next stage." But life after the White House felt like it was "moving in slow motion," he confessed. When his literary agent told him that his publisher wanted to meet with him "right away" about his memoir, he suggested a time the next day. "Oh, no," the agent replied. "It's going to take two weeks to set it up." In the White House, the stakes were incomprehensibly high and urgent. "I had to explain to him," Obama said, "where I'm coming from, 'right away' means if we don't do something in half an hour, somebody dies."

V

CASHING IN

Don't do anything for free.
—George W. Bush

When Harry Truman left office, in 1953, the only income he could rely on was a World War I veteran's pension of about $110 a month. As president he had earned $75,000 a year during his first term and $100,000 during his second, which is more than $1 million in today's dollars. Now he had no Secret Service protection and no money for aides or office space. Truman and his wife, Bess, lived a modest life, and he never wanted anyone to think that he was making money off the presidency. He was so worried that anyone would have the wrong perception that he did not even use brand-name pens when he signed books, because he did not want anyone to think he was getting paid to endorse the brand. But he needed money to run his post-presidential offices in Missouri, so he agreed to a $600,000 contract with *Life* magazine to publish his memoirs. Payment was to be made over the course of five years and, after taxes and expenses, he figured his net profit would be only $37,000 over those five years. He was almost broke and was so adamant that he not appear to be cashing in on the presidency that he had to sell the family farm.

It was because of Truman that an annual presidential pension, with funds for offices and staff, was established. In 1958, Congress enacted the law that allowed for a pension and other entitlements for former presidents. (A president who resigns is entitled to these benefits, a president who is impeached and removed from office after being convicted in the Senate is not.)

Today, former presidents make tens of millions of dollars from book deals and speaking fees, and they receive an annual pension of more than $200,000, plus a six-figure expense account to pay their staffs, rent office space, and travel, among other things. Before Congress granted former presidents pensions, they had to find other ways of making money. George Washington became the country's preeminent whiskey producer. Ulysses S. Grant, the eighteenth president, was bankrupt after the presidency and rushed to finish his memoir as he was dying from throat cancer so that his family could stay afloat after he passed away. Dwight D. Eisenhower got about half a million for his memoir and Lyndon Johnson and Richard Nixon received well over a million each for their memoirs and sold television interviews for six figures. Nixon was hundreds of thousands of dollars in debt when he resigned from the presidency. He hired legendary Hollywood agent Irving "Swifty" Lazar, who got him a $2.5 million deal from Warner Books for *In the Arena: A Memoir of Victory, Defeat, and Renewal*, which became a bestseller. He went on to write eight more books between 1979 and 1992. When he passed away, in 1994, he was worth $15 million, a $13 million jump from his net worth in 1969, when he became president.

Gerald Ford, who was in office for less than one full term, and his wife, Betty, received more than a collective $1 million for their books. He signed a $1.25 million deal with NBC to be a contributor to the network on documentaries. Betty's book *The Times of My Life* outsold her husband's. Ford conceded, "She's a lot more interesting than I am!"

Ford was the first former president to join corporate boards—he sat on more than a dozen, including American Express and the 20th Century Fox Film Corporation—and he began commanding high fees for speeches, making between $15,000 and $50,000 on what he called "the mashed potato circuit." Ford even agreed to back a series of collectors' medals honoring important moments in the presidency, which was a controversial commercialization of the office. When he was criticized for it, his response was "I'm a private citizen now; it's nobody's business." When he became president, his net worth was $1.4 million; when he passed away, in 2006, it had jumped to $7 million.

But while cashing in on the presidency is part of a long tradition, all of these numbers pale in comparison with the increasingly staggering dollar figures of today.

THE BIG BUSINESS OF SPEECHES AND MEMOIRS

Presidents now make $400,000 a year in office, and they quickly discover that there is nothing like leaving the White House to dramatically multiply their net worth. The power might be gone, but the prestige of the office never fades. When he started doing paid speeches, George H. W. Bush called it "white collar crime." His fortune went from $4 million before he became president to $23 million in 2017.

The jaw-dropping surge in the Clintons' net worth is unparalleled (though the Obamas are on their way to matching it or even exceeding it). The Clintons had a net worth of $1.2 million when they moved into the White House in 1993, largely because of Hillary's salary as a lawyer in Little Rock and her positions serving on corporate boards like Walmart's. They had not owned a home since 1982, when they moved into the Arkansas Governor's Mansion for a second time. (Clinton lost his race for reelection in

1980.) She earned far more than he did: as governor of Arkansas, Clinton made $35,000 a year, but as president his income jumped to $200,000. (George W. Bush was the first president to be paid $400,000.) Tax returns show that the Clintons have made an astounding $240 million since leaving the presidency. While campaigning for Hillary in 2008, Clinton said, "When I got elected, I had the lowest net worth of any president of the 20th century." (Harry Truman, in fact, had far less money, and when he was a senator, Truman put Bess on his office payroll so that they could pay the bills.) Hillary said they were "dead broke" because of legal fees when they left the White House. In a 2014 interview with Diane Sawyer, Hillary Clinton said, "We had no money when we got there, and we struggled to piece together the resources for mortgages for houses, for Chelsea's education. It was not easy. Bill has worked really hard. And it's been amazing to me." In a 2018 interview, Bill Clinton said he left the White House $16 million in debt because of legal fees relating to impeachment proceedings and investigations into various scandals.

Two decades on, they have more than made up for it. In his post-presidency, Clinton has kept much busier than Obama or either Bush, and much of his crammed schedule is a frenzy to make money. In the past fifteen years, Bill and Hillary have delivered more than seven hundred speeches, averaging about $210,000 per speech. And they wasted no time: just days after leaving the White House, the president was paid $125,000 for a speech at Morgan Stanley Dean Witter, in New York, according to financial records. He accepted fifty-nine paid speaking offers in 2001 alone, including $550,000 for a three-day trip to Sweden, Austria, and Poland. Between 2001 and 2012, Clinton made $104.9 million in speaking fees, according to an analysis by the *Washington Post*. His astronomical speaking fees led to criticism that he was selling American power and influence to foreign interests, especially when Hillary was secretary of state, which coincided with a surge in his speaking fees. He was paid $500,000 or more each for thirteen speeches delivered around the world, and eleven of those occurred when Hillary was secretary of state, including one in Hong Kong for $750,000 and another in Nigeria for $700,000.

George W. Bush's net worth was $20 million when he began his presidency and is reportedly more than $35 million today. Money matters. Bush's one key piece of advice to a retired member of the residence staff: "Don't do anything for free. If you're doing a speaking engagement you need to insist on getting paid for it." By that point Bush had been retired for the better part of a decade and had become accustomed to the benefits of being a former president. There is one exception to the rule. Jimmy Carter's estimated net worth was around $7 million in 2017, $4.7 million more than it was when he left office—a modest increase as compared with his fellow former presidents; when he delivers paid speeches, he usually diverts the money to the Carter Center instead of his personal bank account.

Another source of cash comes from the increasingly lucrative world of publishing. Writing a memoir has long been considered among the only dignified occupations for a former president because it is not only about making money, it's also about lifting the curtain and sharing how key decisions were made. George H. W. Bush is the only modern president not to write a memoir. Between 2001 and 2015, Bill Clinton was paid an estimated $38 million as an author, a figure that has grown exponentially since his 2018 thriller *The President Is Missing*, co-authored with James Patterson. More than a decade earlier, he received $15 million for his 2004 memoir *My Life*, and Hillary Clinton got a near-record-breaking $8 million advance for her memoir about being first lady, *Living History*.

Though he has said he wants to recede into private life, George W.

Bush has written several books, including *41: A Portrait of My Father* and *Decision Points*, which he was reportedly paid around $7 million to write. His latest book, *Portraits of Courage*, was a collection of his own portraits of people who have served in the military. Bush, like Eisenhower and Carter, has taken up painting in his semi-retirement. The first time he picked up a paintbrush, he was sixty-six. He told his art teacher, "There's a Rembrandt trapped in this body. Your job is to liberate him." Bush makes between $100,000 and $175,000 per speech. He came under criticism in 2012 for charging $100,000 to speak at a charity for wounded veterans who lost limbs in the wars in Iraq and Afghanistan, wars for which he was responsible. (The chair of the board of the charity defended the high speaking fee because, by having Bush there, they raised nearly $2.5 million, more than double what they raised the following year.)

These numbers will only become more staggering as the Obamas use their celebrity status to make a fortune in their post–White House years. "Obama is going to be the first billionaire former president," a former top aide to President Clinton predicted ruefully. The Obamas together were reportedly paid more than $60 million for their memoirs. In May 2018, the Obamas signed a deal with Netflix to produce content through their production company, Higher Ground Productions. Obama reportedly makes around $400,000 a speech, while his wife garners about half that. "They are both trying to put themselves on a good financial footing," said Obama's friend and former aide Chris Lu, in what seems like a massive understatement. "The Netflix deal is an interesting way to generate income without having to make speeches to corporations." But money tends to take over, no matter how well intentioned a former president might be. Obama spends many of his days in his Washington, D.C., office making phone calls to wealthy donors as he raises money for his presidential center in Chicago.

"Right now, I'm actually surprised by how much money I got," the president said during remarks in Johannesburg, South Africa, marking the hundredth anniversary of Nelson Mandela's birth. "There's only so much you can eat," he said with a smile. "There's only so big a house you can have. There's only so many nice trips you can take."

THE OUTLIER

Jimmy Carter is the most relatable of the four living former presidents. In late 1979, Carter and his top aides met for a campaign strategy meeting ahead of the 1980 election, where they would face off against Ronald Reagan. Carter's media strategist, Gerald Rafshoon, was seated next to Bob Strauss, a revered political operative and diplomat. When Carter criticized Rafshoon for a suggestion he made, Rafshoon replied, "Fuck you, Jimmy." The room went quiet for a moment. Strauss eventually said, "Don't you mean 'Fuck you, Mr. President?'" Everyone erupted in laughter, including Carter, and the meeting continued. It is impossible to imagine an adviser saying that to Clinton, Bush, Obama, or, especially, Trump.

When I asked Carter if he thought former presidents are a team, he was not so sure. "You can't put all the presidents in the same box," he said, pausing a moment. "Some make a *lot* of money," he added, arching his eyebrows. He is not one of them, even though Carter desperately needed money when he went home to Plains, Georgia. "My financial circumstances were bad," he said in a 1982 interview with the *New York Times*, "worse than what I'd thought." The farm had been mismanaged when he was in the White House, and when he and Rosalynn returned to Plains—the only place they ever really called home—they discovered that losses from their farm and warehouse businesses, which had been held in a blind trust when they were in the White House, had left them almost a million dollars in debt. Because he was a one-term president, and because he considered profiting off the presidency unseemly, Carter could not get the kinds of speaking fees others could, so he had to write to dig himself out of his financial hole. When the Reagans went on an eight-day tour of Japan and got about $2 million for a few television interviews and speeches, it briefly marred Reagan's reputation. The Gipper even sold a cassette of his best one-liners. The *Los Angeles Times* wrote, "The main impression to be overcome is that he has been inappropriately cashing in on his eight-year presidency." But Carter joked privately that he wanted to know how he could find a gig like that. Carter's main source of income was book writing. He has written an astounding thirty-three books. His 2003 novel about the Revolutionary War, *The Hornet's Nest*, was the first novel published by any American president. He also published a children's book with his daughter, Amy, called *The Little Baby Snoogle-Fleejer.* He writes these books out of a garage he converted into an office.

Writing can take a personal toll, though. The Carters both joke that the closest they ever came to getting a divorce was when they worked on the 1987 self-help book *Everything to Gain: Making the Most of the Rest of Your Life.* Rosalynn Carter is a slow and methodical writer, and her husband writes at a quick clip; neither could appreciate the other's methods and writing style. Things got so bad that the two barely spoke while they were working on the book. Passages in the book are designated "J." and "R.," to indicate who was responsible for which chapter. Getting paid on the so-called mashed potato circuit became less important once the Carters found their true calling. "How much money I make a year is not important to me," Carter said. "I'm determined my life ahead will be just as meaningful to me and, I hope, to the public."

Shortly after leaving office, he came up with the idea for the Carter Center and based the organization in Atlanta, about two and a half hours from his hometown of Plains, to "wage peace, fight disease and build hope." He and Rosalynn have helped treat more than a hundred million people suffering from tropical diseases, and spread the tenets of democracy by overseeing free and fair elections around the world.

Carter has taken an innovative and much less self-serving approach to the post-presidency than fellow former presidents, and it is true that former presidents do not necessarily identify with one another just because they shared the same rarefied job. When asked whether his activism is a new interpretation of the post-presidency that his successors should follow, Carter said, "Each one of us is just as different from one another as radio disc jockeys are, or interviewers, or news reporters, or peanut farmers. So I think a lot of the activism of a former president depends on how old they are when they leave the White House. I was one of the young ones . . . who survived the White House."

$400,000 FOR ONE SPEECH

When President Trump becomes a former president, he will likely profit enormously from his years in office. Trump has famously refused to divest from the Trump Organization, opening himself up to critics who say he is profiting off the presidency. Shortly before taking office, he held a news conference announcing that he would resign from positions directly overseeing his hotels, golf courses, and other businesses and that he would transfer his assets into a trust. Strangely, the president is held to a different standard from other government officials, and there is no legal requirement that he completely divest. While ethics experts said he should put his organization in a blind trust so that he would have no knowledge of how it is being run, he decided to let his eldest sons, Eric and Donald Jr., manage his global business.

"My father made a tremendous sacrifice when he left a company that he spent his entire life building to go into politics," Eric Trump told *Forbes*. "Everything he does is for the good of the American people—he has zero involvement in the Trump Organization and quite frankly to suggest otherwise is outrageous." But Eric said he would keep his father up to date on the state of his business several times a year. This plan has not proven profitable. Trump's divisive presidency has hurt his bottom line. In a 2018 story, *Forbes* estimated that his net worth had plummeted from $4.5 billion in 2015 to $3.1 billion in 2016 and 2017. His name fell 138 spots on the Forbes 400 list in 2018. In 2000, when Trump was considering running for president, he told *Fortune* that it was merely a marketing tool. "It's very possible that I could be the first presidential candidate to run and make money on it." Who would have guessed that, sixteen years later, he would run, win, and lose more than $1 billion in the process?

But once he leaves office, the possibilities are endless. Years before he became president, Trump was paid $400,000 for one speech at New York City's Learning Annex, a continuing education center. It was an astonishing sum for someone who was not yet president, or anywhere close to it. That was not a high enough figure for Trump, who said he was actually paid more than a million dollars for the speech, because he added in the value of the publicity he got from the company aggressively promoting his appearance. The contrast between Trump and Jimmy Carter is stark.

VI

REDEMPTION

Forty-one million, six hundred thousand people don't like me.

—Jimmy Carter

When I asked Jimmy Carter about Donald Trump's commitment to undoing most of Barack Obama's accomplishments, he said it was business as usual. "It reminds me of what Reagan did to us," he insisted. "He said I cut military funding when I didn't, and I called Reagan and he said he didn't say it." Seated next to Carter was his wife, Rosalynn, who was still bitter about the Reagan budget cuts that dismantled the mental health programs she helped shape. But she would not let her husband's comment stand. "He never lied like this," she said, shaking her head, incredulous that her husband would equate Reagan with Trump. Trump had taken the dismantling of his predecessor's agenda to a new level.

Carter is the longest-living U.S. president in history, and he has had the longest and most dynamic post-presidency. He hit the milestone on March 22, 2019, when he turned ninety-four and 172 days, surpassing George H. W. Bush, who died at ninety-four years and 171 days old in 2018. Carter is also unique because he has had the most unorthodox post-presidency and has been critical of each of his successors. He set out wanting to leave behind a legacy in his post–White House years that would overwhelm the flaws of his presidency. Redemption for Carter has meant unburdening himself from the rules of the Presidents Club and being more outspoken, and more politically active, than any other member of the club.

JIMMY CARTER BECOMES A CRITIC

It is never easy to be the recipient of a pink slip, especially when it is delivered by more than half the American electorate. Ronald Reagan defeated Jimmy Carter in a landslide in 1980. Carter won just 41 percent of the popular vote, and it was hard not to take Reagan's victory personally. "When voters decided to change horses in midstream," Carter wrote, "not only had they rejected us, but almost 50 percent had chosen a horse determined to run as fast as possible in the opposite direction."

On Friday, January 22, 1981, Carter woke up after sleeping for what felt like more than twenty-four hours to "an altogether new, unwanted, and potentially empty life." He was jobless at just fifty-six years old, the youngest former president since William Howard Taft, who had embarked on a second career after leaving office. As president, Carter lived in an almost constant state of agitation, brought on by a nation facing double-digit inflation, endless lines at the gas station, and a serious energy crisis. (Rosalynn said her husband kept the residence so cold in the winter—sixty-five degrees—that one of the maids took pity on her and bought her long underwear.) Yet it was a job he loved.

The Iran hostage crisis, and the struggling economy, led to Carter's defeat. The hostage crisis overshadowed the Camp David Accords, the enduring peace agreement he helped forge between Israel and Egypt in 1978, and it left him, and those who served him, exhausted. For 444 excruciating days, he tried everything, including a failed rescue mission that led to the deaths of eight U.S. servicemen, and yet the hostages were not released while he was president. On Inauguration Day, residence staffer Betty Monkman remembered how all the televisions throughout the residence were on as the staff moved the Reagans in and the Carters out. "President Carter had been up in the Oval Office all night long with his staff and barely got over to the house to dress for his 10 a.m. event with President Reagan," Monkman recalled. "Nobody knew what was going to happen. The whole country was waiting." The Iranians released the remaining fifty-two hostages minutes after Reagan was sworn in as the nation's fortieth president— one last dig at Carter, who had worked tirelessly to bring about their release before the end of his administration. As Carter was leaving Reagan's inauguration ceremony on his way to Andrews Air Force Base, he received the call that the hostages were to be released. The next day, he made the journey to greet the fifty-two freed American hostages in Wiesbaden, Germany, with Walter Mondale, who had been his vice president just a day earlier. Carter and Mondale flew together for the first time; they had flown separately as is customary for a president and VP, in case of a plane crash while in office. They spoke with the hostages for about an hour. Some of them felt that Carter's White House had not done enough, and they did not understand how the rescue mission to free them had failed so miserably. It still haunts Carter. "I wish I had sent one more helicopter in that rescue mission," he said, regretfully, decades later.

The morning after the election, Carter's communications director, Gerald Rafshoon, went to visit the president, who was sitting with tears in his eyes in the Oval Office. "Forty-one million, six hundred thousand people don't like me," Carter said. His best friend and chief adviser was his wife, Rosalynn, who said that she was "bitter enough for both of us." Even years later, Rosalynn said, "My biggest regret in life was that Jimmy was defeated."

Rosalynn ends her autobiography, *First Lady from Plains*, with a pointed message: "I'd like people to know that we were right, that what Jimmy Carter was doing was best for our country, and that people made a mistake by not voting for him." And she let her own personal ambition show. "Our loss at the polls is the biggest single reason I'd like to be back in the White House. I don't like to lose." The worst moment for Carter came not when he found out that he had lost the election; it was breaking the news to his wife. "Don't say anything to Rosalynn yet," Carter instructed his staff. "Let me tell her." Rosalynn simply refused to believe the lopsided election results. "I was in such denial," she admitted years later. "It was impossible for me to believe that anybody could have looked at the facts and voted for Reagan." Rosalynn continued with her customary honesty: "I thought our lives had come to an end." She even hoped her husband would challenge Reagan in 1984. As first lady, "you do what you have to do," she said, but once she was a private citizen, she stopped watching the news for six months after they moved back to Plains. The Carters labored in their yard, clearing overgrowth to pass the time, as they tried to figure out what to do next. "By the time we'd get into the house [after working all day], the evening news would be over and I didn't want to see it anyway," Rosalynn said. She could not bear to hear commentators discuss how the Reagans had brought class and grace back to the White House. When an old friend teased her that Nancy Reagan would approve of the tablecloth she had used for lunch, she was not amused. Just because they were from the South, she thought, did not mean that they were not as classy as the Reagans, who hailed from Hollywood.

The Carters were the first president and first lady to move back

to their hometown since Harry and Bess Truman moved home to
Independence, Missouri. The Carters' town of Plains is about 150
miles south of Atlanta, and it was their campaign headquarters in
1976. Going there is like going back in time. Everywhere you go
in town, there is Carter memorabilia, from T-shirts emblazoned
with his famously toothy grin to campaign posters. The town is
just one mile in diameter—even smaller than Independence—
and it is home to Carter's boyhood farm, which had no running
water or electricity. It seemed fitting for Carter to follow Truman's lead: the up-by-his-bootstraps southerner idolized the
plainspoken midwesterner. When he was president, Carter asked
the Truman Library to loan him the original "The Buck Stops
Here" placard that Truman kept on his desk in the Oval Office.
Like Truman, Carter was loyal. "There is no chance I would not
live in Georgia forever," he said. Plains was home, and it would always be home. The Carters built their small ranch house in 1961,
and it was in a state of disrepair when they returned after living
in the governor's mansion in Atlanta from 1971 to 1974 and then
the White House from 1977 to 1981. They have been home for
four decades now, and they still often cook for themselves and
drink cheap chardonnay out of Solo cups with dinner. They even
knocked down a bedroom wall themselves during a renovation
of their home, having become used to doing renovations through
their work with Habitat for Humanity.

The federal government pays for the offices of former presidents. Carter has a modest office in the Carter Center, in Atlanta, that costs $115,000 a year. Not long ago, the Carters put
in a Murphy bed that they can pull down from the wall during
the one week they spend at the center each month—they consider it a small luxury. Carter's post-presidency costs taxpayers
less than half of those of the other living former presidents. According to the General Services Administration, the total annual

bill for Carter is $456,000 a year, including his office, staff, and pension. George H. W. Bush's office, pension, and expenses used to cost taxpayers $952,000 a year, and every other living former president—Clinton, George W. Bush, and Obama—costs more than a million. Obama's 8,198-square-foot office in Washington, D.C., alone costs taxpayers $536,000 a year. Clinton's office costs $518,000, George W. Bush's is $497,000, and George H. W. Bush's was $286,000. Clinton set up his office in Harlem after a public backlash to his original plan to rent offices for his foundation in Carnegie Hall Tower for nearly $800,000 a year. Carter does not even get federal health benefits, as other former presidents do, because of strict rules requiring that recipients spend at least five years working for the federal government—only if he had been reelected would he have served long enough to qualify. Instead, Carter gets his health benefits through Emory University, where he teaches.

In 1981, when Carter left office, not everyone in his family was happy about the move back to Plains. Amy, who was the youngest of the four Carter children by fifteen years, was just thirteen years old at the time and did not like the confines of the small town, so her parents sent her to boarding school in Atlanta. Once he was home, Carter went into a sort of self-imposed exile, as many presidents had done before him. His White House secretary, Susan Clough, moved to Plains to work for him. She spoke with him only a couple of times over a period of nine months. He spent eight hours a day working on his first memoir, which was titled *Keeping Faith*, and doing woodworking, a hobby that became an obsession. He spent hours alone in a converted garage working on coffee tables, benches, and chairs.

But he was left unsatisfied. Like Clinton, Carter always felt like he was in a hurry. Cancer ran in his family: his brother, father, and two sisters all died from pancreatic cancer, and his mother had breast cancer that spread to her pancreas. His family history is so unusual that he has given blood in the hopes of helping doctors understand the genetics of pancreatic cancer. On one white-knuckle flight while he was campaigning in New Hampshire during the 1976 election, which one aide described to me as so turbulent that "everyone was finding God for the first time," Jimmy Carter was perfectly relaxed. That is because of his strong faith. So it was not surprising that he seemed so calm during a 2015 news conference when he announced that, at age ninety, he had melanoma that had spread to his liver and brain. He seemed perfectly content. He had found his true calling during his post-presidential years. "If I had to choose between four more years [in the White House] and the Carter Center, I think I would choose the Carter Center," he said. But, he added, "it could have been both." Carter says he is cancer-free today, and he has seemingly boundless energy, often bringing his wife along on his travels, even when she would prefer to rest at home.

It is not only the Carter Center that has made him so satisfied; it is the freedom to say what he thinks. At a farewell dinner held by his staff in his honor in January 1981, Carter was no longer measuring his words. "We were all among friends, and didn't have to worry about being gracious losers. The good feeling and a few drinks produced a rash of transition horror stories about encounters with Reagan successors. For every anecdote there was someone who could top it: 'Wait'll you hear what happened in *my* department!' It was the same kind of thing that people had said about us four years before. But who cared? It was a chance to snicker and laugh together. Harold Brown talked about the right-wingers coming into the government. 'They are putting people in charge of arms control that are *opposed* to arms control!'"

During the 1980 campaign, Carter and Reagan traded nasty jabs. "Recession is when your neighbor loses his job," Reagan said.

"Depression is when you lose yours. And recovery is when Jimmy Carter loses his." In the months after taking office, Reagan would not send Carter even the perfunctory daily briefings provided to a hundred top government officials until Carter complained to Jody Powell, who had been his White House press secretary. When Powell told Reagan aides that he was getting ready to go to the press unless the briefing papers started arriving, they miraculously appeared. It was especially galling since, when Carter was president, he sent Nixon so many briefings that Nixon pleaded with him not to send them so often.

Even after all that history and baggage, though, there is a mutual respect that Carter and the other former presidents share. In 1986, President Reagan went to Atlanta to be part of the dedication of Carter's library and museum. He called Carter "distinctively and gloriously American." "For myself," Reagan said, "I can pay no higher honor than to say simply this, you gave of yourself to your country, gracing the White House with your passion and intellect and commitment." Carter thanked Reagan with his signature broad grin and said, "I think I now understand more clearly than I ever had before why you won in November 1980, and I lost."

Carter still wants to be a political asset. But in the 1984 presidential election, and most since, his endorsement was not widely sought. When Democrats invited him to the annual Democratic Congressional Dinner, Senate minority leader Robert Byrd and House Speaker Tip O'Neill were privately relieved that he would not be able to make it. Carter thought Reagan should have used him as a Middle East negotiator because of his success at Camp David. He still harbored hopes of being dispatched, in his nineties, to broker an anti-nuclear deal with North Korean leader Kim Jong Un, which is one reason why his criticism of Trump during Trump's first year in office was so measured. "They've been very quiet on the current president," said the Carters' friend Jill Stuckey, a leader at Maranatha Baptist Church, where Carter teaches Sunday school every other Sunday. (He has taught more than eight hundred times.) "They don't want to be seen as constantly criticizing somebody, so they politely smile and avoid the issue."

But what made his initial reluctance to criticize Trump so odd was Carter's refusal to bite his tongue when it came to the other presidents. Seeking to redeem himself and to stay engaged, Carter has created tension with the former presidents by weighing in on their policies, which is considered a cardinal sin in the Presidents Club. Carter says that his best relationship with a sitting president was when President George H. W. Bush was in office. When Bush succeeded Reagan, in 1989, Carter's opinions were solicited in a way they never had been before. Still, he undermined Bush. Carter has maintained his relationships with foreign leaders, and when, after the Iraqi invasion of Kuwait, Bush was building a coalition to oust Iraqi president Saddam Hussein from the country, Carter lobbied members of the United Nations Security Council to vote against U.S. policy. It was a remarkable and unprecedented decision to actively campaign against his own government.

On his own, Carter had done some investigating and thought Saddam Hussein would leave of his own accord if given time, and he wrote a letter saying that he thought Iraq should be given the chance to withdraw before a U.S. invasion. Carter had sent Bush a copy, but the White House did not know that he was also sending the letter to members of the Security Council until Canadian prime minister Brian Mulroney forwarded the letter to Secretary of Defense Dick Cheney. Bush felt betrayed. "It really upset him," said Brent Scowcroft, Bush's national security adviser. Bush would never have undermined another president

like that. Bush said that Carter "always seem[ed] to be siding
with the wrong side when it came to his ostensible support of
dictators and despots." Some Bush aides considered Carter's
actions treasonous. "This guy marches [to the beat of] a different drummer," Bush said. But their relationship survived. Bush
tweeted in November 2017, "In my case, one of the few good
things about becoming the oldest president—or anything—is
seeing my friend President Carter just recently looking strong
and doing so well following a tough diagnosis two years ago. You
can't keep a good man down."

Carter's relationship with Bill Clinton is even more complicated. Both men were remarkably young when they left office—
Clinton at age fifty-four, and Carter fifty-six—and both seemed
to have a lot in common as southern Democrats who did not grow
up with much money. Clinton grew up poor in Hope, Arkansas,
where he was raised by a single mother. Their political careers
set the two men on a collision course; they sometimes helped
each other and they sometimes betrayed each other. When then-
governor Carter was campaign chairman of the Democratic National Committee in 1974, he went to Little Rock to help "this kid
Billy Clinton who was running for Congress." Clinton, as usual,
was forty-five minutes late for their meeting. Carter aide Gerald
Rafshoon was waiting at the hotel with Carter's trusted staffers,
Hamilton Jordan and Jody Powell. "What the hell are you doing?
You're late!" Rafshoon said when Clinton finally walked in. Carter
is never late for anything, a quality Rafshoon credits to his years
at the U.S. Naval Academy. Even though their first meeting did
not go according to plan, the Carters and the Clintons were firmly
in each other's corners back then. But that changed in May 1980,
when Carter, as president, sent twenty thousand Cuban refugees
to be interned at Fort Chaffee, Arkansas. Several hundred broke
out and yelled, *"Libertad! Libertad!"* as they marched through

the streets, sparking a political disaster for Clinton, who was then Arkansas's governor and up for reelection. When Clinton called to ask Carter to move the refugees to another state, he was punted to a midlevel aide. Eventually Carter promised not to send any more refugees to Fort Chaffee, but he broke his promise. Three months before both men faced reelection, Carter moved all the refugees that he had sent to more important political states (like Pennsylvania) back to Arkansas. Both Carter and Clinton lost in 1980. Clinton was convinced that Carter's decision cost him the election.

When Clinton ran for president, he did not see any use in cozying up to the one-term Democrat, whom many perceived as a failure, and Carter's requests to discuss foreign policy with him were never answered. "Jimmy Carter and I are as different as daylight and dark," Clinton said in 1992. The Carters were given bad seats at one of Clinton's inaugural galas, a slight Rosalynn took very personally. Carter vented his frustration in a *New York Times* interview shortly after, breaking the understanding between former presidents to leave their families out of any dispute. Carter said he was "very disappointed" that the Clintons had decided to send their daughter, Chelsea, to the Sidwell Friends private school instead of to a Washington, D.C., public school, as the Carters had done with their young daughter, Amy. He also got in a dig about the Clintons' visit to Georgia the summer before to help the Carters build houses for Habitat for Humanity. "He was obviously not an experienced carpenter," Carter said. Although Carter rarely regrets anything he has said or done, he does feel a pang of guilt for bringing the Clintons' daughter into their rivalry. But he had felt snubbed too often. When Carter went to visit Clinton in the Oval Office, Clinton was late again, just as he had been in 1974, except this time it stung more, because Carter was a former president. "Clinton didn't realize how offensive that is to other people, especially to a former president," said a Clinton aide, who had to sheepishly apologize to Carter.

Carter continued to critique the policies of the sitting president. He criticized the Clinton administration for sanctions on Cuba. When he was president, Carter had lifted travel limitations between the United States and Cuba, and in his 2007 memoir *Beyond the White House* he wrote that he was upset that his successors "have reinstituted and tightened the restraints." During the Clinton years, the Carter Center was a mediator between Fidel Castro and Clinton, but Carter was surprised and disappointed when Clinton signed a 1996 bill that strengthened the U.S. embargo against Cuba. He used his post-presidential power to counter those restrictions. "At the Carter Center, we decided to continue our efforts to bring freedom to Cuba and to encourage friendly relations between Americans and the Cuban people."

When Clinton did find Carter useful, he usually paid a price for it. Carter became known as a freelancing dealmaker. After leaving office, he said, "I look on Washington with equanimity and amusement and an element of deep concern." In 1994, Carter went to North Korea as a private citizen and negotiated a deal with Kim Il Sung, North Korea's founder and Kim Jong Un's grandfather, on their nuclear weapons program. Rosalynn went along as a diligent notetaker. Before the trip, Carter was briefed by the State Department. After hours of briefings, he looked at the assembled diplomats. "None of you have told me what I need to know. You haven't told me what Kim Il Sung wants," he said, then answered the question himself. "What he wants is my respect. And I am going to give it to him." Carter knew that Kim would feel legitimized by a visit from a former American president. Carter went rogue and told Kim that the United States would take the threat of sanctions off the table if he agreed to freeze his nuclear program—something Clinton had not suggested. Carter

brought along a CNN crew and gave an interview before fully
briefing Clinton, who did not know what Carter had discussed
with the North Korean leader until he watched the interview himself on TV. Clinton felt betrayed and he was furious. He began
dispatching aides to go on television to make it clear that sanctions
were still a very real possibility. Carter had clearly overstepped
his boundaries as a former president. "At first I was a hero and
two hours later I was a bum!" he recalled. But Carter's conversation
with the North Korean leader did lead to a framework that would
become North Korea's first deal with the outside world. By 2002,
however, the agreement was declared a failure when North Korea
admitted that it was continuing to develop nuclear weapons and
had been violating the agreement for several years.

That same year, Carter asked Clinton to send him to Haiti to
persuade the leadership of the military dictatorship to relinquish
power to the country's first democratically elected president,
Jean-Bertrand Aristide, who was now in exile. Inside the White
House, there was concern about dispatching Carter. George
Stephanopoulos, a top Clinton aide, "worried about the appearance of subcontracting our diplomacy to a former president." But
Clinton eventually agreed to let him go. The draft of the press
release had Stephanopoulos concerned: "With President Clinton's approval, Jimmy Carter . . ." "We can't say this," said Stephanopoulos, who called the president and changed the wording.
"President Clinton has requested . . ." was much more presidential.
Stephanopoulos's point was simple: "Presidents don't 'approve' national security missions; they 'order' them. We couldn't afford to
give the impression that Carter had backed Clinton into a corner
(even if he had)." This had to look like it was Bill Clinton's idea
and not Jimmy Carter's.

Carter traveled to Port-au-Prince with Georgia senator Sam
Nunn and Chairman of the Joint Chiefs of Staff Colin Powell.

Clinton told the trio they had until noon the next day to strike a deal with military ruler Raoul Cédras to step down. After several frustrating visits with Cédras, Carter—at Rosalynn's suggestion—tried charming his wife, Yannick Cédras. Carter offered to autograph a photograph for their teenage daughter, and he gave their ten-year-old son a Carter Center pocketknife. But talks were slow-moving and, unbeknownst to Carter, Nunn, and Powell, Clinton had already ordered the U.S. military invasion to begin. A dramatic scene unfolded. As they sat with Cédras, one of his advisers ran into the meeting holding a submachine gun and yelled, "General Cédras, my commander in chief, we have to leave here right now. We have been betrayed." Carter also felt betrayed. As the 82nd Airborne started to invade, Carter drew up a watered-down agreement that called for Cédras to abandon power but allowed him to stay in Haiti and granted amnesty for the junta. Clinton called off the invasion and ordered sixty-one C-130s to turn around in the air. Back in Washington, Carter was supposed to stay at the White House and brief the president at breakfast the next morning, but again he decided to do an early-morning interview with CNN first. And once more, Clinton was shocked that Carter would tell the world what had happened without coming to him first. When Clinton, Carter, and Powell were in the Oval Office, Clinton screamed at Carter. Carter screamed back at him and accused him of putting their lives at risk by beginning the invasion while they were still in the country. Nunn finally stepped in and told the current and former president they needed to cool down before the press conference.

Carter had a slightly better relationship with George W. Bush than with Clinton, even though the two men were often on opposite sides of issues. The Carters attended Bush's 2001 inauguration. "Some people commented that we were the only voluntary Democrats present on the reviewing platform," Carter recalled,

Katrina—while Bush was seated nearby. The president and his wife sat onstage near King's flower-draped casket just feet away from Carter as he spoke from the lectern and unmistakably called Bush's leadership into question. "The struggle for equality is not over," Carter said. "We only have to recall the color of the faces in Louisiana, Alabama, and Mississippi—those most devastated by Katrina—to know there are not yet equal opportunities for all Americans."

Carter was considered a problem for Barack Obama also. Carter was expecting to speak at the 2008 Democratic Convention, but there was simply too much baggage. Instead he was asked to make a twenty-minute documentary and travel to the Gulf Coast to show the lingering devastation after Hurricane Katrina. "I spent a day in the area to carry out this assignment, but when we arrived at the convention in Denver, I was told that the film length would be only four minutes and I was requested not to speak, even to greet the delegates (meanwhile the Clintons played major roles in the convention)."

Regardless of the trouble Carter stirred up in his years after leaving Washington, the contributions he and his wife have made are undeniable. To this day, Clinton is "civil and respectful" with Carter but not "close and personal," as he is with the Bushes, said Clinton's former chief of staff and close friend Mack McLarty. Clinton, though, admires what the Carters have managed to accomplish since leaving office. Carter has truly redeemed himself. He has "made a bigger difference than any other of my predecessors," Clinton said. In 1999, Clinton presented Jimmy and Rosalynn Carter with the Presidential Medal of Freedom, the country's highest civilian honor. Clinton said they had "done more good things for more people in more places than any other couple on earth."

GEORGE H. W. BUSH FORGIVES HIMSELF

After his devastating 1992 defeat, George H. W. Bush invited Clinton to the White House for the customary meeting between the newly elected president and the departing president. He laid out the most worrisome policy matters that Clinton would be inheriting in a matter of weeks, including the violence between the Bosnian Serbs and Croats in the former Yugoslavia. Bush then turned to Clinton and said, "Bill, I want to tell you something. When I leave here, you're going to have no trouble from me. The campaign is over, it was tough and I'm out of here. I will do nothing to complicate your work and I just want you to know that." Later, in 1999, Bush wrote, "With few mild exceptions, I feel I've stuck to this pledge." When I asked, no one from Bush's office could even recall what the "mild exceptions" were that he was referring to.

Clinton's reaction to the majesty of the White House, according to Bush, was simply "wow." But residence staffers were not taking the transition well, because they were devastated to see the Bushes go. Though they try not to get too attached to whoever is in office, the staffers often seem to be pulling for the incumbent to be reelected, whether Democrat or Republican. When Clinton defeated Bush, White House pastry chef Roland Mesnier described the outcome as a "veritable disaster" and he said that Inauguration Day inside the White House was a "little short of funereal." Mesnier had grown so close to the Bushes that he was unsure whether he would be able to serve another president. He wasn't alone: when other residence staffers called in sick after President Clinton's election, the joke was that they had caught the "Republican flu." For the residence staff, the Bushes were a dream to work for. Even before she moved into the White House, Barbara Bush assured Chief Usher Gary Walters that she wouldn't be making any changes in the kitchen. "I've never had a bad meal [at the White House], so you just have the chefs put whatever they want to on the menu every evening and we'll be surprised at what we eat each night." It was a welcome change after Nancy Reagan, who always wanted to be in absolute control.

While Bush blamed himself for his 1992 defeat, Barbara and George W. mostly blamed Clinton. "There was the inevitable finger-pointing when the campaign was over about 'Whose fault was it?'—Ross Perot? The media? The campaign?" Bush senior wrote in an addendum to his book of letters, *All the Best*. "I will always feel it was mine because I was unable to communicate to the American people that the economy was improving." That first day after his father left office, George W. Bush, who had worked tirelessly on his campaign, said he did not know what his father would do. "I've asked him the question myself and he said, 'I don't know.' I just don't think he's worked it out."

On January 20, 1993, the day of Bill Clinton's inauguration, Bush revealed a hint of resentment at just how much change the Clintons were bringing to Washington. He called his wife, Barbara, "popular and wonderful" and wrote about his amazement at how "suddenly she is eclipsed by the new wave, the lawyer, the wife with an office in the White House; but time will tell and history will show that she was beloved because she was real and she cared and she gave of herself." While they joked about what a bad cook Barbara was and what life would be like with no valets to take care of them, they knew they would be fine back home in Houston, just as they had been before. They rented a two-story white colonial for seven months while their new home was being built in an upscale Houston suburb. "On January 20, we woke up [at the White House] and we had a household staff of ninety-three," Barbara Bush recalled. "The very next morning we woke up and it was just George, me, and two dogs—and that's not all that bad."

Their first day back in Texas, coffee began brewing at 5 a.m., they read the newspaper in bed, and by 7:30 Bush was on his way to his new ninth-floor office in a nondescript building in Houston. As the elevator doors opened, he told a photographer who had accompanied him, in the nicest way possible, that he wanted some space. "I've been in public life for more than twenty years, now I just want a little time for myself." He was not twiddling his thumbs. More than five hundred letters came in daily, and he had to get to work on his $83 million presidential library and museum at Texas A&M, in College Station, about ninety minutes from Houston.

Because so many people were driving by the Bushes' Houston home, the Texas Legislature enacted a law that allowed gates to be installed on streets leading to the private residences of former presidents. The Bushes bought a Mercury Sable wagon, and, after twelve years of not driving, Barbara enjoyed buying her own groceries. When people approached her in the store and asked, "Aren't you Barbara Bush?" she'd answer, with her famously dry wit, "No, she's much older than I am."

For Bush, redemption was personal and private, and he started seeking it when he was still in the White House. A week after he lost to Bill Clinton, the president visited the Vietnam Veterans Memorial to mark its tenth anniversary. It was the day before Veterans Day at 11:35 p.m. when Bush woke Barbara up and told her his plan. He knew she would want to go with him. White House usher Chris Emery and a small number of Secret Service agents accompanied them on the short ride. It was important to Bush to recognize those who had served.

As a World War II veteran, visiting the Vietnam memorial, with the names of more than 58,000 fallen and missing service

members etched on its black granite wall, was especially moving for Bush. He wanted to quietly and privately read the names
of some of the fallen without any press around to document it.
"There's not much time left to say what is in my heart, but one
thing I care about is Vietnam," he wrote in his diary before the
visit. "It's going to be emotional."

It was close to midnight when they arrived, and Bush, wearing
a leather aviator jacket with the presidential seal, approached a
small group gathered around the stage listening as people read
the names of friends and loved ones who were killed or missing in action. One woman was just about to read her husband's
name when she spotted the Bushes. She told the president that
she would be honored if he would read her husband's name instead. Bush agreed, and he and Barbara went up onstage. "They
let us cut in line," Barbara told me as she recalled that night. Bush
read a dozen names and then he and Barbara left quietly. They
signed autographs, including one for a vet who had lost both his
legs. ("If you can move your beard just two inches, I can sign right
here," Bush said before signing the shoulder of his tattered denim
jacket.) On the ride back to the White House, Emery spotted a
tear in the president's eye. Bush wanted to pay his respects as the
sitting president who had sent soldiers into war—cameras or not.
That sense of honor and pride never left him, and the nagging
feeling that he could have done more had he won was always
there. But, as the years passed, Bush learned to forgive himself
for losing.

BILL CLINTON STAYS IN THE GAME

Bill Clinton is Gladys Knight and not a Pip, joked former Clinton
aide Jamal Simmons. It is not easy for a president to leave office
and find himself a supporting character in not one but two of his

wife's presidential campaigns. "The great thing about being a former president is you can say whatever you think," Clinton said several years after leaving office. "Of course, nobody cares anymore."

The saxophone-playing, celebrity-loving president who ushered in a new era of laid-back cool in the White House (always careful not to let his titanic temper show) was now wearing hearing aids (from too many campaign rallies) and watching worriedly as his left hand started trembling (a result of signing so many autographs and not a sign of Parkinson's disease, according to his doctor). Clinton still stays up late chewing cigars, playing cards, reading voraciously—aides packed up eight thousand books when he left the White House—and finishing off the *New York Times* crossword puzzle religiously. But it is his restless spirit that concerns some of those closest to him. A reporter who traveled with Hillary Clinton as first lady joked to Bill that going on an international trip with him as a former president was like traveling with her when she was first lady: quick ceremonial meetings with heads of state, panel discussions, and treks to rural areas to see how people live. Clinton laughed, seemingly resigned to his fate as the spouse and not the person elected. "We've reversed roles," he said.

Clinton has been out of office more than twice as long as he was in it, so he should be comfortable with some of the changes by now. But he and Hillary have never felt at ease on the outside looking in. Hillary said that even after eight years of living in the residence, and enduring agonizing times there, she still views the White House "with the same awe I felt as a little girl pressing my face up to the gate to get a better look." Her husband's outsize personality can never be completely reined in. In the years since leaving office, he has spent more than half his time on the road, doing fund-raisers and global awareness events. He has spent lots of time with wealthy womanizing bachelors, including the controversial California supermarket billionaire Ron Burkle, whose personal Boeing 757, which includes a private bedroom suite, Clinton often used. It is known by the decidedly unpresidential moniker "Air F**k One" by Clinton aides and gossip columnists. He also maintained a friendship with the now-deceased disgraced financier Jeffrey Epstein, who was accused of sexually abusing young girls and who donated to the Clinton Foundation. Clinton took several trips on Epstein's private plane, which had its own disturbing nickname: the "Lolita Express." Given Clinton's past, it was unseemly at best to be spending so much time with these men, which not only fueled rumors that he was still cheating on Hillary but also called into question his judgment and morality.

But once Clinton left office, he made a list of global problems that he wanted to address, and, through his foundation, he has done a lot of good, including getting low-cost medicine to more than a million AIDS patients and working with subsistence farmers and doctors in Rwanda. Rwanda is especially important to him as he seeks redemption because in 1994, when he was president, the United States did not step in as Hutu extremists murdered hundreds of thousands of Tutsis and moderate Hutus.

But when it comes to Bill Clinton, nothing is black and white. He has also used his role as a former president to lend credibility to dubious business deals. His friendship with Canadian mining magnate Frank Giustra is problematic. In 2005, Clinton traveled to Kazakhstan on Giustra's MD-87 jet and had dinner with President Nursultan Nazarbayev, who was accused of human rights abuses. At their meeting, Clinton said he supported Kazakhstan's effort to head the Organization for Security and Co-operation in Europe, an international organization that monitors elections. By backing their bid, Clinton was going against U.S. foreign policy. Not long after their meeting, the company Giustra was working with secured the rights to Kazakhstan's uranium deposits, and Giustra donated more than $30 million to the Clinton Foundation.

dents and transformative presidents," like Franklin D. Roosevelt, Kennedy, and Reagan. He did not mention Clinton's name. Of course, this was upsetting; Clinton had, after all, balanced the budget for the first time in decades, passed the North American Free Trade Agreement, and overhauled welfare, but, like Carter, he felt that he got no respect.

Over the past 140 years, only two other Democratic presidents, Harry Truman and Jimmy Carter, have been alive long enough to witness another Democrat in the White House, and Clinton desperately wanted to be useful. "Clinton does absolutely everything for his legacy," one former Clinton aide told me, "and he really wanted to be of use to Obama." Obama, though, was never interested in long, meandering conversations, which are Clinton's specialty. But Obama knew when he needed help. After the "shellacking" he took in the 2010 midterm elections, when Republicans won control of the House and made huge gains in the Senate, it was time for Obama to call on the wisdom of the Presidents Club.

In December 2010, a month after the election, Obama invited Reagan aides to the White House to ask them how Reagan had dealt with self-doubt and the challenges he faced as president. He also asked Clinton to come for a White House visit to get his advice on an important tax deal. But more than advice, Obama wanted Clinton, the great salesman who was fast becoming a Democratic elder statesman, to sell the package and get out in front of reporters and television cameras to make the case to liberal Democrats who thought Obama was giving away too much to Republicans. Clinton was happy to oblige—this was what he'd always wanted. After their Oval Office meeting, the two men were alone because the rest of the staff was at a holiday party in the residence. They wandered the halls in the West Wing outside the Brady Press Briefing Room, and when they tried to open the door to the briefing room, they were surprised to find it was locked. They had to track down Press

Secretary Robert Gibbs to unlock it, and they asked him to turn on the microphone on the sleepy Friday afternoon. A staffer quickly announced over a loudspeaker that reporters—many of whom had left early or were working on stories in the small cubbies near the briefing room—should take their seats right away.

When Obama and his surprise guest approached the microphone, there was an audible gasp. Seeing a former president and the sitting president standing side by side was remarkable. "I have reviewed this agreement that the president reached with the Republican leaders," Clinton told the hastily assembled group of reporters. "The agreement taken as a whole is, I believe, the best bipartisan agreement we can reach to help the most Americans."

Obama barely said anything and eventually chimed in, "I've been keeping the first lady waiting."

"I don't want to make her mad," Clinton said, happy to stay behind and linger. "Please go."

After Obama left, Clinton gamely answered questions for another twenty minutes. When a reporter asked if he enjoyed offering advice more than governing himself, he said, "Oh, I had quite a good time governing. I am happy to be here, I suppose, when the bullets that are fired are unlikely to hit me, unless they're just ricocheting." But the truth was, he desperately missed being president. While in office, Clinton had read the Twenty-second Amendment closely, hoping to find a loophole that might let him run again, but there was no way to interpret it as anything other than a two-term limit for any president. Just as he was getting comfortable in the job, he was forced to leave it.

Clinton, like his sometime nemesis Jimmy Carter, has found redemption by staying in the game. "I like my life now," he has insisted. "I loved being president and it's a good thing we had a constitutional limit or I'd have made the people take me out in a pine box, probably."

VII

AMERICA'S PYRAMIDS

AND THE WEIGHT OF LEGACY

@flfw.com ("former leader of the free world")
—George H. W. Bush's playful email domain name after leaving office

The archivist of the United States, David Ferriero, works closely with former presidents to make sure as much material as possible from their administration is available for study. But there is tension between what to make available to the public, where to make it available, and how quickly to make it available. Presidential libraries live on long after presidents have passed away, and raising money for them and determining what will be in them takes up time and energy for former presidents. Their legacies mean everything to them—even when they insist they do not.

Obama appointed Ferriero to the post, and one of his first assignments was to go to Dallas in the fall of 2009 to meet with George W. Bush to review the plans for his impressive brick-and-limestone library as they were coming up on groundbreaking. Ferriero was "amazed and delighted" at how involved Bush was in the project, he told me. Laura Bush, a former librarian, played a huge role in the design of the interior and the exterior, and her thinking "touched every square inch of it," said Bush's best friend

Don Evans. She had special influence over the first exhibit, on education and children. It seemed like she was just as interested in cementing her husband's legacy as he was. The fact that Bush left office so deeply unpopular made their mission even more important. The former presidents are self-conscious about the contrived nature of their libraries, which are essentially homages to themselves. "I told President Obama," Bill Clinton said at the Bush library opening, "that this was the latest, grandest example of the eternal struggle of former presidents to rewrite history."

Presidents play the long game when it comes to their legacies, and they understand that history will ultimately be the judge of their decisions long after they have passed. Bush, for example, has defended the most controversial aspects of his presidency, including the wars in Iraq and Afghanistan, Abu Ghraib, and the use of waterboarding. "I truly believe," he said, "that the decisions I made will make the world a better place. Unfortunately, if you're doing big things, most of the time you're never going to be around to see them. . . . And I fully understand that. If you aim for big change, you shouldn't expect to be rewarded by short-term history."

Bush was especially proud of the fact that his library would include 210 million email messages. He leaned over his desk with a big grin and pointed at Ferriero. "You know, not one of those was mine," he announced triumphantly. Giving up the ability to email friends and family members was painful when he was president, but it made life much easier. At Bush's library there is a box on the wall with letters written to him while he was in office. When Bush saw it, according to a close friend, he said, "Well, these are all letters from people who liked what I was doing and thought I was doing a great job. Where are the other letters? I got plenty of those. Those need to be included here, too. That's what leadership is about: it's about making the tough decisions regardless

[of] popularity." (When Obama was president, he asked to see ten letters every day, all unfiltered, so that he could see what was on people's minds. He took those "10LADs"—some very heartfelt, asking for help, and some very critical of his presidency—to read at the end of his briefing book every night in the residence.)

REIMAGINING THE POST-PRESIDENCY

Jimmy and Rosalynn Carter have together revolutionized the post-presidency. Like George H. W. Bush, Jimmy Carter does not even like being called "Mr. President," because, he says, there is only one president at a time. (In the White House, Carter would not let "Hail to the Chief" be played, because he thought it was ostentatious.) When he left Washington, he estimated that he had a life expectancy of twenty-five more years—it has been fourteen more than that and counting—and both Carters wanted to do something meaningful with their lives.

They came up with the idea for the Carter Center suddenly. In January 1982, Jimmy Carter shot up in bed in the middle of the night, startling his wife, and said he knew what he wanted to do with his library—he wanted to do something entirely different. "We can make it into a place to help people who want to resolve disputes," he told her. "There is no place like that now." In the early 1980s, they also began devoting time to Habitat for Humanity. Their lives as a former president and first lady bore little resemblance to the five-star service of the White House. While they worked on fixing up a tenement building on the Lower East Side of New York City, they stayed in dorm-like rooms in Hell's Kitchen. They have helped renovate 4,300 homes. Carter became the first former president to win a Nobel Peace Prize. (Theodore Roosevelt, Woodrow Wilson, and Barack Obama were awarded the prize while they were in office.) Fully a third of the space in Carter's presidential library is devoted to his post-presidential years. Though Rosalynn insists that he was an underrated president—she said that "the thing that bothered me most was that no one knew what Jimmy had done in office"—it is clear that they consider their years out of Washington to be their greatest contribution.

The Carters have four children, twelve grandchildren, and several great-grandchildren, and they are committed to making sure that the Carter Center, which has a $600 million endowment, lives on long after they are gone. After leaving the White House, the Carters typically traveled to Africa several times a year together—their last trip to the continent was in 2014. Rosalynn spoke emotionally when describing a visit to a village where Guinea worm has been eradicated because of their work. "It's just so wonderful," she said to me tearfully, "just to see the hope on their faces that something good is happening."

LIBRARIES BORN OF SADNESS AND FRUSTRATION

The two most recent tragic ends to a presidency were when Richard Nixon resigned over Watergate and when the larger-than-life figure of Ronald Reagan became afflicted with Alzheimer's. Nixon raised $21 million to fund his library even as he argued with the government over the release of some 150,000 pages of documents and three thousand hours of White House tapes. Up until a few days before his death, Nixon was filing lawsuits to keep control of the records. The private library is now part of the federal system, and the National Archives has been making some of the tapes public since 1980. About eight hundred hours are deemed "private-personal" or "private-political"; at some point the latter will all be made public.

After his two terms came to an end, Reagan would live and

work in Los Angeles for the next fifteen years. His 13,939-square-foot thirty-fourth-floor office suite in the Fox Plaza building, on the Avenue of the Stars, cost $18,000 a month. He was so used to working every day that he showed up on the first day he was back home in California, before the phone line was set up properly. When calls came through, they went directly to him instead of the receptionist. "Ronald Reagan's office," he answered. "Ronald Reagan speaking." Friends got together and bought the Reagans a 6,500-square-foot, $2.5 million mansion at 666 St. Cloud Road, in Bel-Air, and leased it to the Reagans for $15,000 a month. (Nancy Reagan was superstitious and a believer in astrology, so the house address, 666 St. Cloud Road, was changed to 668 because of the number's association with the devil.)

Nancy made it her mission to make sure her husband would be remembered as one of the great presidents, even as Alzheimer's took hold of him. She was largely successful, and helped create a legacy so strong that Republican presidential candidates perpetually jockey to be the one most like Reagan. She raised nearly $60 million to build what was the most expensive of the nine presidential libraries run by the National Archives at the time. The 153,000-square-foot building in Simi Valley, California, sits atop a mountain and has jaw-dropping views of the Pacific. Nancy passed away in March 2016. Her funeral was held at the library. Not surprisingly, she planned every detail of the service, down to the guest list, which blended her love of Washington with her love of Hollywood. It included then–first lady Michelle Obama, Hillary Clinton, Tom Selleck, Arnold Schwarzenegger, and Caroline Kennedy. Former Canadian prime minister Brian Mulroney read a moving letter written by President Reagan and addressed to "Mrs. R" on Christmas Day 1981. In it, Reagan wrote to his wife, "There could be no life for me without you." Before she died, museum staff would sometimes see her sitting alone at her husband's grave with a Secret Service agent standing nearby. As was the case with Jimmy and Rosalynn Carter and George and Barbara Bush, the legacy Ronald Reagan left behind was intertwined with the woman who stood by his side all those years and who helped him shape it.

CREATING A DYNASTY, LIKE IT OR NOT

Aides sometimes called George H. W. Bush "F.L.F.W."—for "former leader of the free world." It started shortly after he left office, when his staff was setting up an internet domain name and an aide suggested the acronym. Bush had an irreverent sense of humor and took an immediate liking to it. He always thought the L-word, "legacy," was going to take care of itself, in part because he believed he'd made the best decisions he could as president and because he lived so long it enhanced what people knew of him. "Forty-One never let us use the word 'legacy' around him, as it connotes some sense of entitlement, which he did not like," said his spokesman, Jim McGrath, who worked for Bush up until his death. The Bushes raised more than $630 million for charity and were very involved in Houston's MD Anderson Cancer Center, a cause they held dear, especially because they lived through the devastating illness of their daughter Robin, who died of leukemia at three years old.

According to friends, Bush felt at peace in the final years of his life. He was still engaged in politics during Trump's first year in office, and he talked privately with Dan Coats, who was an old friend and Trump's director of national intelligence at the time. He asked Coats about the nuclear threat posed by North Korea and what the administration was doing about it. But he was always wary of predicting how history would view him, or any other former president. He said he was a "nervous wreck" on Election

Day whenever his sons were on the ticket. When, in 1998, Jeb won his race for governor of Florida and George W. was reelected governor of Texas, they were the first siblings to govern two states at the same time since Nelson Rockefeller was governor of New York and Winthrop Rockefeller was governor of Arkansas in the 1960s and early '70s. Bush 41 sought to distance himself from the idea of a dynasty, though, and said he was nothing like Joseph Kennedy, who pushed his children into politics. "This is not about vindication or legacy or entitlement. It's about the love of a father for his son and about the love of a mother for her son." When W. ran for president, he told donors, "This is not going to be George H. W. Bush, Part Two. It's going to be George W. Bush, Part One."

A COMPLICATED LEGACY

Bill Clinton's legacy has driven everything he has done publicly out of office. He privately hopes that the Monica Lewinsky scandal won't become his lasting legacy. The Clintons hated to leave the White House. George W. Bush's victory made the departure a little more painful, because he had beaten Al Gore. On their last full day in the White House, the whole family, including Chelsea, took advantage of their private theater one last time to watch the movie *State and Main* well after midnight. Clinton, a night owl, was up until 3:30 a.m. Relishing the last vestiges of power, he created eight new national monuments and nominated nine federal judges. He wanted to do everything he could to cement his legacy, especially since he knew that a Republican successor could undo much of what he had put in place. He told friends he worried about fading "into oblivion," and he seemed in a state of denial that January 20 would indeed mark the end of his political career.

When presidents meet privately with their successors in the

Oval Office after the election, they warn them about the most pressing national security issues facing the country. When they leave office, they receive their final national security report on their last morning, a dramatic acknowledgment that they will never bear the great responsibility of the presidency again—or the great honor, power, and prestige. Bill Clinton met with George W. Bush just as Bush's father had met with Clinton eight years earlier. Bush 41 had told Clinton that he thought the biggest issues facing the country were national missile defense and Iraq. Clinton told Bush 43 that he saw things differently. In order of importance, he said the biggest national security issues were Osama bin Laden and al-Qaeda; the tumult in the Middle East; the tension between nuclear powers India and Pakistan; the Pakistanis' relationship with the Taliban and al-Qaeda; North Korea; and finally Iraq. He told Bush he had come close to ending North Korea's missile program but that a president "probably would have to go there [North Korea] to close the deal."

Before the Bushes could start choosing furniture, however, they had to deal with a most unexpected complication: the 2000 recount, which kept the outcome of the election a mystery until December 12, more than a month after the votes were cast. Perhaps no one, aside from the candidates themselves, was watching the unfolding drama of the election quite as closely as the residence workers. On Election Night 2000, the Bushes were together in Austin, and George H. W. Bush felt more anxious than he had for his own elections in 1988 and 1992. He called his son's advisers all the time asking them for updates. Bush told him to stop watching the news. "I'm at peace," he said. On November 9, the Clintons hosted a dinner at the White House celebrating the two hundredth anniversary of the mansion, bringing together Lady Bird Johnson and three former first couples: the Fords, the

Carters, and the Bushes. Presidential grace prevailed over partisanship as the fraternity of presidents and the sorority of first ladies waxed nostalgic about their shared privilege of living in the White House. They all wondered who would be the next inhabitant. "It's the most nervous time in my entire life," George H. W. Bush said. White House chief usher Gary Walters scoured the news constantly, anxious to learn whom they would be catering to: George W. Bush or Al Gore. After the decision was handed down—and George and Barbara Bush wept with relief at the controversial outcome—Laura Bush had half the normal amount of time to prepare for their move. But it was a smooth transition. "You could hardly take a breath and it was done," White House florist Bob Scanlan said of their move-in.

The Clintons wanted to make the most of every remaining minute they had in the White House. "The fun of that night left them so tired that when Barbara, Jenna, and I glanced over at Bill during George's inaugural address, he was dozing," Laura Bush recalled. The night before, not only had Clinton stayed up watching a movie with his family, but he had been so consumed granting eleventh-hour pardons that he had to do so much last-minute packing that he was opening dresser drawers and dumping their contents straight into boxes. White House valets who were helping him were worried he would not get everything packed up in time. He later said his biggest mistakes were made when he was completely exhausted; aides worried that he might faint during a farewell meeting at Andrews Air Force Base on January 20. The last-minute flurry of activity was intense, even for Clinton.

On Inauguration Day 2001, when the traditional worship service was over at St. John's Episcopal Church, a church built in the early nineteenth century and attended by every president since James Madison, the Bushes and the Cheneys got in their motorcade. It would be a short ride across Pennsylvania Avenue to the

White House for the breakfast that the outgoing president and first lady always host for the incoming president and first lady. But instead the Bushes and the Cheneys "sat there, and waited and waited and waited," a still-miffed Dick Cheney told me. Cheney, who would become vice president in a matter of hours, asked the Secret Service what the holdup was, and they replied, "Well, the president is not ready to receive you yet." Cheney was fuming. "I don't care how much they're messing around—at high noon our guy's going to be president." They eventually got to the White House for the reception, after which, in the motorcade to the Capitol for the swearing-in ceremony, Cheney sat next to Vice President Al Gore in a limousine behind Clinton and Bush. He asked him what had caused the delay. "Bill was up there signing pardons," Gore said and shrugged. Eight years later, Cheney would wish his boss were doing the same.

Clinton would use his power up until the very end, no matter how poorly it reflected on his legacy. According to Article II of the Constitution, presidents have the power "to grant reprieves and pardons for offenses against the United States, except in cases of impeachment." In a nineteenth-century case, the Supreme Court concluded that their power "is unlimited." The ability to have federal felony convictions pardoned gives the president a dizzying amount of responsibility, and it can become an all-consuming obligation in the final days of the presidency. But for Clinton it became an act of personal retribution. When he took his final trip on his beloved Air Force One for a quick stop to his hometown of Little Rock, Arkansas, he walked up and down the aisles of the plane, looking in on conference rooms and stopping by the press compartment at the very back of the plane. "You got anybody you want to pardon?" he asked reporters, to their amusement. "Everybody in America either wants somebody pardoned or a national monument."

Of the 140 pardons that Clinton granted late into the night and the next morning, the most controversial one was for the fugitive financier Marc Rich, who was the ex-husband of Denise Rich, who had written huge checks to the Clintons, including a $450,000 contribution to Clinton's presidential library fund. Rich had been indicted on charges of tax evasion and was splitting his time between Israel and Switzerland. Clinton later regretted the Rich pardon. "It was terrible politics," he said, and it had not been "worth the damage to my reputation." In his first interview as a former president, in an April 2002 issue of *Newsweek*, he said, "I was just angry that after I worked so hard and after all that money had been spent proving that I never did anything wrong for money, that I'd get mugged one more time on the way out the door."

But in his 2004 memoir, *My Life*, Clinton wrote that he wished he had pardoned more people, including Webb Hubbell. He planned to personally apologize to Hubbell, who was a longtime friend of Hillary Clinton's and who President Clinton named associate attorney general. Hubbell was eventually sent to prison for his role in the Whitewater scandal. Clinton was keeping score, and for the most part he thought he had done nothing wrong: "President Carter had granted 566 clemencies in four years. President Ford had granted 409 in two and a half years," he wrote. "President Reagan's total was 406 in his eight years. President Bush had granted only 77, and they included the controversial pardons of the Iran-Contra figures." Clinton issued 396 pardons, 61 commutations, and two other types of clemency—a total of 459.

Clinton left the White House with a 66 percent approval rating, but in the following weeks he watched helplessly as those numbers plummeted. In exile, he watched television obsessively and worried about what people were saying about him. Puttering around his suburban home, not surprisingly, was not a good fit for the former president, who grew increasingly restless during those first few weeks away from the center of political power. In February, less than a month after leaving office, he wrote an op-ed for the *New York Times* called "My Reasons for the Pardons," filled with righteous indignation. But his op-ed had stretched the truth. The *Times* decided to add an editor's note to clarify his misstatements, particularly Clinton's assertion that three prominent lawyers, who were former lawyers for Marc Rich, had reviewed and pushed for the pardon. The editor's note stated that the three lawyers denied any involvement.

But the Rich pardon was not the only thing plaguing Clinton in those final days. He wanted to come to an understanding with the special prosecutor to put an end to the legal issues that had consumed his presidency. Eventually he agreed to a deal that included a five-year suspension of his Arkansas law license, but first he would have to admit that he had not provided a judge with honest testimony in the Lewinsky matter. He had to make the admission while he was still in office. On his last full day as president, January 19, 2001, Clinton "accepted and acknowledged" that "he knowingly gave evasive and misleading answers" to a judge "concerning his relationship with Ms. Lewinsky," and that "he engaged in conduct that is prejudicial to the administration of justice" in relation to the Paula Jones sexual harassment case against him. With that he was suspended by the Arkansas Bar Association for five years and ordered to pay a fine of $25,000. It was remarkable for a sitting president to have his law privileges stripped away in his home state—a state he served as governor for five terms. He was furious and joked to friends (though it did not always come across as a joke) that the Republicans who were investigating him reminded him of Iran's mullahs.

Another scandal plagued the Clintons in the days after they left the White House. They were accused of taking $190,000 worth of what they believed were gifts, including, china, rugs, and flatware, to furnish their newly purchased homes in Chappaqua and Northwest Washington. Unlike most presidents, the Clintons did not have a home to go to while they lived in the White House. When they did finally become homeowners in 1999, rumors circulated that Hillary had registered for household items at luxury department stores like a new bride. The reports in the *Washington Post* were deeply embarrassing, including the fact that $28,000 worth of gifts were actually meant for the White House and not for the Clintons. Worse still, $7,375 worth of tables and chairs were from Denise Rich. Jimmy Carter, as usual, was completely unafraid and unrestrained when it came to criticizing Clinton. He called the Rich pardon "disgraceful" and said that "some of the factors in his pardon were attributable to his large gifts." The story dragged on, and a year after they left the White House, Republican congressional investigators released documents that showed the Clintons had not accurately reported the value of some of the gifts they received. The total value was more like $360,000, not $190,000. Less than a month after leaving office, the Clintons paid the government $86,000 for the items they had taken with them. They returned several things that belonged to the White House and eventually paid for the rest.

On Inauguration Day in 2001, Clinton stood on the inaugural platform with George H. W. Bush, the man he'd beaten in 1992, and his son, the man who vowed to undo much of the work he had done in office. As Clinton was leaving the inaugural platform, he was faced with the guilt of knowing that he was partly to blame for Gore's loss—Gore would not turn to him for help because of the baggage he carried. He also had the bittersweet feeling of watching Hillary leave him behind to walk into the Capitol for lunch as a new senator representing the state of New York. She would be the Clinton in elected office from then on.

Clinton soon found himself alone in the cedar-shingled white Dutch colonial nestled in the quiet New York suburb of Chappaqua. A sign hung outside: THE CLINTONS, EST. 1999. He was not content to spend his days as a former president "taking pills and dedicating libraries." At first Clinton's former chief of staff and close friend Mack McLarty was concerned about him, he said. It turned out that adjusting to normal life was harder for Clinton than it was for George H. W. Bush, George W. Bush, or Barack Obama. "Before President Clinton started focusing on his book, he was worried about what he was going to do the next day," McLarty said. He went from being the most powerful person in the world to wandering around a mansion in suburbia while his wife fulfilled her ambition to embark on her own political career in the Senate.

The low point came when his beloved chocolate Labrador, Buddy, died. Buddy had been his companion during the tumult of the Lewinsky scandal. In a famous image from his presidency, Clinton held Buddy's leash in his right hand and Chelsea's hand in his left as they walked out to Marine One to go to Martha's Vineyard for summer vacation the day after he admitted his affair with Lewinsky on national television. Hillary was humiliated and upset in dark sunglasses as she held Chelsea's other hand. Hillary had bought the dog for Bill in 1997, knowing that he would struggle being an empty nester once Chelsea went away to college on the West Coast. Her instinct was right, proving the old adage "If you want a friend in Washington, get a dog." Buddy slept in the Clintons' bedroom and was a constant companion on hikes, a kind of salve for Clinton's loneliness. Buddy was hit by a teenage girl on Route 117, near the Clintons' cul-de-sac. Clinton called Buddy's death "by far the worst thing that happened in the first year" out of office. He got another dog, a nephew of Buddy's, but it was not the same, since he had become so attached to Buddy during those difficult final days in the White House.

Clinton was lonely. He asked his White House valet, Oscar Flores, to work for him in Chappaqua. Flores was sometimes the only other person in the house with Clinton, and he became a link to Clinton's past life. Before he came up with the idea for the expansive foundation and annual conference that would come to define his post-presidency, Clinton, a quintessential extrovert who feeds off of interacting with people, became obsessive about his presidential library in Little Rock. When he walked through the replica of the Oval Office, a centerpiece of presidential libraries, he said, "The ceiling is too low." Staff measured, and, of course, he was right—it was several inches too low. The ceiling was quickly replaced.

Clinton also became obsessed with winning over his enemies. He called former Speaker of the House Newt Gingrich—who led impeachment proceedings against him and who once compared the Clinton White House to *The Jerry Springer Show*—on the night his mother died to express his condolences. Trent Lott, a Republican and the former Senate majority leader from Mississippi, called Clinton when he had a heart attack. "He and I still talk," Lott said at a 2009 public event. "You know, when he had a heart attack, I really got worried about it. I was afraid he was going to kill himself. I called him and told him so."

He might have felt isolated in Chappaqua, but he also hated being in Washington. In February 2001, Clinton called a friend and said he could not stand staying in the capital even briefly and he was heading to Chappaqua that night to get away. Hillary was mad at him, because his half brother Roger had been arrested for drunk driving and disorderly conduct after Clinton had pardoned him for a drug conviction. She was also angry about news reports that he paid almost half a million dollars to her brother Hugh for legal work he had done for applicants requesting presidential clemency. It was a mess, and Hillary was in the Senate and having to answer questions about her husband's decisions at the tail end of his presidency. "He wanted to get out of town," his friend told me. "He was a pariah."

Clinton eventually began using his bona fides and celebrity status as a former president to travel the world and use his influence. Even after leaving office, when a former president goes abroad and meets with foreign leaders, the message he carries is incredibly consequential. The world is the former presidents' clubhouse. A foreign leader meeting with a former president can help provide legitimacy after a contested election, and support from a former president for a specific policy can help influence voters. Former presidents follow a tradition of asking the sitting president for permission before they get involved. When George W. Bush was in office, Clinton reached out to Bush's national security adviser Condoleezza Rice, whom he knew personally from when she was a provost at Stanford University and Chelsea was a student there. The Bush administration was negotiating the release of twenty-four detained servicemen after their aircraft was forced down over China in April. Clinton had been asked to give a speech in Hong Kong; he said he needed the money. But he also knew that his old friend Jiang Zemin, the Chinese president, would be there. He did not want to get in the way of the Bush administration's negotiation efforts. Clinton called up Rice and made a blunt plea: "I need to give a speech, they're gonna pay me a ridiculous amount of money and you guys nearly bankrupted me. I'm an American first and here's the problem, Jiang Zemin is going to be there and the airplane's still on the island and I cannot go there without seeing him. He's my friend and I will not insult him or be rude or do anything. So you have to tell me what to do. If you don't want me to go, I won't go. If you want me to go, I'll deliver the message and I will make sure he knows it's President Bush's message, not mine. There's only one president at a time, whether I agree with it or not."

Rice called him back and said, "We'd like for you to go."

Clinton replied, "Okay, what am I supposed to say?" The country is always more important than the person sitting in the Oval Office.

Clinton wants to be seen as an asset to the Democratic Party, and among his most notable moments was the rousing speech he gave in support of Barack Obama at the 2012 Democratic Convention. But after nearly two decades out of office, and with the #MeToo movement exploding, his popularity has sunk below 50 percent after reaching a peak of 69 percent in 2013. During most midterm elections since he left office, the more events he would do, the better he would feel, because it meant that he was still considered an important and impactful elder statesman. He always kept track of the number of events he did each cycle, and if there was a dip he noticed it. But the #MeToo movement has caused people to reassess his past, and Hillary's 2016 loss has somewhat diminished the Clinton brand. When Clinton was promoting a political thriller he wrote with author James Patterson in 2018, his book tour was consumed with questions about Lewinsky. When he said he would not handle the fallout from the affair any differently today than he had back then, it showed that he did not understand how much the culture had changed, especially for the liberal Democrats who were vowing to reshape the party. "I have never talked to [Lewinsky], but I did say publicly on more than one occasion that I was sorry," Clinton said in a *Today* show interview. "Do you think President Kennedy should have resigned? Do you believe President Johnson should have resigned?" He seemed woefully out of touch and completely out of step with the new era of accountability.

In 2017, at the dawn of the #MeToo movement, several women accused Bush 41 of touching them inappropriately in the past. One woman said that in 2006, when she was running for a seat in the Maine State Senate, she posed with Bush, who "grabbed my butt and joked saying 'Oh, I'm not THAT President [referring to Bill Clinton].'" Bush's office released a statement apologizing. "To anyone he has offended, President Bush apologizes most sincerely." There is no such thing as anonymity in the post-presidency. For better and for worse.

During the 2018 midterms, the Democrat in the closest congressional race in Arkansas did not ask Clinton, who was once governor and attorney general of that state, to campaign for him. No longer "explainer-in-chief," in 2018, Clinton appeared at a small number of private fund-raisers for midterm candidates. Even though Clinton called him to offer his congratulations after he won the Democratic primary, Andrew Gillum did not ask him to help in his race for governor of Florida. Clinton, it seemed, was becoming radioactive.

Donna Shalala was a former president of the Clinton Foundation and the longest-serving health and human services secretary in history when she served in Clinton's cabinet, so when she decided to run for Congress in south Florida, it seemed logical for her to ask Clinton for his help. She did not. The scars from the Lewinsky scandal were deep. She had been the chancellor of the University of Wisconsin–Madison and the president of Hunter College, and when she went to a cabinet meeting with Clinton shortly after the Lewinsky scandal started coming to light, she said she "blew up" at him. "It was the young person thing," she said. "It just hit against every principle I've had in my life and the world that I come from. I have zero tolerance with a faculty member with this kind of behavior. I've fired tenured professors over this, and it was just unacceptable. . . . It was that it was a young person and an intern."

But she was happy to have Hillary Clinton campaign for her in south Florida, even referring to her as "Wonder Woman." Bill Clinton was another matter altogether.

OBAMA'S CONTROVERSIAL LIBRARY

The reason Barack Obama spends a significant amount of time raising money for his library is simple: presidential libraries cost astronomical sums to build. But donors can begin giving money while a president is in office, and while most libraries disclose some of their donors, there is no requirement for them to reveal that information. The Obama Foundation lists its donors, but the sizes of their donations are given in ranges. Almost seventy donors, some well known, like the Oprah Winfrey Charitable Foundation and the Bill & Melinda Gates Foundation, have donated more than $1 million each. Many presidents make decisions that seem tied to raising money for their libraries and the preservation of their all-important legacies. Clinton, who pardoned Marc Rich, whose ex-wife made a hefty contribution to his library, is not an outlier. In 1993, Edwin Cox Jr., who had been convicted of bank fraud, was pardoned by George H. W. Bush, who later received hundreds of thousands of dollars for his library from Cox's father, a wealthy GOP donor.

Presidential libraries preserve the history of each president, both as museums and as research facilities. The presidential library system began when FDR donated his papers to the federal government and started building a library close to his home in Hyde Park, New York, while he was still in office. The library is located in a picturesque setting high above the Hudson River. It is modest compared with the giant behemoths of Reagan, Bush 41, Clinton, and Bush 43. Libraries are built with private funds raised by the president's foundation. Like the dollar figures on the speaking circuit, the price tag to build a presidential library has surged. Once presidential libraries are complete, the keys are handed over to the National Archives and Records Administration (NARA), staffed by the government. But Barack Obama's library will not be a library at all, it will not hold any of Obama's presidential records, and it will not be run by NARA. The enormous four-building "working center for citizenship" will be built on nineteen acres on the South Side of Chicago, and it will be more like an urban center, complete with a gym and a recording studio, than a traditional quiet academic setting. The Obama Foundation will run the museum.

In addition to the recording studio, Obama's presidential center will include a 235-foot-high museum tower and a sledding hill, and it will cost an estimated $500 million. Its construction is being met with complaints from the Chicago neighborhood in which it is being built as critics voice their concern that the center will displace residents. Another point of contention: the Obama Foundation plans to do something no other library has done and digitize the more than thirty million pages of unclassified paper records from his administration, including more than 275 million emails and more than three million digital photographs, a process that will take years and years. Presidential historians are concerned that this won't have the stated effect of democratizing the records by making them available online, but that instead the process of giving access to information will be dramatically slowed down. Records from presidential libraries are invaluable for historians and journalists, who can physically hold documents the presidents once touched and uncover new and important information about how they made decisions in office. Obama's presidential center will have a staff of approximately twenty-five to thirty archivists to work on the immense project; 275 million emails divided among twenty-five to thirty archivists is approximately ten million emails per person. If these workers can review five hundred emails in a single day—and work 365 days a year—it will take them an astonishing fifty-five years to finish. The archivists will also have to look through paper documents and they will be assigned file boxes roughly the length of three football fields to review. If one archivist can get through a full inch of documents in a single day, and that person also works 365 days a year without a break, it will take her twenty-nine and a half years to get through her allocation.

There is also a concern that records not be selectively digitized, and historians worry that Obama's library will set the precedent for future presidential libraries. Pulitzer Prize–winning historian Robert Caro, who is best known for the thousands of pages he has written chronicling Lyndon Johnson's political career, said, "I don't want anyone deciding what's going to be digital. I don't want anything standing between me and the papers. I think the younger generation doesn't know what it's like to hold the actual thing in your hand. . . . To see that cable traffic, to hold in your hand what Johnson was reading? I can't even explain it to you." Defenders argue that the bulk of Obama's presidential records are already digital and that the handwritten notes and cables of the Johnson era are no longer a good comparison because emails, Word documents, and JPEGs have taken their place. And most people cannot travel to what Caro affectionately calls "America's pyramids," making Obama's approach more accessible to the general public.

And then there is the concern that the foundation, a private

VIII

*Everything was returned to normal. Everything was
basically reset, like we were never there.*

—The Obamas' social secretary, Deesha Dyer

In the days surrounding President George H. W. Bush's state
funeral at Washington National Cathedral, the sprawling Bush
family stayed at Blair House, the cream-colored guesthouse for
visiting dignitaries located across Pennsylvania Avenue from the
White House. Melania Trump extended an invitation to former
first lady Laura Bush and many of the Bushes' children and grandchildren to stop by the White House and see the Christmas dec-
orations the day before Bush's funeral. She met Laura Bush, the
only former first lady with whom she has any relationship, in
the East Wing and offered her hot chocolate and cookies. More
than a dozen Bush family members posed in front of a portrait
of George H. W. Bush that was draped in black fabric, a White
House tradition when a former president dies. The Bushes were
grateful to be invited to stay at Blair House, and they credit Melania and her chief of staff, Lindsay Reynolds, who had worked in
the Bush White House, with the invitation.

The only genuine interaction between George W. Bush and
Donald Trump has been through their wives, who are part of a

small and selective sisterhood (now only five women strong) who understand the pressure, and near-constant criticism, piled on first ladies. Laura Bush's White House chief of staff, Anita Mc-Bride, said that when Bush visited Melania at the White House shortly after Trump's election, she tried to comfort her. "As first lady you're faced with the realization that history does not end with you," she said. During the December visit with Laura, Melania was consumed with worry about the negative public re-action to the dramatic bright red trees she had displayed in the White House for the 2018 holiday season. The trees were being compared to the red costumes from the popular Hulu series *The Handmaid's Tale*, based on the dystopian thriller about a future world where women have lost their rights—for some viewers a not-too-subtle nod to the Trump administration. But Laura tried to reassure Melania and told her to let it go. "People will go after you no matter what," she told her.

Laura Bush was touched by the visit, and while she was back at the White House she asked to meet with members of the resi-dence staff who had worked for her family when she lived there. Months earlier, Melania had invited retired White House maître d' George Hannie and current White House butler Buddy Carter to fly on Air Force One to attend Barbara Bush's funeral in Hous-ton, because she knew how close the two men were to the Bush family, and to Barbara Bush especially. Neil Bush said he and his wife walked up to Melania at his mother's funeral to intro-duce themselves. "She's engaging, she asks questions, and she's thoughtful," he told me. "I was very impressed with her. I don't know what I was expecting, but it wasn't that." After that White House visit, in the afternoon, the Trumps took an eight-vehicle motorcade 250 yards across Lafayette Square to meet with the Bushes at Blair House to pay their condolences, which seemed rather extravagant. Melania wore towering stilettos and Laura

Bush wore simple black flats. Laura and Melania may be friendly, but the Trumps, as members of a rival Republican clan, stayed for just twenty-three minutes. It was the only time George W. Bush and Donald Trump had ever spoken in person.

WELCOME TO THE CLUB

The first lady has an incredible opportunity to draw attention to issues she cares about, but she also faces an unparalleled level of scrutiny. It can be hard for presidents to deal with the constant media glare and sometimes even harder for their spouses, who are often trying to also protect their children. That is why leaving the White House can be especially liberating for first ladies. It is not easy wearing a semi-permanent poker face and exercising extraordinary self-control when their husbands—or their own looks—are being criticized.

Susan Porter Rose, who worked for Pat Nixon, Betty Ford, and Barbara Bush, recalled times when Barbara Bush refused to read the newspapers and "tuned out" because what was being said about her husband was too negative. Rose called it a form of "self-preservation." It happens to every first lady, regardless of political party. Eleanor Roosevelt, the first activist first lady, was told to "stick to her knitting" by one member of her husband's administration; Pat Nixon's shy demeanor was mistaken as standoffish, and she was derided as "Plastic Pat"; Rosalynn Carter earned the nickname "the Second President" because she sat in on her husband's cabinet meetings and quietly took notes. When Barbara Bush was first lady, 150 students at the all-women's Wellesley College signed a petition saying they were "outraged" by the decision to have her speak at their graduation, arguing that she was chosen only because of the man she had married. Critics dubbed Michelle Obama's signature campaign to end childhood obesity the "food police." Every first lady has been reprimanded at one point for being too outspoken or too reserved, too controlling or not ambitious enough. Even after they leave the White House, they are held to exacting standards. Jackie Kennedy was vilified for marrying the billionaire Greek shipping magnate Aristotle Onassis five years after her husband's assassination with headlines blaring, "Jackie, How Could You?" and "Jack Kennedy Dies Today for a Second Time."

These women have challenging roles and often feel like they are walking on a tightrope, trying to be effective without offending anyone. During times of crisis, it is the first lady who acts as the consoler in chief. Whether it is a devastating natural disaster or a heart-wrenching meeting with the parents of fallen soldiers, first ladies have been called upon to meet family members who have lost loved ones. One East Wing aide put it best when she told me that the East Wing, where the first lady's office is located, is the heart of the administration and the West Wing is the head.

Now that Barbara Bush and Nancy Reagan have passed away, Laura Bush has taken on the role of the grande dame of the former first ladies. (Rosalynn Carter is the eldest, but she is more involved in the Carter Center and Habitat for Humanity than she is in the sorority.) And, like all the other first ladies, Laura Bush has experienced having her words twisted. Anita McBride told me that Laura was "so happy to write her memoir and say things that would have been skewed as political or self-serving before. She is not the loudest voice in the room, but people listen when she speaks." Barbara Bush always liked her daughter-in-law, for good reason. Laura famously got Barbara's son George W. to quit drinking, something that Barbara and George senior were always grateful to her for. Barbara said her daughter-in-law followed "a great philosophy in life—you can either like it or not, so you might as well like it."

Barbara Bush told Laura to keep any policy disagreements she had with her husband private. That was not always easy. The day before her husband's 2001 inauguration, Laura slipped during an interview with Katie Couric. She said she thought that the *Roe v. Wade* Supreme Court ruling legalizing abortion should not be overturned, as some in her husband's party wanted, and when it came to gay marriage, she said she had reminded him that they had many friends who were gay or had gay children. "There was, from the start, a desire by some in the press and many of the pundits to discover any point of disagreement between us," she said. Of course, her statement supporting *Roe v. Wade* made headlines. In 2005, she was asked whether she wanted her husband to name a woman to the Supreme Court to fill Sandra Day O'Connor's spot, and she replied, "Sure, I would really like for him to name another woman. I know that my husband will pick somebody who has a lot of integrity and strength. And whether it's a man or a woman, of course I have no idea." That remark became the attention-grabbing headline "First Lady Wants New Female Justice." (Bush tried to put his White House counsel, Harriet Miers, on the bench, but her nomination was withdrawn. He ultimately appointed two men to the court, Samuel Alito and John Roberts.)

The rules of the First Ladies Club are similar to those for the Presidents Club, the most important being that the sitting first lady is rarely the object of direct criticism from other members. Two weeks after Trump's election, Barbara Bush wrote a letter to Melania. (She had prepared a funny note to Bill Clinton, too, assuming Hillary would win—"Welcome to the First Ladies Club, we can't wait to initiate you," it read—but that letter would never be sent.) Melania was facing questions about when, or even if, she would move into the White House with the Trumps' then-ten-year-old son, Barron. In the letter, Bush welcomed Melania to the

"First Ladies very exclusive club" and said, "Living in the White House is a joy and their [the residence staff's] only job is to make you happy. If you decide to stay in NYC that will be fine also. When you come to the White House let your son bring a friend. That is my unasked for advice."

In 2012, Barbara and Laura attended a conference at the LBJ Presidential Library. Library director Mark Updegrove introduced them. "Laura Bush has graciously allowed me to call her Laura for the evening, so I will be referring to her as Laura and you as Mrs. Bush." Barbara shot him a withering glance and said, "I would certainly hope so." The audience burst into laughter. For the most part, Laura was "very deferential" to her mother-in-law, said McBride. "She knows that that's Bar." Ultimately, Barbara and Laura were bound by their shared love of George W. Bush. When Laura was asked at the conference what the biggest misconception about her husband was, she said, "That he was sort of a heedless, cowboy caricature." Barbara cut in, "Don't mention it to me, it makes me so mad." When Barbara was asked for the biggest misconception about her husband, George senior, she said, "There was none, he is a saint."

"Sometimes I'm reminded of things that I've said and I'm mortified," Barbara said when a staffer reminded her of how she had told her husband that he needed to lose weight. But it was that kind of candor that earned Barbara the love of the White House residence staff, whom she teased constantly. She was the same way with the press. On a foreign trip, a reporter asked her, "Are you going to be buying pearls in Bahrain?" She looked at the reporter and said, "Not as long as [costume jewelry designer] Kenneth Jay Lane is alive."

Like her mother-in-law, Laura Bush has a great respect for the tradition of the First Ladies Club and does not openly criticize any of the other women who have occupied the position. In a

2018 interview, she said she thought Melania had "done a lovely job" and that she was a "wonderful representative for the United States." For Laura Bush, being married to the son of a former first lady and being first lady for eight years has made her aware of how bound together all of these women are. Veteran White House reporter Ann Compton said Laura told her that she almost burst into tears when her Secret Service agent informed her that all of the former first families were secure in the terrifying hours after the 9/11 terrorist attacks.

"WHEN THE BATTLE'S OVER AND THE GROUND IS COOLED . . ."

Lady Bird Johnson, who was first lady from 1963 to 1969, said a first lady needs to be a "showman and a salesman, a clotheshorse and a publicity sounding board, with a good heart, and a real interest in the folks" from all over the country, rich and poor. She must take up a cause that's deemed weighty enough that it is worthy of her time but not controversial, and she must plan Christmas parties, governors' balls, Easter Egg Rolls, and dozens of luncheons and events, all while looking flawless. No easy feat. First ladies can get attached to living in the White House; it is their home for four to eight years, after all. During the stress and strain of the move out of the White House, first ladies have been seen on the morning of the inauguration stealing a quiet moment to themselves.

First ladies have always been able to relate to one another as wives, mothers, and political spouses. Those jobs, of course, do not end when they leave the White House. Often their relationships have nothing to do with the political party they have come to represent. The unexpected friendship between Jacqueline Kennedy and Nancy Reagan began with a 1981 visit that Rose

Kennedy made to the White House, the first time she had been back since her son John's death. The Reagans had a wonderful time with Rose and later, in 1985, went to a fund-raiser at Senator Ted Kennedy's house in McLean, Virginia, to help raise money for the John F. Kennedy Presidential Library. "He was a patriot who summoned patriotism from the heart of a sated country," Reagan told the crowd of wealthy donors on that summer night. "Which is not to say I supported John Kennedy when he ran for president, because I didn't. I was for the other fellow. But you know, it's true: when the battle's over and the ground is cooled, well, it's then that you see the opposing general's valor." The Reagans tried to talk with every member of the Kennedy family they could, and after his remarks, Jackie approached President Reagan and said, "That was Jack." He had summed him up perfectly. Ted Kennedy sent the president a letter the next morning expressing his appreciation: "Your presence was such a magnificent tribute to my brother."

The day after Ted Kennedy died, in 2009, Nancy Reagan did a telephone interview with Chris Matthews on MSNBC's *Hardball*. "We were close," she said of the Kennedys, "and it didn't make any difference to Ronnie or to Ted that one was a Republican and one a Democrat." Jackie did not care if Nancy was a Republican or a Democrat, either; she had a genuine respect for her. According to Gustavo Paredes, the son of Jackie's personal assistant Providencia Paredes, Jackie appreciated Nancy because she brought glamour back to the White House after four years of the decidedly less fashion-conscious Rosalynn Carter. Jackie also liked that Nancy invited cultural icons like Ella Fitzgerald and Frank Sinatra to perform there. Like Jackie, Nancy was appalled when she saw the state of the White House. She raised $800,000 to redecorate it, with most of the money going to updating the second-floor residence, mirroring what Jackie had done two decades earlier.

(Reagan was well aware that she was called "Queen Nancy" in the press and candidly wrote in her memoir that she "won the unpopularity contest" among the other first ladies "hands down.")

Though during their years in the White House they can feel like they are living in a fishbowl (in 2015 Hillary Clinton told the National Automobile Dealers Association that she had not actually been behind the wheel of a car since 1996), it is striking how many presidential families choose to replicate the rooms of "the People's House" when they become private citizens, as the Clintons did in their Chappaqua home. When Jacqueline Kennedy moved her two young children into an eighteenth-century Georgetown town house after JFK's assassination, she asked her decorator to copy the bedrooms the children had lived in in the White House so they would be just like the rooms they had slept in when their father was alive. Pat Nixon's fierce devotion to her husband during Watergate was reflected in the decor of their California home. Their daughter Julie wrote, "When he was defeated, Mother upheld him." Pat rearranged the photos at Nixon's office at Casa Pacifica exactly as they had been in the Oval Office. In the Obamas' Washington, D.C., home, the living room furniture is arranged just how it was in the White House and the house is sprinkled with mementos from their time there, including a book autographed by Nelson Mandela "that reminds us it was all real," Michelle Obama said. The Obamas' daughters, sentimental about their old lives, moved their beds from their White House bedrooms into their parents' new home.

ROSALYNN CARTER AND THE CLUB

It is a rite of passage for 2020 Democratic presidential candidates to make the trip down to Plains, Georgia, to get the blessing of Jimmy and Rosalynn Carter. But, just as Jimmy Carter is an outlier in the Presidents Club, his wife is also sometimes excluded from the First Ladies Club. Rosalynn told me that if Michelle Obama asked her for advice about life as a former first lady—which she has not—she would tell her that she still has a great opportunity, and responsibility, to create change. "You still have the resources," she said. "You can still call anybody in the world." Like her husband, she has resented not being asked for her advice as often as she would like. Rosalynn's signature issue was mental health, a subject that dominates the news decades later. As first lady, she wanted mental illness to be treated like any physical illness, and one month after taking office, President Carter created the Mental Health Commission because of her. Even so, when the Obamas held a mental health summit at the White House in 2013, Rosalynn was left off the guest list. "I got really mad," a former Carter aide said. Mrs. Obama's chief of staff, Tina Tchen, said it was an oversight. According to President Carter's aide, Rosalynn did not believe them and felt intentionally excluded. When asked in an interview if Hillary Clinton had sought her input when crafting health-care legislation or if either Michelle Obama or President Obama had asked for her advice when developing the health-care overhaul, given her extensive work on mental health issues, Rosalynn said simply, "The answer to both of these questions is no."

When the Carters left the White House, in 1981, and returned to Plains, Rosalynn became an integral part of redefining the post-presidency as a vehicle for real change around the world. She serves as a deacon at the Maranatha Baptist Church and has worked to revitalize the working-class town, revamping the local inn and adding a butterfly garden. But she and her husband are most famous for their work with the Carter Center, to which they devote fifty-one weeks out of every year, with the remaining week spent working for Habitat for Humanity.

Father and son, who came to be called "Bush 41" and "Bush 43", fishing off the coast of Kennebunkport in the summer of 1991. "Nothing can ever be written that will drive a wedge between us," George H. W. Bush wrote to his sons George W. and Jeb, "nothing at all."

The Clintons and four former presidents and four former first ladies attend Richard Nixon's funeral in 1994. In his eulogy, Bill Clinton paid homage to his unlikely mentor. "May the day of judging President Nixon on anything less than his entire life and career come to a close," he said.

A National Day of Prayer was held at Washington's National Cathedral three days after 9/11. The presidents and first ladies were seated according to protocol in chronological order. George H. W. Bush asked Bill Clinton if he would switch seats with him so that he and his wife could comfort their son. "It was just a beautiful gesture," George W. Bush recalled.

Laura Bush and former first ladies (from left) Rosalynn Carter, Hillary Clinton, and Barbara Bush at the dedication of Bill Clinton's presidential library in 2004. First ladies have their own very private and exclusive club.

George W. Bush tapped his father and Bill Clinton to lead the humanitarian mission after the 2004 Indian Ocean tsunami that killed nearly a quarter million people. It was the start of a long and genuine friendship. Here they are in Thailand reviewing recovery efforts.

The Bushes, the Clintons, and the Carters hold hands at a memorial service for Coretta Scott King in 2006. During the funeral, Carter, who never played by the rules of the Presidents Club, took a swipe at George W. Bush's mishandling of Hurricane Katrina. "The struggle for equality is not over," he declared.

George H. W. Bush took up skydiving in his seventies. The first time that Barbara Bush met one of her husband's skydiving partners, she warned him, "If you hurt him, I will kill you."

When he presented
the Carters with the
Presidential Medal
of Freedom in 1999,
Bill Clinton said they
had "done more good
things for more people
in more places than any
other couple on earth."
Here they are in Ghana
checking on the country's
progress eradicating
Guinea worm disease.

President George W.
Bush speaks with
President-elect Barack
Obama in the Oval
Office on January 7,
2009. Bush, acting on a
suggestion by Obama,
invited the former
presidents and the
president-elect for lunch.
It marked the first time
since 1981 that all the
living presidents had
been together at the
White House.

George W. Bush leaves
the Capitol after Barack
Obama's inauguration.

President Obama's first call after al-Qaeda leader Osama bin Laden was killed was to George W. Bush. "Protecting our country is neither the work of one person nor the task of one period of time," he said. Here Bush and Obama stand at the National September 11 Memorial on the tenth anniversary of the terrorist attacks.

Three former presidents share a laugh with President Obama at the dedication of the George W. Bush Presidential Library in 2013.

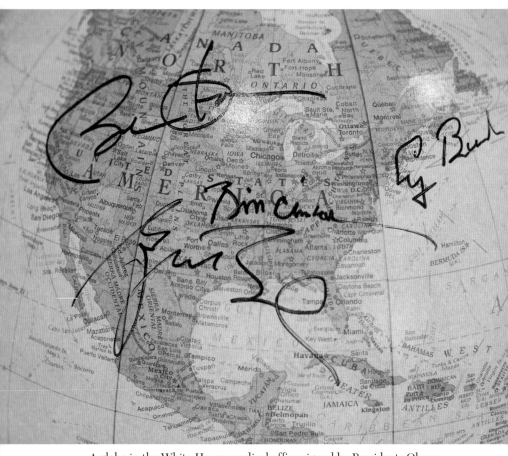

A globe in the White House medical office signed by Presidents Obama, George W. Bush, Bill Clinton, and George H. W. Bush.

The Carter Center has a $600 million endowment and oversees elections around the world. The center has treated more than seventy million people globally for different disease, and Rosalynn has been active in it from its inception. She has worked to eradicate river blindness, a parasitic disease caused by blackflies in Africa and South America, and Guinea worm, which is contracted by drinking stagnant, contaminated water—there were only twenty-eight cases in 2018 in large part because of she and her husband's work. In 1986 an estimated 3.5 million people had the disease. Carter Center staff have observed more than a hundred elections in more than thirty-eight nations since the center's founding, in 1982. No matter how much they have accomplished in the decades since leaving office, the disappointment of being a one-term president and the bruising defeat that accompanies that reality have never left them. In a 2016 interview, Rosalynn reflected on her nearly four decades after leaving Washington. "I missed having Jimmy in the Oval Office taking care of our country," she told me. "I have never felt as safe as I did when he was there. I still have a bully pulpit to work on issues I like, and because he was president, I have unlimited opportunities. It is a good life."

During a 2018 interview in the living room of the Carters' modest ranch-style home in Plains, Rosalynn reminisced about her time as first lady and the relationships she had formed with the handful of women she had known who have held the position. "I think about Betty [Ford] a lot," she told me. She was closest to Ford and Lady Bird Johnson. She famously sat in on her husband's cabinet meetings, and she was the first first lady to routinely use her East Wing office. Dubbed the "Steel Magnolia" by the press, she transformed herself from a shy woman into a powerful and influential first lady. She was there to absorb, understand, and communicate to voters what her husband's administration was doing when she was out on the road campaigning for him. In 1980, she spent nearly all her time campaigning for Carter's reelection while he stayed behind in the White House working on tense negotiations to release the Americans held during the Iran hostage crisis.

Longtime Carter family friend and White House aide Gerald Rafshoon remembered Rosalynn as a close adviser in the White House. "We'd be in a meeting with the Carters, and if the subject was a little bit touchy, all of a sudden they'd start speaking to each other in Spanish," he said, laughing at the memory. "And *none* of us spoke Spanish." Carter's vice president, Walter Mondale, put it bluntly in a 2016 interview: "Whatever secrets there were, she knew about all of them."

She was just as critical to the Carter White House as Mondale was. Maybe more so. Her predecessor Betty Ford told her to do what she felt was right, because she would be criticized no matter what she did. Rosalynn took that advice to heart and repeated it to the women who followed her in the daunting position.

After touring a Cambodian refugee camp in Thailand, she learned that an infant she had held had died. She sobbed on the plane, and when she got home she told the president that the United States needed to give more aid to Cambodian refugees. "One night we were campaigning during the 1978 midterms and flying very late at night after several stops," her press secretary, Paul Costello, recalled. "I was in the front cabin with Rosalynn, and while everyone else was asleep, including Secret Service agents and all of her staff, I opened my eyes and there is Rosalynn sitting with her overhead light on, studying her Spanish. It embodied to me who she is: a serious, disciplined, and studious person." She herself was a natural politician who enjoyed talking to her husband's advisers about polling data and other detailed information.

The Carters have been married more than seventy-three years, longer than any president and first lady, and it is not surprising that she is incredibly loyal to him. At Carter's presidential library, a monogrammed compact that he gave Rosalynn before their wedding is on display. It is engraved with sweet initials they would use for the rest of their lives together: "ILYTG" for "I love you the goodest."

They have had a longer post–White House tenure than any former first couple, and since leaving Washington, when they were both in their fifties, they have done more good around the world than any other former president and first lady. On his seventieth birthday, Barbara Walters interviewed Carter and asked him what part of his life had been the best: Was it his work as a submarine officer, a farmer, a businessman, a governor, or a president? He replied, "By far, my best years are those I'm enjoying now, since Rosalynn and I left the White House."

Rosalynn has traveled to hot spots around the world with her husband, including visits to Cuba, Sudan, and North Korea. The Carters arranged peace talks between Ethiopian leaders and Eritrean rebels and denounced the rigged elections in Panama. Jimmy Carter won the Nobel Peace Prize in 2002, and some of their friends believe she should share the prize. "The Carter Center is a shared legacy. She's been there digging latrines right next to him," said their close friend Jill Stuckey. "Most of us in the church would jump in front of a bullet to protect either of them." She said the couple, both now in their nineties, exercise and eat well, and they read their Bible every day. They are trying to do everything they possibly can to live as long as they can, because they know the impact they have. When they are apart, they are on the phone four or five times a day. And when they are together, they are usually holding each other's hands. When Rosalynn was undergoing treatment for a health problem and was unable to attend church, Carter looked lost. "You just wanted to hug him," Stuckey said. They do everything with a level of passion and commitment that few other presidential couples share. When she was working on her memoir, Rosalynn affixed a sign to her office door that read, NINE TO NOON—DO NOT DISTURB. No one would dare knock on her door then.

Costello said that campaigning for her husband in 1976 gave her a newfound confidence. "This is someone who used to vomit before she spoke when her husband first got into politics, and she had blossomed into this fascinating, interesting, sophisticated person." And she would be that same empowered woman for the rest of her life.

Spouses of presidents are presented with an impossible task when they become first ladies. They are asked to embody a feminine ideal, take up an important but noncontroversial cause, and publicly support their husbands without being involved in their husbands' actual policies. The expectations are unfair, but for many of these women the reward is the post-presidency, when they can pursue ideas they care about without worrying that every word they utter could be a liability to their husbands. Once they move out of the White House, they are finally allowed to become more themselves and embrace their powerful perches as former first ladies.

LAURA AND MICHELLE:
"EMPOWERED AND UNLEASHED"

"This needs to be perfect," Michelle Obama told her East Wing aides ahead of George W. Bush and Laura Bush's 2012 visit to the White House for the official unveiling of their portraits. It was the first time they had been back to the house they had lived in for eight years. The residence staff, at Michelle Obama's direction, had a long table set in the elegant Red Room, on the State Floor, for the Bushes' large extended family. Fourteen Bushes had a meal together and were served by the same butlers who had attended to them for years in the upstairs residence. After the event, staff who worked for the Bushes gathered in the East Room in a receiving line to see them again.

It was a sentimental event. Bush joked about First Lady Dolley Madison saving the portrait of George Washington—another George W.—when the British Army burned the White House to the ground in 1814. "Now, Michelle," he said, pointing to his freshly unveiled portrait, "if anything happens, there's your man." When things got difficult and he did not have an answer to a tough situation, Bush said, Obama could always "gaze at this portrait and ask, 'What would George do?'" Laura Bush was in on the lighthearted event and said, "Nothing makes a house a home like having portraits of its former occupants staring down at you from the walls." Years before, when Laura Bush gave Michelle Obama her first tour of the White House, she was eager to assure Michelle that a life could be made there for her daughters. During that first meeting, Laura took her hands and said, "Please call me Laura." Bush 43, Michelle recalled, had "a magnanimous Texas spirit that seemed to override any political hard feelings."

But there were strict protocols to follow that Michelle did not yet understand. Laura wanted the tour to be special and private, even though Michelle had brought along a staffer. "This is really for Michelle and me," Laura told Michelle's aide. "You can meet with my staff, but this is a private visit for us." Unlike the president, who leaves a note behind with advice for his successor, the first lady traditionally uses the tour of the second and third floors to impart words of wisdom. When asked if she had left a note behind for Nancy Reagan, Rosalynn Carter said, "I did not leave her a note. I didn't think about it. Betty Ford didn't leave me one."

The transition from the Bushes to the Obamas is considered the smoothest in modern history, though Laura had to put aside some ill will during that visit. As she wrote in her memoir, "It is easy to criticize a sitting president when you are not the one in the Oval Office, when you are not responsible for the decisions that must be made," she wrote. "I thought of that when I heard the daily rants from the campaign trail. It got so that even the weather seemed to be George's fault." Obama, she said, was more consumed with attacking her husband than he was with going after his rival for the presidency, John McCain. But, like the first ladies who came before her, Laura did not wallow in her anger. While their husbands met in the Oval Office, she continued the great tradition of taking the incoming first lady on a tour of the residence. She showed her the dressing room window, which has a view through the Rose Garden to the West Wing, where first ladies can occasionally catch a glimpse of their husbands at work. It was the same spot Barbara Bush had shown Hillary Clinton and Hillary Clinton had shown Laura.

When they leave the White House, first ladies feel unshackled from the constraints of trying to please everyone all the time. Sometimes they are willing to say things that their husbands cannot or will not say because of the code among former presidents. Ten years after leaving the White House, Laura Bush, the quiet former librarian who told her husband she would marry him only if she would never have to make a campaign speech on his behalf, would speak out in a bold way that no one expected. On June 17, 2018, the *Washington Post* published an op-ed Laura wrote calling on President Trump to stop separating children from their parents at the border with Mexico. It was a spur-of-the-moment decision, but she felt she had to say something.

"I live in a border state," she wrote. "I appreciate the need to enforce and protect our international boundaries, but this zero-

tolerance policy is cruel. It is immoral. And it breaks my heart."
It was entirely her initiative, an aide said, and she went so far as
to compare the camps to the internment camps where Japanese
Americans were taken during World War II. A member of Bush's
staff told me, "She decided to write it on a Sunday morning, and
it ran in the *Washington Post* that evening. She decided it was the
right thing to do. When we think about speaking out, our default
setting always is: Don't do it. She looked at it through the lens
of whether it will make a difference. She decided that it might
move the needle, which turned out to be right, because other
first ladies followed and it led to this public outcry." Her op-ed is
"something Bush 43 would *not* have done," George H. W. Bush's
spokesman Jim McGrath, who knows the family well, told me.
"He believes strongly that there is one president at a time."

Laura declined interview requests after the story ran—she
felt she had said what she'd had to say. But every other former
first lady felt compelled to speak up. Michelle Obama retweeted
Laura's message and added, "Sometimes truth transcends party."
Even Melania Trump issued a less partisan statement saying that
she "hates to see children separated from their families." Hillary
Clinton joined the chorus on Twitter and wrote, "Every parent
who has ever held a child in their arms, every human being with a
sense of compassion and decency, should be outraged." Rosalynn
Carter was the last to weigh in, but her statement was among the
most powerful: "When I was first lady, I worked to call attention
to the plight of refugees fleeing Cambodia for Thailand. I visited Thailand and witnessed firsthand the trauma of parents and
children separated by circumstances beyond their control. The
practice and policy today of removing children from their parents' care at our border with Mexico is disgraceful and a shame
to our country."

Laura Bush feels "empowered and unleashed," said McBride.

"When they leave the White House, they're different from when they entered it." Michelle Obama, too, has been more outspoken after leaving office. During a 2019 interview with Gayle King, she described what it was like leaving the White House: "That day was very emotional and then to sit at that inauguration and to look around at a crowd that was not reflective of the country, and I had to sit in that audience as one of the handfuls of people of color, all that I had to hold on to over those last eight years, and it was a lot emotionally."

WHITE HOUSE KIDS

Barbara Bush had worried about the Clintons' daughter, Chelsea, and how she would handle living in the White House as an only child, just as she would when Barron Trump moved in with no siblings close in age. In her memoir she wrote, "That afternoon Hillary Rodham Clinton came by the White House for her tour. She was very easy to be with and, I believe, we had a good visit. We talked about the office, the mail volume, and Chelsea. I suggested that she might bring a cousin or a best friend to spend the first year and go to school with Chelsea. It's a big lonely house for one little girl."

But Bush had no reason to worry; the Clintons had spent years preparing Chelsea for life in the White House. In 1986, when Bill was running for reelection as governor of Arkansas, the Clintons sat Chelsea down at the dinner table and shared some hard truths. "We explained that in election campaigns, people might even tell lies about her father in order to win, and we wanted her to be ready for that," Hillary Clinton said. "Like most parents, we had taught her it was wrong to lie and she struggled with the idea." Then they "explained that now her daddy was going to pretend to be one of the men running against him. So Bill said terrible things about himself, like how he was really mean to people and didn't try to help them." Chelsea burst into tears when she heard these staged attacks, but eventually she stopped crying. She was six years old.

When tabloids printed stories about her father's rumored affairs, Hillary took her to the supermarket to look at them. It turned out to be very good training. In a 1992 "Wayne's World" skit on *Saturday Night Live*, Mike Myers, playing the goofy Wayne, gibed that adolescence "has been thus far unkind" to Chelsea, adding, "Chelsea Clinton—not a babe." The skit infuriated the Clintons, and the remarks were edited out of rebroadcasts. Myers even wrote a letter of apology to the Clintons. "I really find it hilarious when they make fun of me," Bill Clinton said in an interview. "But I think you gotta be pretty insensitive to make fun of an adolescent child."

Every president and first lady grapple with how to protect their children from a world eager to know everything about them. "What we determined was, if it's a picture of the children at a public event, it's fair game, or if it's a picture that has their father in the frame," said Katie McCormick Lelyveld, Michelle Obama's first press secretary. Most journalists stuck to the understanding that Sasha and Malia, who were just seven and ten at the time they moved in, were largely to be left alone. When a photo ran of Sasha racing down the colonnade to greet her father after Marine One landed on the South Lawn, Lelyveld talked to editors at the news outlets that had run the photo to admonish them and tell them once again that the Obamas' young daughters were off-limits. "It was a reminder that the White House is an office, a home, and a museum."

Before the Obamas moved into the White House, they lived in the Hay-Adams, a luxury hotel nearby, but after two years on the campaign trail they were eager to settle into their new home.

"Living in a hotel for two weeks, I kind of did that for two years," Obama said. Like many kids, Sasha and Malia had one request of their parents during the grueling campaign: at the end of it all, they wanted a dog. The Obamas followed through, and three months after they moved into the White House, a six-month-old Portuguese water dog named Bo came into their lives, a gift from Senator Ted Kennedy. Early in Obama's second term, they added another puppy of the same breed, named Sunny. Sasha and Malia loved the dogs, and they also became useful as a way to at least try and satisfy a curious and seemingly insatiable media appetite for stories about Obama family life. Because the Obamas' daughters were not made available to the media, Michelle Obama said she got regular requests in her evening briefing book for a "Bo and Sunny Drop-By" so the dogs could fill the void and entertain members of the press by providing some comic relief, instead of the Obamas' daughters, who were busy leading their own lives.

For families, it can be a relief to live in the White House, because then the president is truly *living above the store* and is more available than they may have been when they were campaigning around the country or serving as governors, members of Congress, or businessmen. Michelle Obama was happy that her husband was finally showing up for dinner on time, instead of commuting to Springfield, Illinois, where he was a state senator, or later when he was a senator flying back and forth to Washington, or when he was traveling around the country during the 2008 presidential campaign. "We had access, at long last, to Dad," she wrote. "At 6:30 p.m. sharp he'd get on the elevator and ride upstairs to have a family meal, even if he often had to go right back down to the Oval Office afterward." When he came back from trips as president of the United States, he did what many working parents do and brought home souvenirs: globes for Sasha and keychains for Malia. Their lives were strangely more manageable inside the White House than they ever had been before. Of course, it helped to have chefs, housekeepers, and butlers available at all hours.

But things were undeniably different. "It was awkward to explain to people that before Sasha could come to little Julia's birthday party, the Secret Service would need to stop by and do a security sweep," Michelle Obama explained. "It was awkward to require Social Security numbers from any parent or caregiver who was going to drive a kid over to our house to play." And she felt guilty at times: "You want your kids to grow up normal. You want them to be able to have wonderful experiences privately. And you want them to be able to fail and stumble privately, like any other kids," Michelle said in an interview. "When they're not allowed to do that, it's unfair and you feel guilty about it. Because they didn't choose this life."

Malia took driving lessons with the Secret Service and Sasha took swim lessons at American University, not far from the White House. On Monday and Wednesday nights Sasha's famous mom would slip in, often unnoticed, to watch her practice. Obama wrote, "She wore a navy-blue swim cap and a one-piece bathing suit and diligently motored through her laps, stopping once in a while to take advice from the coaches, chatting merrily with her teammates. . . . For me, there was nothing more gratifying than being a bystander in these moments, to sit barely noticed by the people around me and witness the miracle of a girl—our girl—growing independent and whole." When Malia played tennis, Michelle stayed behind in a Secret Service van, watching her matches from a window, because she was worried she would cause a scene if she sat courtside. It is easy to become spoiled when your parents are so famous that you get a birthday serenade from Janelle Monáe and Kendrick Lamar (which happened to Malia in 2016) or when the chief usher of the White House flies to South Dakota to inspect a swing set that will be erected on the South Lawn just for you (which happened for both girls in 2009, shortly after the Obamas moved in). But that did not happen to the Obamas' daughters.

Presidents and first ladies grow to rely on the people who work in the residence as lifelines to the outside world. The Obamas stayed in Washington so that their younger daughter, Sasha, could finish high school at Sidwell Friends, from which she graduated in June 2019. The Obamas were the first first family to stay in Washington in nearly a century—since President Woodrow Wilson in 1921. They grew particularly attached to one residence staffer, former usher and Air Force One chief flight attendant Reginald Dickson, whom they asked to work for them after they moved into their $8.1 million eight-bedroom mansion located, ironically, around the corner from Ivanka Trump and Jared Kushner's house. Like Clinton, they wanted a familiar face who had proven his discretion and loyalty. The Obamas could trust Dickson, who was the first person to tell Michelle about the seven bullets that were fired at the residence while she and her husband were traveling and while her mother, Marian, and daughter Sasha were home in the residence. The frightening incident happened in 2011 when a White House maid discovered a broken window and a chunk of white concrete on the floor of the Truman Balcony. Because of her discovery, the Secret Service investigated and realized that someone had fired at least seven bullets at the residence several days before. The president was still traveling, but the first lady had arrived back at the White House earlier that morning and was taking a nap. Dickson went to check on her and to discuss what had happened, assuming she had already been told about the shots fired into her home, but she had not. Top Obama aides had decided they would tell the president first and let him tell his wife about the frightening incident. She was understandably angry about being kept in the dark and thankful that Dickson had told her. He proved he would always be looking out for the first lady.

Small things matter almost more than ever in the White House, because families cling to a sense of normalcy. For instance, Michelle asked the florists to label all the flowers in the arrangements in their living quarters so that she and her daughters could learn the different names. The first lady also asked beloved longtime butler Smile "Smiley" Saint-Aubin, who was from Haiti and spoke beautiful French, to speak in his native language when serving her daughters so that they could start learning the language. By all accounts, Sasha and Malia were very polite. White House florist Bob Scanlan wanted the Obamas to have a special first Christmas season at the White House (they spend the holiday itself in Hawaii), so he made boxwood Christmas trees and put one on Malia's dresser and one on Sasha's mantel. Malia especially liked hers. When Scanlan went into her room to check on the tree, he found a sticky note waiting for him: "Florist: I really like my tree. If it's not too much to ask could I please have lights on it? If not, I understand." Her sign-off was a heart. Scanlan took the note off the dresser and brought the tree down to the flower shop. "Now you tell me, how could I *not* put lights on that tree?" He laughed.

But maybe the most precious bond for the Obamas was the friendship their daughters formed with the two sisters who had lived in the White House just before they did and who were always in their corner. "I love those girls," Michelle Obama said of the Bushes' twin daughters, Jenna and Barbara. "I will love them forever for the kind of support they provided to my daughters. . . . If someone went after them in the press, Jenna would get in there and say something and Chelsea would send a tweet out. That made a big, big difference." Attacks on her daughters hit Laura Bush hard. "The Clintons took a hard line, and the press was shamed into leaving Chelsea alone," Laura recalled. "The press did largely the same for Barbara and Jenna, although reporters from the tabloids and from more mainstream publications frequently called their friends, trying to entice them to talk about the girls."

There are only a handful of people alive who know what it's like to grow up in the White House, which reinforces the bond between the former first children. "At the White House, there is no off-season hiatus or a director to yell, 'Cut, that's a wrap.' The demands of not just the nation but of the world are fierce and unrelenting," Laura said. "I am certain that all presidents have moments when they simply ask God, 'Please do not let anything happen today.'" For the Obamas' two daughters—Sasha, who was the youngest person to live in the White House since newborn John F. Kennedy Jr., and her big sister, Malia—they became so used to the constant presence of the Secret Service that they took to calling them the "secret people." (Michelle Obama called them "stone-faced softies" because of how serious they looked on the outside but how much fun they would have joking around with her family behind the scenes.)

When the Obamas left the White House, in January 2017, Barbara and Jenna Bush, who had been starting college when their father became president, recalled what it had been like when they gave the Obama daughters their first tour of the White House eight years earlier. "We saw both the light and wariness in your eyes as you gazed at your new home," they wrote, remembering the frigid November day after Barack Obama was elected president in 2008, when they met Sasha and Malia on the steps of their beautiful and intimidating new house. "We left our jobs in Baltimore and New York early and traveled to Washington to show you around. To show you the Lincoln Bedroom, and the bedrooms that were once ours, to introduce you to all the people—

the florists, the grounds-keepers and the butlers—who dedicate themselves to making this historic house a home." They recalled how they showed Sasha and Malia how to slide down the banister of the Solarium, an informal family room on the third floor of the White House, and how they did the same. "As 20-year-olds chasing our youth, your joy and laughter were contagious."

The Bush twins could relate to the Obama daughters in a unique way as sisters. "And through it all you had each other. Just like we did." Now they welcomed the Obama daughters to the "rarefied club" of former first children. "You stood by as your precious parents were reduced to headlines," they wrote, reflecting on the Obama daughters' experience during their father's eight years in office. "Your parents, who put you first and who not only showed you but gave you the world. As always, they will be rooting for you as you begin your next chapter. And so will we."

MICHELLE AND MELANIA: "NO SYMPATHY!"

The Trumps are not going to fit into this elite club, mostly because of how viciously the president has attacked his predecessors, but also because of Melania. She has not asked her most recent predecessor for advice. During the Trumps' visit to the White House two days after the election, Michelle and Melania had tea in the Yellow Oval Room in the residence, and they talked about what it is like raising children in the White House. Michelle and White House curator Bill Allman gave Melania a tour of the residence, including a stop on the Truman Balcony to admire the view of the South Lawn. But it was all pro forma with not a lot of chemistry between them.

The relationship between Michelle and Melania is the most complicated in modern history because of the vitriolic nature of the campaign, when Trump went after Obama and the Clintons with a level of fervor and personal animosity—all put on public display—that has never been seen before. During a 2016 interview on *The Late Show with Stephen Colbert*, then–first lady Michelle Obama said she had "no sympathy" for Melania on the campaign trail. "You have to be in it," Michelle said, in a not-so-subtle dig at Melania. "Bottom line is, if I didn't agree with what Barack was saying, I would not support his run."

It was Donald Trump's role as the most famous member of the so-called birther movement, which questioned President Obama's citizenship and therefore whether he was a legitimate president, that most outraged Michelle and has never stopped infuriating her. Melania's decision to support the birther movement has stayed with Michelle. "It's not only Donald who wants to see [Obama's birth certificate]. It's the American people who voted for him and who didn't vote for him. They want to see that," Melania said in a 2011 interview. Michelle Obama's first campaign stop for Hillary Clinton happened to come on the same day Donald Trump finally acknowledged that her husband was born in the United States. Michelle said, "There were those who questioned and continue to question for the past eight years, up through this very day, whether my husband was even born in this country." During her passionate remarks, she called Trump "erratic and threatening," without ever speaking his name. In her 2018 memoir, Michelle wrote that she would "never forgive" Trump for his role as a leader of the birther conspiracy, which she said had put her family's safety at risk. ("She got paid a lot of money to write a book, and they always expect a little controversy," Trump told reporters gathered on the South Lawn of the White House. "I'll give you a little controversy back, I'll never forgive [President Obama] for what he did to our U.S. military.")

The change between administrations has been stark. The Obamas' social secretary, Deesha Dyer, walked through the eerily quiet halls of the East Wing late at night on Obama's last day in office. The first lady's domain is in the East Wing, located along a quiet corridor on the second floor next to the calligraphers, who write elegant invitations to formal White House events. "Everything was returned to normal," Dyer recalled. It felt like running a marathon for eight years that abruptly ended. "Everything," she said, "was basically reset, like we were never there. All the furniture is moved and the photos are gone." Dyer described how things have changed now that she is no longer the most popular and influential party planner in town. "It's tough coming out of that role when everybody wants to be your best friend and on January 21 they're like 'Who are you?'" she told me, laughing but perhaps a bit hurt by the transactional nature of Washington.

Social secretaries are typically well-connected socialites or event planners who feel at home in the rarefied atmosphere of stuffy state dinners, but Dyer, who was the second African American to hold the job, had an unconventional résumé. She grew up in a tough neighborhood in West Philadelphia, dropped out of college, and took a freelance job writing about Philadelphia's hip-hop scene. She went back to school at twenty-nine, graduated from Community College of Philadelphia, and started working in the White House's Office of Scheduling and Advance as a thirty-one-year-old intern in 2009. Michelle Obama promoted her to the prestigious post during the final two years of the Obama presidency, a time when loyal aides are often rewarded for their hard work and given opportunities that could help launch new careers after they leave the White House. The first lady "instilled confidence in me—she always believed in me and believed that I was good enough for the job," Dyer said. After the election, Michelle told her, "This chapter in your life is over, but you have to believe in yourself and you have to believe that you can do anything."

The first lady had tears in her eyes as she said goodbye to staff on that final morning on Donald Trump's Inauguration Day.

Later that morning, Melania Trump showed up at the White House with a big Tiffany & Co. gift box (a frame was inside), but no one had told the staff that she would be bringing anything. If they had known, Dyer would have been outside for the handoff. The result was a confused Michelle Obama looking around for someone to hand the box to. Eight years earlier, Michelle had brought a gift for Laura Bush, but because their relationship was so much better, the scene was far less tense and Mrs. Bush discreetly tucked the gift box behind her back when they posed for photographs. The odd part, according to Michelle Obama's aides, was not that Melania had brought a gift but that the gift was so obviously from Tiffany that it seemed like a paid advertisement. "That's not something that we do—we don't really give gifts that say 'Dior' or other brands on the side," an aide to Michelle Obama told me.

Once inside the White House, the Trumps, Obamas, Bidens, and Pences had the traditional coffee in the Blue Room. Thankfully for all involved, it lasted only about thirty minutes, so any tension was brief. "The Obamas are not mean people," Dyer said. "President Trump probably talked to other people in the room more than he talked to President Obama. Mrs. Trump was totally polite." Michelle was concerned about Vice President Mike Pence's daughter Charlotte. She took her aside after Trump's speech on the steps of the Capitol and told her, "Hold tight to each other. You're all you have now." No one understands the loneliness and isolation of the position better than people who have lived it.

In an April 2019 interview promoting her memoir in London, Michelle made it clear that her view of Trump had not changed. "We come from a broken family, we are a little unsettled," she said. "Sometimes you spend the weekend with divorced dad. That feels like fun, but then you get sick. That is what America is going through. We are living with divorced dad. In 2016, the country decided to put its faith in the hands of a fun but careless caretaker who let his kids gorge on ice cream and stay up late, regardless of the consequences." Her strong feelings about Melania's husband make it impossible to imagine the two ever forging a relationship like the one Michelle has with the Bushes.

BUSH 43 AND MICHELLE:
"THEY HAVE BECOME *BEST* FRIENDS"

Before Barbara Bush's April funeral at her beloved St. Martin's Episcopal Church, in Houston, George W. Bush hosted a brunch for VIPs. "He was effusive about greeting everyone, but it's possible that Michelle Obama got the biggest hug of all," said George H. W. Bush's chief of staff, Jean Becker, of the friendship between the Democratic former first lady from the South Side of Chicago and the former president from the country's most prominent Republican family. When I asked if Michelle Obama and George W. Bush have become friends, Becker said without hesitation, "They have become *best* friends." Because of protocol at library openings and funerals, traditional events that bring the former first families together, Michelle Obama is always seated next to her husband's predecessor, George W. Bush. Former presidents are almost always seated next to former first ladies—Barbara Bush used to sit next to Jimmy Carter, and after events she would recount their conversations: *Jimmy said this* and *Jimmy said that.* Even former presidents and first ladies appreciate gossip—they may, in fact, *especially* enjoy gossip—but the relationship between Obama and Bush is different and, somehow, deeper. She has described Bush as a "beautiful, funny, kind, sweet man."

Their embrace at the dedication of the National Museum of

African American History and Culture in September 2016 went viral in a world seeking that kind of genuine empathy and bipartisanship. Lonnie Bunch, the founding director of the museum, was seated a few feet away from Bush and Obama when they hugged, and Bush seemed to almost nuzzle into the first lady's neck. He smiled contentedly as she wrapped her arms around him. "You saw that there was a sense of friendship, I'd almost say family, between them," Bunch said.

Since then the pair have been seen talking like old friends. It was not their first sweet interaction. The two have held hands at memorial services, including at a funeral for five Dallas police officers who were ambushed and killed by a lone gunman in July 2016 that was believed to be in retaliation for police shootings. Liz Allen, who served as Obama's deputy communications director, remembered helping to plan Obama's trip to Dallas for the memorial service. Aides gathered in a conference room at the Eisenhower Executive Office Building on a Saturday morning to discuss the logistics. It was decided that they should invite the Bushes, since the shooting had happened in their hometown of Dallas. They accepted immediately. The Obamas and the Bushes felt it was important to have a bipartisan show of solidarity.

Bush's message was powerful and one of the key moments from that day. "Too often we judge other groups by their worst examples, while judging ourselves by our best intentions," he said, "and this has strained our bonds of understanding and common purpose." At the funeral, Bush tried to comfort the families of the slain police officers and he grabbed Michelle Obama's hand and swung her arm during "Battle Hymn of the Republic," which some people thought was too jubilant a gesture at a memorial service but not unusual for the retired president, who quickly gets caught up in the emotion of events.

At John McCain's funeral, the moment when Bush handed

Michelle a cough drop and she mouthed the words "Thank you" went viral. He did the same thing at his own father's funeral three months later. "He is my partner in crime at every major thing where all the 'formers' gather. So we're together all the time," Obama has said. "I love him to death, he's a wonderful man, he's a funny man. It was a simple gesture. He was getting a cough drop from Laura and I looked over and I said, 'Hand me a cough drop.'"

Bush and Barack Obama may have an easy relationship—once, when Bush was having trouble taking a selfie with a family at an event, he handed the phone to Obama and asked him to take it—but Bush and Michelle Obama are more simpatico in many ways. These relationships come down to personalities meshing, or not. And the former first lady and Bush simply have fun together. Bush tells friends, "I've got an irreverent sense of humor and not everyone appreciates it. Laura is sick of it, but Michelle gets it and I'm grateful." Bush said, "I needle her a little bit . . . I'm fairly lighthearted. [The Obamas] are around serious people all the time and we just took to each other."

They also use their public platforms in similar ways. The Bushes' work on veterans' issues is in line with Michelle's Joining Forces program, one of her major initiatives as first lady. "Party doesn't separate us; color, gender, those kinds of things don't separate us," Michelle Obama has said. "If we're the adults and the leaders in the room and we're not showing that level of decency, we cannot expect our children to do the same . . . I think about the next generation, every single time."

Bush's White House press secretary, Ari Fleischer, told me that some of Bush's outward affection for the Obamas is done with a specific purpose. "President Bush is particularly mindful that at events, when he and his predecessors and successor are together, it is important to help create images that are unifying. That's why pictures with Michelle and Hillary go viral." Bush believes it is a good thing for the country to see those organic, sweet moments, especially given how toxic politics has become. The viral photo of Bush and Michelle embracing at the opening of the Museum of African American History made him especially happy.

Michelle was no fan of most of Bush's policies when he was president, but, like her husband, she appreciates how Bush has approached the next chapter of his life and how he refrained from criticizing her husband when he was in office. "We've become a culture where the nasty sells," she said in an interview with Bush's daughter Jenna Bush Hager on NBC's *Today* show. "So people are just gonna keep feeding that. We're all Americans. We all care about our family and our kids and we're trying to get ahead." Bush Hager said she got a text from her dad before the interview that said, "Send Michelle my love."

"I was like, 'Don't you call her Mrs. Obama?'"

"He's like, 'No, I call her . . . Michelle,'" Bush said.

"That's your dad . . . you know your dad," Obama replied with a smile.

The political differences between the Bushes and the Obamas are what make the story of their friendship so much more significant, because it is their shared empathy and humanity that bind them.

HILLARY CLINTON:
"SUSIE'S HERE, NOW I CAN CRY"

Since no woman has been president, vice president, or even White House chief of staff, the first lady is the most visible office in the White House held by a woman. And Hillary Clinton intended to make it much more than it had ever been before. But her efforts to expand the role in unprecedented ways made the public deeply uncomfortable.

Fifty-seven percent of voters approved of her when she and her husband moved into the White House, in 1993, but six months later that number had plummeted by double digits as she led the administration's failed efforts to reform health care. As the Whitewater scandal consumed the White House, those numbers only fell more, as they did during much of her tenure as first lady, which is unusual, since first ladies are usually more well liked than their husbands. The only time her popularity approached what it had been in the early days of her husband's presidency was when the details of his affair with Lewinsky became public and sympathy surged for a first lady who had been humiliated and betrayed by her husband. The public felt more comfortable with Hillary the victim than Hillary the politician.

She was slow to come to terms with this reality. Clinton told Michelle Obama privately that she'd "misjudged the country's readiness to have a proactive professional woman in the role of First Lady." Clinton had "tried to do too much too quickly, it seemed, and had run straight into a wall." Many first ladies find themselves running into that wall as they try to use their education and professional experience to make real change and discover that there is very little appetite among the public for them to weigh in on politics. These presidential spouses are not elected officials, and the backlash over Clinton's involvement in her husband's health-care reform effort served as a warning to all her successors. Hillary even told Laura Bush that if she could turn back time, she would not have had an office in the West Wing but would have stayed in the traditional East Wing, away from politics and policymaking. (Trump has not learned from her example and has installed his daughter Ivanka and her husband, Jared Kushner, as top West Wing aides.) Clinton also said she wished she had not turned down invitations just because her schedule was too packed. She'd always felt particularly guilty about having declined an invitation from Jackie Kennedy to attend the ballet. (Jackie died a few months later.) Her advice to Laura Bush: *Don't let small obligations overwhelm you and get in the way of the important things.* Hillary never lost the feeling of complete reverence for the White House. Even after eight years as first lady, which included many painful days there, she still viewed the residence with absolute reverence.

Unlike every other first lady, with the possible exception of Rosalynn Carter, Hillary Clinton's years since the White House have surely been more fascinating than her tenure as first lady. She is the only former first lady to run for office, including two successful runs for the Senate and two unsuccessful bids for the presidency. Because of her personal political ambition, she stands apart from every other woman to fill the role, with the possible exception of Eleanor Roosevelt, who was an activist in the White House and beyond, and whose photograph Hillary kept on a table in her office. She often asked herself: *What would Eleanor do?* Hillary's projected answer from her idol seems to be: run. She did not want to spend the rest of her life being referred to as "former first lady."

Harry Truman named Eleanor as a delegate to the United Nations General Assembly, and she helped draft the UN's Universal Declaration of Human Rights, an unprecedented role for a former first lady. Hillary intended to be even bolder than her idol. She had helped save her husband's presidency, sticking by his side during devastating revelations and fighting on his behalf during the Senate impeachment trial. She helped win him the support of the Democratic caucus by arguing before its members as dispassionately as possible that what he had done was wrong but not impeachable. And now it was her turn. On the same day that the Senate was voting against impeachment, Hillary was meeting with New York politico Harold M. Ickes, who had been her husband's deputy chief of staff, to plot her run for the Senate. "After eight years with a title but no portfolio," she said, "I was now 'senator-elect.'"

The 2008 Democratic primary caused a deep rift between the Clintons and the Obamas, though Michelle Obama occasionally felt sorry for her husband's challenger. "Her voice was interpreted as screechy; her laugh was a cackle," Obama wrote, saying that while she did not feel "especially warmly" toward her at that time, she could sympathize with how she was being diminished because of her gender. But then, after Barack Obama won the primary and then the White House in 2008, he tapped Clinton as his top diplomat, following his idol Abraham Lincoln's lead and creating a "team of rivals" for his cabinet. She served as secretary of state for almost four years and visited more countries than any of her predecessors. Her approval rating peaked at 59 percent in February 2009. Her position in Obama's cabinet drew the two most powerful Democrats in the country closer together. As she charted her own course, Clinton was occasionally defensive about her husband's influence on her decision-making. During a trip to Africa in 2009, she was angered by a question from a student who asked her for her husband's opinion about a local issue. She paused for several seconds and said sharply, "Wait, you want me to tell you what my husband thinks? My husband is not the secretary of state. I am. So you ask my opinion, I will tell you my opinion. I'm not going to be channeling my husband."

Both Barack and Michelle Obama campaigned for Clinton in 2016. Michelle famously stirred crowds when she responded to Trump's campaign with the rallying cry "When they go low, we go high," and Barack Obama argued that Hillary was more qualified for the job than he and Bill Clinton ever were. At the same time, it was impossible to overlook her shortcomings. "The truth is, is that Hillary and I have become friends, but we're not bosom buddies," Barack Obama said in an interview on CBS's *Face the Nation*, four months before the election. "We don't go vacationing together. I think that I have got a pretty clear-eyed sense of both her strengths and her weaknesses." While he went on to praise her knowledge of policy and her hard work, there was always an understanding that she did not have his, or Trump's, ability to captivate an audience.

Hillary has a midwestern steeliness. During the Lewinsky scandal, Bill Clinton called his adviser and friend James Carville and said, "Good God. She is not going to forgive me." Hillary is a devout Methodist, and during that dark period she confided to a friend, "I have to take this punishment. I don't know why God has chosen this for me. But He has, and it will be revealed to me. God is doing this, and He knows the reason. There is some reason." It seemed she felt the same after the 2016 election: there was nothing she could do but accept the pain and, this time, the sting of defeat.

"When I saw her the morning after the election," recalled her close friend Susie Tompkins Buell, a top Democratic fund-raiser, "she said, 'Susie's here, now I can cry.'" She's been going through the stages of grieving, Buell told me, and relying on her Methodist faith to get through it. "She's the most resilient human being I've ever known." Buell remembered talking with Clinton in the early days of the 2016 general election campaign, when Clinton told her, "I'm the only thing standing between you and the apocalypse." At the time, that seemed extreme, but now Buell says it does not seem as far-fetched. "She's always doing what she's supposed to do. I always tell her she's not the kind of girl I would have been friends with when I was little. I liked to make mischief."

Hillary is not just the only former first lady ever to run for office; she is in a unique position in the sisterhood because she is among the most high-profile Democrats, and since her 2016 defeat she has been expected to be a torchbearer for the party. In March 2019, Hillary said the United States is going "through a full-fledged crisis in our democracy" where "racist and white supremacist views are lifted up" in the White House.

"This is a time, my friends, when fundamental rights, civic virtue, freedom of the press, the rule of law, truth, facts, and reason are under assault," she said as she accepted an award at an event in Selma, Alabama, commemorating the fifty-fourth anniversary of Bloody Sunday. Just because there are not "tanks in the streets," she said, does not mean that the times are not as serious as they were during the civil rights era.

In the days following her stunning loss, Hillary sought solace in nature and took long walks in the woods in her hometown of Chappaqua, sometimes running into stunned and awestruck hikers who took selfies that quickly went viral. In 2017 she told a crowd gathered in Scranton, Pennsylvania, "I am ready to come out of the woods." She has voiced her disbelief at Trump's brash and unorthodox approach to the presidency. "Literally you can't make this stuff up," she said. "A dozen times a day your head is spinning." But some Democrats wonder why the Clintons are still clinging to the spotlight. It is a criticism Hillary has no patience for. "I noticed that there were no articles telling Al Gore to go away or John Kerry to go away or John McCain or Mitt Romney to go away," she said. "Mitt Romney is going to the Senate, that's where he's going."

The Clintons have built a barrier around themselves after decades of being celebrities. Hillary has said, "I'm probably the most famous person you don't really know." And that sense of not knowing who she really is has left a void that has been filled by outrage over her private email server, among other things. The legal challenges the couple faced during Hillary's 2016 campaign and the questions surrounding her email practices echoed the

Whitewater investigation of the 1990s, which led to Clinton's affair with Monica Lewinsky becoming public in the Starr Report. The drama of the 1990s is never far behind them. *The Clinton Affair*, an A&E documentary series that aired in November 2018, particularly bothered Bill Clinton, whose womanizing had made him a target of the #MeToo movement, in which powerful men were being held accountable for sexual misconduct. And his behavior has once again complicated Hillary's life. Until Donald Trump became president, the last White House to be consumed by personal scandal was Bill Clinton's. "The most difficult decisions I have made in my life were to stay married to Bill and to run for the Senate from New York," Hillary wrote in *Living History*.

Nearly twenty years later, Donald Trump would capitalize on Bill Clinton's past and weaponize it against his wife when he brought accusers, including Juanita Broaddrick, who claimed that Clinton had raped her in 1978, to a 2016 debate. The same thoughts of two decades before must have been running through Hillary's mind, only this time her humiliation was more profound because she was seeking the presidency and there was nowhere to hide. Back in 1998, when she was alone with her husband's press secretary, Mike McCurry, in Martha's Vineyard, the day after Clinton testified before a grand jury about his relationship with Lewinsky, Hillary revealed her private agony and asked five rhetorical questions aloud:

"Do I feel angry?"

"Do I feel betrayed?"

"Do I feel lonely?"

"Do I feel exasperated?"

"And humiliated?"

On Election Night in 2016, she undoubtedly felt all these things.

IX

"WEIRD SHIT" STRIKES THE PRESIDENTS CLUB

It particularly enraged him.

—Barack Obama's reaction to Donald Trump's allegation
that he wiretapped his phones during the campaign

Some presidents have been able to relax after grueling years in the White House—for example, Gerald Ford averaged four days a week on the golf course. But things are more complicated now; the mantle of decency that used to rest with the sitting president has now fallen to the men who used to hold the job. The uncertainty Trump breeds has infected the club.

Trump fires off incendiary tweets daily, sometimes hourly, starting at 4 or 5 a.m. (Twitter executives are thrilled that he uses their platform.) Some of his tweets are directed at the men who sat in the Oval Office before him, and some are reserved for Hillary Clinton, who he has said should be put in prison. Trump routinely attacks Obama—who hardly ever takes the bait—and criticized his health-care policy, which he is trying to dismantle; the Iran nuclear deal, which he did dismantle; and Russia's intervention in the 2016 campaign, which he blames on Obama. Trump has said that he can do things no other president has been able to do, including working with Russian president Vladimir Putin, whose country, U.S. intelligence agencies have concluded, interfered in the 2016 election. "Bush tried to get along, but didn't have the 'smarts.' Obama and Clinton tried, but didn't have the energy or chemistry," Trump tweeted.

Many of his tweets take aim specifically at his most immediate predecessor. After a solar eclipse, Trump retweeted a series of photos showing his face moving to cover Obama's. "THE BEST ECLIPSE EVER!" he wrote. Obama is fair game, Trump and his aides say, because they think that his predecessor has abandoned the rules of former presidents by attacking Trump directly. In what was a kind of proxy fight between Trump and Obama ahead of the 2018 midterm elections, Obama campaigned for Democratic candidates and said that Trump lies "blatantly, repeatedly, baldly, shamelessly."

Trump sees himself as the first president in decades who has confronted the hard issues. "I was extremely popular in Europe, but now I'm not very popular in Europe because I'm saying, 'You've got to pay for your military, your deficits are too big,'" he told me. "I fully understand that Europe can't love that, but other presidents should have said the same thing."

INAUGURATION DAY

"That was some weird shit," George W. Bush grumbled after Trump delivered the bleakest inaugural address in history. Bush and his wife, Laura, sat behind the Obamas and next to Hillary Clinton on the dais on the West Front of the Capitol on the cold, rainy day. Bush's epic struggle with his unruly poncho quickly became an internet meme, lightening the mood on what Trump considered a day of reckoning for his predecessors. The new president's attack on "the establishment" and the men sitting behind him was pointed: "For too long, a small group in our nation's capital has reaped the rewards of government while the people have borne the cost." Jimmy Carter flinched, and Michelle Obama did not plaster on the customary smile expected from departing first ladies no matter how bitter the election. She looked decidedly disgusted. "I stopped even trying to smile," she said later. She had compared the White House to a "really nice prison" and was happy to be leaving, but she was deeply worried about the man who was taking over.

Bill Clinton told friends that he was surprised by the darkness of Trump's address and found it difficult to sit through. Hillary Clinton said it was "one of the hardest days of my life." George H. W. Bush was the only living former president who did not attend Trump's inauguration—not out of any personal animosity but because, at ninety-two, he was in and out of intensive care battling pneumonia. Barbara Bush also did not attend for health reasons, so George W. Bush was representing his parents at the inauguration. Bush 41 spokesman Jim McGrath told me there was not any deeper meaning behind the Bushes' absence: "The fact that the 43s [George W. Bush and Laura Bush] were attending made them feel less guilty about missing the festivities. Forty-One had total and abiding respect for the office of the president of the United States, so much so it was almost woven into his DNA to show respect for the office and the occupant." In customary Bush fashion, he sent Trump a lighthearted letter on January 10, 2017, days before the inauguration, with good wishes and an offer to be of help: "Barbara and I are so sorry we can't be there for your Inauguration on January 20th. My doctor says if I sit outside in January, it likely will put me six feet under. Same for Barbara. So I guess we're stuck in Texas." But the Bushes were baffled by Trump's popularity, and their staffs still seem shellshocked, years later, by his election victory. The Republican Party looks very different today than it did during Bush 41's presidency.

"From this day forward a new vision will govern our land,"

Trump announced. "From this day forward, it's only going to be America first." When he was working on his address, he asked historians which presidents had delivered the best speeches—he was not familiar with them. Inaugural addresses usually call upon Americans to do more, as Kennedy did in 1961 when he famously said, "And so, my fellow Americans: ask not what your country can do for you—ask what you can do for your country," or inspire the country with a message that things will get better, as Ronald Reagan did in 1981 when he said, "The economic ills we suffer have come upon us over several decades. They will not go away in days, weeks, or months, but they will go away. They will go away because we as Americans have the capacity now, as we've had in the past, to do whatever needs to be done to preserve this last and greatest bastion of freedom." There was also the unifying message Jimmy Carter shared when the first thing he said in his inaugural address was about the man he defeated, Republican Gerald Ford: "For myself and for our nation," Carter said, "I want to thank my predecessor for all he has done to heal our land." At the time, Ford was so moved by the kindness of the gesture that he stood up and shook Carter's hand.

The inaugural addresses of the past stand in stark contrast to Trump's message, which was hopeless and divisive, casting blame on the men sitting behind him on the steps of the Capitol. He spoke of "rusted-out factories scattered like tombstones across the landscape of our nation" and "the crime, the gangs, and the drugs" that he said were rampant around the country. But the pivotal line was the most jarring: "This American carnage," he said, "stops right here and stops right now."

Trump said triumphantly that his Electoral College victory was the result of a movement "the likes of which the world has never seen before." He is constantly looking for praise; in private meetings Trump offers guests a compliment and then waits for that compliment to be returned. If it is not, an awkward moment follows. The former presidents go to great lengths to follow the rules of the Presidents Club, and they try hard not to criticize Trump. George W. Bush learned how to be "sphinxlike" with this president, according to an aide, and Obama has mostly followed suit. But other former government officials are less reluctant. "I think they view Trump as damaging to the office of the presidency," Obama's former secretary of defense, Leon Panetta, told me. "Maybe deep down they feel that if they can create that bond by being close to one another, maybe they can somehow get America through this administration." They are all institutionalists, and that would be their biggest problem with Trump—what he's done to the FBI and the intelligence community, Obama's deputy secretary of state, Tony Blinken, told me.

George W. Bush's best friend, Don Evans, does not see Bush's approach changing: "It's an exhausting run being in the White House; it's a ten-year run because of the campaigning that starts two years before. I think President Bush made a very principled and clear decision that it wouldn't have been in the best interest of the country for a former president sitting in the stands chirping away at what he thinks the current president is doing wrong. He didn't do that when President Obama was in office and he's not doing it now. He's staying on the sidelines because that is the appropriate role for a former president."

OBAMA AND WIRETAPPING

The most glaring example of how Trump has affected the Presidents Club came when Trump, in a series of tweets early on a Saturday morning in March 2017, accused Obama of wiretapping his offices in Trump Tower ahead of the 2016 election (a tactic he claimed harkened back to McCarthyism). He said Obama had taken the nation to "A NEW LOW!" Obama did not immediately respond to the charge directly because, as his aides told me, they worried that would satisfy Trump's need for an enemy. Instead he had his spokesman issue a public statement. According to someone who worked for Obama at the time, this attack "particularly enraged him." He wanted to push back unequivocally and asked for a stronger statement than the original one his aides had put together. The integrity of the office and the integrity of his White House were being challenged, and he had to defend himself.

The response Obama and his advisers settled on was clear. "A cardinal rule of the Obama administration was that no White House official ever interfered with any independent investigation led by the Department of Justice," said Kevin Lewis, an Obama spokesman, in a statement that afternoon. "As part of that practice, neither President Obama nor any White House official ever ordered surveillance on any US citizen. Any suggestion otherwise is simply false." Several former Obama administration officials, including former director of national intelligence James Clapper, came out on Sunday morning talk shows to fight back against the explosive claim.

Then came Trump's chaotic family separation policy in the summer of 2018, which led to about three thousand immigrant children, some just babies, being taken from their parents at the U.S. border with Mexico, with no clear plan for how to reunify them with their families. After two months and an intense and sustained public outcry, Trump signed an order to end the policy. On World Refugee Day in 2018, Obama posted a message on Facebook, clearly directed at Trump and the situation: "Imagine if you'd been born in a country where you grew up fearing for your life, and eventually the lives of your children. . . . That's the reality for so many of the families whose plights we see and heartrending cries we hear. And to watch those families broken apart in real time puts to us a very simple question: are we a nation that accepts the cruelty of ripping children from their parents' arms, or are we a nation that values families, and works to keep them together?"

Can Obama and Bush imagine Trump being welcome in the club when he leaves office? Absolutely not. If they wanted to embark on some joint relief effort, as George H. W. Bush and Bill Clinton did after the devastating 2004 tsunami, they would not be waiting for Trump to organize the humanitarian effort. "The code among this group of people is you avoid criticizing your successor, because you've been there and you understand how impossible it is for anybody on the outside to get a full comprehension of the pressures you are under inside the Oval Office," said Russell Riley, co-chair of the Miller Center's Presidential Oral History Program, who took a leading role in collecting interviews with officials from the administrations of George H. W. Bush, Bill Clinton, and Jimmy Carter. "It's a combination of gentlemanly courtesy and a refined sense of institutional propriety, that the institution survives better if the former presidents do not avail themselves of their First Amendment rights by making a fuss if things are going badly, except in the most extraordinary circumstances." Which makes it all the more incredible that former president George W. Bush, the last Republican president before Trump was elected, often jokes that President Trump's White House makes his own administration look "pretty good." His approval rating has nearly doubled, and now, instead of protesters, he gets standing ovations when he enters a room. According to Gallup, Bush's approval rating was 34 percent when he left office. Two years into Trump's administration, it was above 50 percent *among Democrats*—an extraordinary feat for a president who was deeply polarizing just a few short years ago.

43 AND 44 VERSUS 45

George W. Bush enjoys retirement and was never openly critical of Obama, but he has publicly reprimanded Trump for pulling the United States out of the Iran nuclear deal, withdrawing troops from Syria, and building the wall on the U.S. border with Mexico. He warned against the "dangers of isolation." "America is indispensable for the world. The price of greatness is responsibility," he said at an awards ceremony hosted by the Atlantic Council, a nonpartisan foreign policy think tank, which was giving him an award for his work to end HIV/AIDS in Africa. "One cannot rise to be in many ways the leading community in the civilized world without being convulsed by its agonies and inspired by its causes."

In October 2017, less than a year into Trump's presidency, Bush 43 and Obama, the forty-fourth president, made speeches about Trump and the threat they believed the forty-fifth president posed to democracy, all without ever mentioning his name. Bush denounced the "casual cruelty" of the administration during a speech in New York. "We've seen nationalism distorted into nativism, forgotten the dynamism that immigration has always brought to America," Bush said. "We see a fading confidence in the value of free markets and international trade, forgetting that conflict, instability, and poverty follow in the wake of protectionism. We've seen the return of isolationist sentiments, forgetting that American security is directly threatened by the chaos and despair of distant places." He added that bullying in public life has corroded "the moral education of children."

"If you have to win a campaign by dividing people, you're not going to be able to govern them," Obama said at an event in Richmond, Virginia. "You won't be able to unite them later if that's how you start."

At a March 2019 event where broadcast television networks

publicize their new slate of shows, George W. Bush was there to promote the History Channel. He criticized "America first policies" and the ways immigrants were being treated, and he talked about how much he enjoyed reading history, which is not one of Trump's favorite hobbies. "The presidency is more important than the one who occupies the office," he said. "I understand a lot of people are concerned right now, but let me take you back to 1968"—that cataclysmic year that saw the assassinations of Martin Luther King Jr. and Robert Kennedy. After 9/11, he said, "people would come up to me and say, 'Oh, man, you had the worst presidency ever.' I said, 'Read about Lincoln.'" It is that sense of history and perspective that the former presidents worry Trump does not possess or care to understand.

In her memoir Laura Bush wrote, "Our presidents have overwhelmingly been good and decent men, men who did the best they could under the circumstances they faced, with the knowledge they had. They loved their country and wanted the best for it and for the office they held." At George W. Bush's presidential library dedication, in 2013, when all the living former presidents were gathered together, Obama said, "We've been called 'the world's most exclusive club.' . . . But the truth is, our club is more like a support group. . . . Because as each of these leaders will tell you, no matter how much you may think you're ready to assume the office of the presidency, it's impossible to truly understand the nature of the job until it's yours, until you're sitting at that desk. And that's why every president gains a greater appreciation for all those who served before him; for the leaders from both parties who have taken on the momentous challenges and felt the enormous weight of a nation on their shoulders." And because of that common understanding, they can sometimes forgive mistakes. Jimmy Carter apologized to George W. Bush at his library dedication for being too tough on him, especially for his outspoken criticism of the war in Iraq. "Oh, hush," Bush replied. Bush could forgive Carter for criticizing his policies, but he could not forgive Trump for attacking his family.

The current politics of rancor makes the work of the former presidents more difficult, because everything is now seen through a political lens; even things that used to be relatively innocuous have taken on new meaning. Immigration reform is part of the work of the Bush Institute, a nonpartisan policy center at the George W. Bush Presidential Center that holds naturalization ceremonies for new U.S. citizens. "Because of the nature of President Trump, when we talk about the same things that we've been talking about ever since President Bush left office, they are automatically viewed as criticism of the current president," said an aide to the former president, who asked to remain anonymous because of the sensitivity of the subject. "President Bush said something about a free press and suddenly it's a challenge to Donald Trump. No, he's been saying this forever."

At a March 18, 2019, ceremony at the Bush Center, President Bush could not avoid this highly charged issue. Forty-nine people from more than twenty countries were there to be sworn in as United States citizens. Bush celebrated the "spirit of self-reliance" that "runs deep in our immigrant heritage." "I hope those responsible in Washington can dial down the rhetoric, put politics aside, and modernize our immigration laws soon," he said. "As president, I worked hard on comprehensive immigration reform, and I regret that our efforts came up short. Today, emotions can cloud the issue."

Unlike Obama and Clinton, who haven't spoken with Trump since the inauguration, George W. Bush and the president have a relationship that has "progressed a lot," according to a Trump aide, in part because of Trump's nomination of top Bush White House aide Brett Kavanaugh to the Supreme Court. Bush and

Trump spoke about Kavanaugh's appointment twice on the phone, and Bush called members of Congress to try to push for the confirmation of the controversial nominee, who was accused of sexual assault. But one former senior Bush aide, who is in touch with Bush regularly, disputes that telling: "Trump doesn't reach out for advice often, but President Bush's door is always open. Kavanaugh thawed some of the ice, but the ice is coming from one side." Any implication that the two are close is far-fetched, according to another close current aide to Bush. They are not sworn enemies, but their relationship is far from strong. Bush 41 said, "I don't like him" of Trump in Mark Updegrove's *The Last Republicans*, and added that he thought Trump was a "blowhard." Trump, the younger Bush said, "doesn't know what it means to be president."

But Bush's relationship with Trump is certainly better than Trump's relationship with his most immediate predecessor. When he was president and Trump was leading the birther movement, Obama called Trump a "carnival barker." Now he tells friends that Trump is "nothing but a bullshitter." After Trump won the election, Michelle Obama joked that she would be in mourning for a couple of years and wear all black. One former Obama aide said the ex-president wanted to be remembered for his great accomplishments but now he might simply be remembered as a good human being in contrast with Trump.

CHARLOTTESVILLE

When deadly violence erupted in Charlottesville, Virginia, in August 2017, Trump's response was not presidential. The violence was ignited by a crowd of white nationalists who were taking part in a "Unite the Right" rally originally premised on protesting the planned removal of a statue of Confederate general Robert E.

Lee in the center of the bucolic college town. The angry crowd
of torch-bearing young white men shouting "blood and soil," an
English translation of a Nazi slogan, became worldwide news. A
woman who was part of a counter-protest was killed and dozens
of her fellow counter-protesters injured when a car intentionally
plowed into a crowd. The country needed a president who would
denounce this heinous violence, console a troubled nation, and
empathize with the people affected by it. But Trump equivocated
and laid blame with both the counter-protesters and the people
they were protesting against. He came under heavy criticism for
denouncing "hatred, bigotry, and violence on many sides," without specifically calling out the white nationalists who had caused
the bloodshed.

Two days later, as the public grew more and more aghast at his
comments, Trump called out white supremacists by name, saying, "Racism is evil, and those who cause violence in its name
are criminals and thugs, including the KKK, neo-Nazis, white
supremacists, and other hate groups." But the very next day he
doubled down on his original argument that both sides were to
blame, during what was meant to be a statement on infrastruc-
ture at Trump Tower. "You had some very bad people in that
group, but you also had people that were very fine people, on
both sides," he said during an impromptu press conference. The
whiplash-inducing statements were certainly not in keeping with
how presidents respond to national crises.

The former presidents were shocked by Trump's reaction. It is in
these moments of profound national stress that presidents are expected to unify the country. On the day of the Charlottesville rally,
Obama tweeted, "No one is born hating another person because of
the color of his skin or his background or his religion," along with
a photograph that showed him smiling at four children of different
races. It became one of the most liked tweets ever. A few days later,

on the day of the memorial service for Heather Heyer, the woman who was killed, George W. Bush and George H. W. Bush issued a joint statement calling on Americans to "reject racial bigotry, anti-Semitism, and hatred in all forms." The statement ended with the kind of call for unity normally made by the sitting president: "We know these truths to be everlasting because we have seen the decency and greatness of our country."

There was a sense of urgency to the Obamas' campaigning during the 2018 midterms; he endorsed almost 350 Democratic candidates, including close races for governor and state legislatures. Michelle Obama co-chaired a nonprofit called When We All Vote, and she made stops around the country, including in Ohio and California. "This moment in our country is too perilous for Democratic voters to sit out," said Obama spokeswoman Katie Hill. At a September 7 speech during a campaign stop at the University of Illinois at Urbana-Champaign, Obama was much less scripted and careful than usual when he said, "This is not normal. These are extraordinary times, and they are dangerous times. But here is the good news: In two months we have the chance—not the certainty, but the chance—to restore some semblance of sanity to our politics." Obama began using the president's name, which he had avoided doing before: "It did not start with Donald Trump. He is a symptom, not the cause."

The former presidents would not forget Trump's divisive words after Charlottesville. Two months after the events, Bush 43 said, "Bigotry or white supremacy in any form is blasphemy against the American creed." Obama echoed Bush's bewilderment and outrage at the president's reaction. "How hard can that be? Saying that Nazis are bad," he said at a September 2018 speech ahead of the midterm elections, more than a year after Charlottesville. Trump's reaction to Obama's remarks: "I'm sorry, I watched it, but I fell asleep. I found he's very good. Very good for sleeping."

CARTER AND TRUMP

When I met with Jimmy and Rosalynn Carter at their home in Plains, Georgia, in the spring of 2018, Carter was still harboring hopes of being dispatched by President Trump to negotiate the nuclear deal with North Korean leader Kim Jong Un. It was a plan that always seemed far-fetched. In 2013, taking a dig at Obama, Trump wrote, "Former President Jimmy Carter is so happy that he is no longer considered the worst President in the history of the United States!" In *The Art of the Deal*, Trump wrote that Carter had come to his office to ask for a $5 million donation to his presidential library. He was surprised that Carter had "the nerve, the guts," to ask for something so "extraordinary." Needless to say, Trump did not give it to him. "He bragged about it," Carter said. "That was one of his major selling points: 'I turned down Jimmy Carter.'"

But Carter was one of the first people to call Trump to congratulate him on his election victory in 2016 (a gesture Trump clearly appreciated), and, friends say, he is reluctant to attack Trump in part because the Carter Center needs to work with the State Department. In 2016, the Carters voted for Bernie Sanders and not Hillary Clinton in the Democratic primary, and they do not feel much warmth toward the Obamas. They were clearly disappointed that the Obamas had not sought their advice on how to lead an effective post-presidency, and Carter felt that Obama did not pay him the proper respect when he was president. When Carter called Obama to offer advice or to brief him on a foreign trip, he would often get a call back from Tom Donilon, the president's national security adviser, who had been an intern in the Carter White House. For a former president, that was the ultimate humiliation. During Obama's reelection campaign in 2012, a friend said to Rosalynn over lunch, "You must be excited." Rosalynn, ever the loyal wife, shook her head and replied, "He won't return any of Jimmy's phone calls."

Carter was measured in his criticism when I met with him in 2018, and he said he disagreed with George W. Bush's first inaugural address just as strongly as Trump's. "I thought President Bush's address was just awful." Rosalynn is less restrained, however, and she spoke more candidly than her husband about President Trump. "He is a train wreck," she told me. "It's Trump's lies that are the worst part."

Trump felt more partial to Carter as a fellow outsider. Carter has spent so many decades being ostracized from the Presidents Club that he has developed a thick skin. Trump is sympathetic to the way Carter has been treated by the other former presidents, which is why Carter is the only living former president he has sought advice from. One quiet Saturday night in April 2019, as the former president was about to serve himself at the buffet table at a friend's house, a call came in from a White House operator announcing that President Trump wanted to talk to him about China and trade. Carter set his plate down at the buffet table and picked up the phone. Trump spoke for most of the call, but Carter was able to ask about the status of talks with North Korea, and he advised the president to "be flexible" with the North Korean leader. Carter got in a dig about Trump's then–national security adviser, John Bolton, a staunch supporter of the war in Iraq, to which Trump replied, "I call the shots." According to a person in the room, the ten-minute call left Carter "unmoved," and after they hung up he went back to the table, piled with platters of food, and quietly filled his plate as though nothing had happened.

Later, when it was clear that Trump would not be sending him to broker any deal with the North Koreans—or anyone else— Carter didn't pull any punches. "I think he's a disaster," he said unequivocally. At a Carter Center event in June 2019, he went further, saying that a full investigation "would show that Trump didn't actually win the election in 2016. . . . He was put into office because the Russians interfered."

Any chance of the two developing a relationship was over. When Trump was asked to respond to Carter's assessment of him a day later, Trump replied witheringly, "He's a nice man. He was a terrible president. He's been trashed within his own party. He's been trashed."

"THEY CAME TO MY WEDDING"

Before things devolved, Trump had a mutually advantageous relationship with the Clintons. He got affirmation from the presence of the former president and sitting U.S. senator at his 2005 wedding to Melania at Mar-a-Lago, where Hillary Clinton sat in the front row. "I had a very good relationship with both Clintons, actually. They came to my wedding to the first lady, they were there," he told me, which of course I knew because I'd seen the much-discussed, surreal photograph that showed the Clintons and the newly married Trumps beaming. The Clintons, in turn, got money. Trump made a $100,000 donation to the Clinton Foundation and other donations to Hillary's Senate campaigns, before the two embarked on the most jaw-dropping, no-holds-barred political feud in history.

Bill Clinton may have been the reason Trump ran in the first place. He called Trump in late May 2015, a month after his wife announced her candidacy, and reportedly told him that he thought his message was resonating with frustrated conservatives. He was intrigued when Trump confided in him that he was considering running for president. Clinton told Trump that he was tapping into a big part of the Republican electorate that was tired of career politicians. ("It's a complicated story," Trump told me when I asked him directly whether Clinton encouraged him to run for president.) Trump announced his candidacy weeks later. Clinton was a member of Trump National Golf Club, in Briarcliff Manor, New York, six miles from the home the Clintons bought in Chappaqua after leaving the White House. Trump told *New York Times* columnist Maureen Dowd that he renovated the club in 1999 specifically to entice Clinton to join. It worked. "I'm proud to have him," Trump said when Clinton joined in May 2003. "He's a great gentleman, a good golfer and a wonderful guy." Hillary even played golf there with her husband as part of his sixty-fifth birthday present. Remarkably, Bill Clinton still had a locker at the club during the heat of the campaign in the summer of 2016.

TRUMP VERSUS BUSH 43

In January 2019, at the height of the partial government shutdown, Trump held court at a wide-ranging Rose Garden news conference. He talked about the more than $5 billion he was seeking for the wall at the U.S. border with Mexico in order to end the shutdown: "This should have been done by all of the presidents that preceded me and they all know it. Some of them have told me that we should have done it." The only problem was that every single one of them denied ever talking to Trump about a border wall. Jimmy Carter said, "I have not discussed the border wall with President Trump, and do not support him on the issue." Bill Clinton's spokesman Angel Ureña said Clinton "never said that" and added that "they've not talked since the inauguration." George W. Bush's spokesman Freddy Ford said that Bush and Trump had never discussed the wall, and Obama has been openly critical of the wall. "A nation ringed by walls would only imprison itself," he said in 2016.

Trump has isolated himself from the Presidents Club, including the last Republican president to sit in the Oval Office. In a November 9, 2017, tweet, he said, "I don't blame China, I blame the incompetence of past Admins for allowing China to take advantage of the U.S. on trade leading up to a point where the U.S. is losing $100's of billions. How can you blame China for taking advantage of people that had no clue? I would've done same!" During presidential campaigns, it is expected that the candidates will go after each other. On August 10, 2015, when Jeb Bush was still seen as a formidable contender, Trump used his father and brother to attack him. Trump tweeted, "Enough is Enough—no more Bushes!" with a link to an Instagram video showing President George H. W. Bush saying, "Read my lips: no new taxes," a promise he broke, which led to his 1992 defeat. On October 16, 2015, Trump tweeted: "The W.T.C came down during his watch," referring to President George W. Bush.

But it is his attacks since taking office that threaten to upend the Presidents Club once he is in it. A president unraveling his predecessors' policies is nothing new, but Trump does everything with unprecedented grandiosity. When he moved the U.S. embassy in Israel from Tel Aviv to Jerusalem, he tweeted, "I fulfilled my campaign promise—others didn't!" At a closed-door event with Republican donors in March 2018, Trump called the 2003 U.S. invasion of Iraq "the single worst decision ever made." He said Bush's decision threw "a big fat brick into a hornet's nest." He continued, "Here we are, like the dummies of the world, because we had bad politicians running our country for a long time."

Bush has long defended the Iraq War and insists that the 9/11 attacks "changed the equation" in Iraq. "I'm very comfortable that when people fully analyze my decisions in the proper context, they will understand why my foreign policy—not in the principles of U.S. leadership but in the application—was

different." Bush's vice president, Dick Cheney, attacked Obama
in office because Bush refused to, but it was nothing like
Trump's actions. "I criticized Obama when he was president, but
he is an easygoing fellow," Cheney told me with a chuckle. It is the
fact that there is no dialogue between Trump and his predecessors that worries Cheney most. For a time, Vice President Mike
Pence had a good relationship with former vice presidents Joe
Biden and Cheney, who serve in a very informal Vice Presidents
Club. Pence and Biden talked at least once a month, and Cheney
helped Pence in the initial months of the Trump presidency. In
2018 Cheney told me, "There have been no conversations with
Trump. I think there are things you can learn by talking to your
predecessors."

Trump's attacks on Bush have cut far deeper than anything
Obama said during the heat of the 2008 campaign, and there
are rare moments when Bush has let his frustration show. Bob
Scanlan, who was a White House florist when George W. Bush
was in office, recalled being invited to a 2016 lunch at the Bushes'
Florida vacation home shortly after Trump won the election.
When Trump's name came up, Bush abruptly ended the conversation and said, "Can we stop talking about him and enjoy our
lunch?" Even Bush's brother Neil told me he has not heard him
talk much about Trump. But one former Trump official, who is
friends with Bush, had a very different interaction with him.
When he told Bush that he did not want to say anything in public
that was critical of Trump, Bush replied, "Why not?"

"Well, out of loyalty," the official said.

"Oh, yeah," Bush said sarcastically, "because he's been so loyal
to *you*."

There are many subtle ways former presidents can play positive roles. In 2017, the Golden State Warriors did not celebrate
their NBA championship with a visit to the White House, as they

had when Obama was in office, because their invitation was re-scinded by the president when teammates and coaches criticized his administration. Two star players, Stephen Curry and Kevin Durant, said they would not go even before the invitation was extended. They did not even discuss going to the White House to celebrate their 2018 NBA title. In January 2019, the defend-ing NBA champions instead met with Obama when they were in Washington. George W. Bush made a political statement during the partial government shutdown in 2018–19 when he brought pizza to his Secret Service detail, who were working without pay. In a rare Instagram post, he wrote, "@LauraWBush and I are grateful to our Secret Service personnel and the thousands of Federal employees who are working hard for our country without a paycheck. It's time for leaders on both sides to put politics aside, come together, and end this shutdown." The Clintons served din-ner to furloughed workers in their library. The former presidents have aligned against Trump.

"DOWNCAST" AND "DEFENSIVE"

Obama was forty-seven years old when he was sworn in as pres-ident and fifty-five when he left office and joined the ranks of Jimmy Carter and Bill Clinton among the youngest former pres-idents. He has made the decision to largely stay out of politics, and he has avoided criticizing Trump in part because he believes that when he gets involved it only emboldens Trump's support-ers. He does not want to be Trump's foil, and he made it clear from his first meeting with his post-presidential staff that he did not want to do regular statements and would respond only in very select cases, as he did after Trump's wiretapping accusation. A few months after Obama called Republican Arizona senator Jeff Flake, Flake announced his retirement. "We joke that it's the kiss of death for Obama to befriend any Republicans now," an Obama aide told me.

He has about twenty people and a dozen interns working for him in his private office, located in the World Wildlife Fund headquarters building, about a mile from his home and only two miles from the White House. Obama is in the office, which he shares with his wife, several times a week. He meets with donors to his foundation and works on his widely anticipated book. One aide described the office to me as "the East Wing meets the West Wing meets the Oval Office." The former first lady's office and the former president's office are next to each other, and their staffs hold joint weekly meetings. At times the office can feel like a war room, where aides meet to plot their response to Trump's attacks. When issues like health care or deporting so-called Dreamers—children who were brought to the United States illegally—come up, they meet to decide which former cabinet secretaries should write op-eds and do television interviews to defend Obama's policies. "Everybody gets on the phone, we talk to Bush people, there is no baggage," said an aide who worked for Obama after he left office. "Trump doesn't call anyone. He is an island."

Obama has said that if Dreamers were deported, he would consider it an attack on American "core values." His administration protected more than 700,000 of them from deportation with the Deferred Action for Childhood Arrivals program, or DACA. At a final news conference before leaving office, Obama said, "The notion that we would just arbitrarily or because of politics punish those kids, when they didn't do something themselves . . . would merit my speaking out." When Trump and the Republican-controlled Congress were trying to repeal the Affordable Care Act, Obama's signature achievement in office, he posted on Facebook asking people to call their representatives and tell them "what this means for you and your family." But, as always, Obama was careful not to mention Trump by name. (After Senator John McCain cast the deciding vote against repeal, Obama called to thank him.)

Many Democrats want to see him do more. "Obama is over-thinking it," said one former Obama White House aide. "Even now, he's surrounded by a small cadre of long-timers who act like he's still president and put out long statements vetted by several people. There's too much hand-wringing." The reality, this person said, is that during the 2016 election Obama did "put his thumb on the scale by not putting his thumb on the scale." His decision not to let the public know more about Russian interference played a role in Trump's victory. Obama strongly disagreed with how his FBI chief, James Comey, handled the Hillary Clinton investigation, in particular Comey's announcement eleven days before the election that the FBI would be reexamining her emails for classified information. While he tries to follow the post-presidency of George H. W. Bush, it is impossible. He has been privately counseling Democrats, including his former vice president and friend Joe Biden, who is running against Trump, and he talks candidly with them about the personal toll of a presidential campaign. He tells Democrats to talk to voters who are not necessarily part of their base, because if they are going to beat Trump, they will have to win back formerly Democratic voters who voted for him.

Luis Miranda was Obama's director of Hispanic media, and he remembers seeing a different Obama when they met at an event in the summer of 2018. Miranda said Obama seemed "downcast," and other former Obama aides described him as "defensive." Obama told Miranda that he was working more than he had expected to and that he recognized that he is getting criticized for not being more outwardly critical of Trump. But Obama said, "If

I go out there it's a distraction and not helpful." Miranda told him he was doing the right thing. "He was down," Miranda told me. "He introduced the topic of Trump unprompted to justify himself for not being more of an active presence in the Democratic Party." Obama wants to be a private citizen again, but no former president can ever really get his old life back, especially when his successor brings him up at every opportunity.

X

TRUMP IN THE CLUBHOUSE

We had a very good relationship, but things change
when you choose the path that I chose.

—Donald Trump on his friendship with Bill Clinton

There was a time when Donald Trump desperately wanted to be accepted by this group of powerful men, who, though they receded from the daily headlines, would always have an exalted place in history as former presidents. Former first lady Pat Nixon watched Trump in a December 1987 episode of *The Phil Donahue Show*, and she could see the appeal of the young, handsome businessman, brimming with confidence. "Dear Donald," Richard Nixon wrote, "I did not see the program, but Mrs. Nixon told me that you were *great* on the Donahue show. As you can imagine, she is an expert on politics and she predicts that whenever you decide to run for office you will be a winner!" That he was being taken seriously by a former president and first lady was an important moment for him. He still craves acceptance. After he won the election in 2016, Trump tweeted a photo of himself shaking hands with the late President Reagan.

But Nancy Reagan was not a fan of Trump's. Although she was happy that her husband had emerged as an important historical figure, she did not appreciate candidates, on the right or the left, using his legacy for their own political ends. "She didn't see any of them as being the reincarnation of her husband," the Reagans' son Ron told me. And she did not hesitate to call friends and offer her opinion on the state of the Republican Party during the 2016 election. When Trump's name came up, she had one devastating adjective to describe him: "Silly." Memos at the Reagan Presidential Library show how Reagan aides tried to handle Trump's "large ego" and his wishy-washy willingness to donate to politicians from both parties.

After the 2016 election, Trump was as stunned as anyone that he was no longer fighting the establishment—he *was* the establishment. Pat Nixon turned out to be a brilliant political prognosticator.

CHAOS AND GRIDLOCK

The groundwork for the fraught and vitriolic relationship between Trump and all of his most recent predecessors was set long before he ever sat down at the Resolute desk in the Oval Office. After his stunning election victory, the chaotic transition stood in stark contrast to the peaceful transfer of power between George W. Bush and Barack Obama. "It was remarkable," said Chris Lu, who began working for Obama in 2005. "The Bush people clearly preferred the McCain people in their heart of hearts, but they never dealt with us in anything other than a completely aboveboard, impartial way." When it was time to leave office in 2009, after Obama won the presidency and his family was preparing to move into the White House, the Bushes promised to have the best transition in history. And by all accounts they fulfilled their promise. Michelle Obama's first chief of staff, Jackie Norris, said that she will "never forget the intense camaraderie and loyalty that the first ladies and members of the first ladies' staffs have for each other." After Obama's election, Norris sat down in Laura Bush's office with Laura's East Wing team, including Laura's chief of staff, Anita McBride. Michelle's staff was given what amounted to a blueprint as Laura's staff told them what missteps they had made along the way, which parties and luncheons were important, and which could be safely skipped. "What they wanted was to completely set aside politics and to help us succeed and to help Michelle Obama succeed as first lady. They were all in this unique position to understand just how hard her role would be."

The Trump campaign, and Trump himself, did not think they would win. And it showed. The transition was such a haphazard affair that no one on his campaign team had even taken the time to put together an acceptance speech. New Jersey governor Chris Christie had volunteered to head up Trump's transition in April, seven months before the election. The endeavor was, like most things Trump, drama-filled. Christie and his longtime deputy Rich Bagger had a detailed process in place, which they took seriously as they tried to fill the top five hundred federal government jobs, should they win. They sent profiles of each potential hire to the transition's executive committee—which included Jared Kushner, Ivanka Trump, Donald Trump Jr., and Eric Trump. Kushner was referred to as "the kid" inside the campaign. Even after Christie was in charge of the transition and there was a semblance of professionalism, the aversion to learning from the past, and hiring people who had served in the most recent Republican administration, was an issue. "It was a problem throughout: whether it came from Trump or whether it came from someplace else, there was always a skeptical eye on not having too many [George W.] Bush people," Bagger told me, still sounding perplexed. "They would ask for Reagan people and fewer Bush people. Bush people didn't fit into their populist insurgency." By contrast, Obama's chief of staff, White House counsel, treasury secretary, attorney general, and homeland-security secretary all had worked for Clinton, while his secretary of state, of course, was married to him.

Before the election, Bagger said he had several meetings with senior White House aides in the office of Obama chief of staff Denis McDonough. They spoke to Trump and Clinton transition team members to discuss details of how the massive bureaucracy would be handed over, so as not to look like they were favoring one or the other. Obama aides were told to turn in the final drafts of their thick transition manuals, each describing in detail the work of their particular departments, by the early fall, because they wanted them done before they knew who was going to win the election. The manuals from each department are the ABCs of how to run the office, including details as small as the voice-mail pass code for the office phone. The binders are turned in to the White House counsel's office, which then goes through and edits out anything that reveals sensitive internal communications. They are left behind in each office for whoever wins. One Obama aide compared the binders to *What to Expect When You're Expecting*, a popular primer for pregnant women. They go into so much detail that the Obamas' Visitors Office director, who was in charge of events like the Easter Egg Roll and visits from foreign leaders, included a reminder in the binder that if there is a presidential trip and tents are set up on the South Lawn, the president has to motorcade to Andrews Air Force Base instead of taking Marine One, because there is no room for the presidential helicopter to land when the tents are set up. "There is a domino effect to the decisions you make," an Obama aide said. "You realize the enormity of this operation." But Obama aides had no one to hand their carefully curated briefing books to. "We tried to do the same thing the Bush people had done for us, but there was no one on the other end," said Obama's deputy secretary of state, Tony Blinken, who met with members of Trump's State

ition team was about to be summarily disbanded. The day after
the election, referred to by aides as "day next," about 130 full-time
team members with credentials and badges were ready to get into
offices and get to work. They were prepared to be part of so-
called landing teams that would go into the agencies within a few
days of the election. But when Christie and Bagger went to present more than a hundred names to the executive committee for
top positions, they were surprised to find retired Army lieutenant
general Michael Flynn sitting at the table with Jared and Ivanka.
They knew Flynn wanted to be Trump's national security adviser,
which is among the most influential positions in the White House,
but they had managed to keep him at bay. Until now. "Michael
Flynn was the major sticking point," Bagger recalled.

"Flynn basically said, 'All of your recommendations stink,'
and Ivanka said, 'General, how would you like to serve?'" Bagger
said, still sounding appalled by the sudden change of course.
"Flynn said, 'It's not about me, it's about the country, it's about
service. But I would like to be secretary of state, secretary of defense, or national security adviser.'" It was shocking how quickly
the tide had turned and Christie and his team had lost control.
Trump adviser Steve Bannon took Christie aside and delivered
the news: *It's over.* Vice President–elect Mike Pence would be
taking over the transition. Jared Kushner had always deeply disliked Christie, who, as U.S. attorney for the District of New Jersey in 2005, had put his father, Charles Kushner, in jail for tax
fraud and witness tampering. In a bizarre and scandalous twist,
the senior Kushner had hired a prostitute to seduce his brother-
in-law, whom he thought was cooperating with Christie, and
sent a videotape of the encounter to his own sister. It was tawdry
stuff that led to a simmering resentment between Kushner and
Christie. All the work they had done over the previous several
months was literally thrown away, including dozens of binders

full of recommendations meant to serve as instruction manuals for the landing teams, with background for cabinet nominees and details about each government agency. For instance, before Christie and Bagger were summarily dismissed, the Commerce Department had a Day 1 plan, for the day after Trump's inauguration, all the way through to a Day 100 plan. After their dismissal there was nothing, and Pence reportedly outsourced the vetting of Trump's cabinet to the Republican National Committee.

Trump decided they needed to revisit every decision and put a hold on everything moving forward. It was chaos: ten different people in power centers needed to sign off on everything, and critical positions were left unfilled. In some cases, they hastily announced positions before completing background checks, including FBI checks and preliminary security clearance checks. Bagger said he was surprised that no one on Pence's team called him. "I was expecting to get a lot of calls from people on the transition, but I got none." Career government employees waited at the Department of Energy, the Department of Commerce, and all across the sprawling bureaucracy. They wanted guidance— they wanted to know who their new bosses were and how their jobs would change in a Trump presidency—but they got nothing. In fact, some high-level employees waited and waited until, after weeks of silence, they assumed they were no longer employed, and packed up their offices.

"SO THAT HAPPENED"

—President Obama to an aide, stunned after Trump's 2016 victory

In his memoir, Rhodes recalled how he and top speechwriter Cody Keenan sat alone in Keenan's Washington, D.C., apartment on Election Night. After Trump was declared the winner, Obama emailed Keenan to tell him he would call him through the White

House switchboard to go through what he would say the next day. "So that happened," Obama said once he was on speakerphone with Keenan and Rhodes. Rhodes compared the tone of Obama's voice to someone who had just received a grim diagnosis and was trying not to dwell on it. Obama went through what he wanted to say as Keenan typed: *Congratulate Trump, praise Hillary, and end on an optimistic note meant for young people who might be in despair over the results.* "Do you want to offer any reassurance to the rest of the world?" Rhodes asked.

"What do you have in mind?" Obama replied.

"Something for our allies, for NATO. That the United States will continue to be there for them."

"No," Obama said after a pause. "I don't think that I'm the one to tell them that." From the very beginning, Obama was wary of breaking the unwritten rules of the club.

In 2008 the Obama campaign had used some of the same tactics to defeat Hillary that Trump had used to win. Now they were left with a new and unexpected reality. Obama's former White House aide and friend Reggie Love told me that Obama watched cable all the time in the White House and was well aware of views on the other side when he was president. He is still very much a media consumer now, not only reading the *New York Times* on his iPad but also watching Fox News and other conservative outlets occasionally. "Everyone is racist and sexist to some extent," Love said. So the way that Trump was able to seize upon a broad suspicion and intense dislike of Hillary Clinton, who would have been the first female president, was not surprising. But there was something else: Obama thought she did not want it enough. "To win, [Obama] told us, you have to have a core reason why you're running, and you need to make it clear to everyone how much you want to win," Rhodes said. Hillary had not done that successfully.

The morning after the election, Obama received the President's Daily Brief, or PDB, a top secret document with the most pressing national security concerns of the day, and headed into Chief of Staff Denis McDonough's office. The morning routine was like any other, but everything had changed. "This country will get through this," Obama told McDonough and other senior advisers. The normally stoic group was obviously emotional and worried that the work they had done would be upended. Obama had heard that his press secretary, Josh Earnest, was talking to press aides, most of whom were in their twenties and thirties. Many of them were crying. Obama summoned them to talk to him in the Oval Office. "The sun is shining," he told them calmly. "We have to remember—history doesn't move in a straight line, it zigs and zags." He told them they must try to do for Trump what Bush had done for them. Michelle Obama gathered her team in her small East Wing office and did much the same thing. Most of her staff were women and minorities, and some of them were in tears. "They'd poured themselves into their jobs because they believed thoroughly in the causes they were furthering," she wrote in her memoir. "I tried to tell them at every turn that they should be proud of who they are, that their work mattered, and that one election couldn't wipe away eight years of change. Everything was not lost. This was the message we needed to carry forward."

It was such a different world than it had been when they came into office. Eight years earlier, after Obama won the election in November 2008, his press aides Jen Psaki and Bill Burton went to the White House to meet with Tony Fratto and Dana Perino, who led President Bush's press team. Psaki had never been to the White House before, and the whole experience was equal parts exciting, bewildering, and terrifying. "We were there for hours," she recalled. "President Bush's staff walked us through everything, they even showed us how to send press releases." It was the first transition since 9/11, and it was happening during the worst financial crisis since the Great Depression, so Bush was adamant that information be shared. He viewed Obama as a partner, even if Obama had won in part by denouncing Bush and the Iraq War. Perino and Fratto were warm and welcoming.

Eight years later, Trump, now the president-elect, followed tradition and went to the White House to meet with President Obama. There was no love lost between them. Obama had called Trump "uniquely unqualified" to be president during the campaign. "I ran against John McCain, I ran against Mitt Romney. I thought I'd be a better president, but I never thought that the republic was at risk if they were elected," he had said at a North Carolina rally days before the election. The meeting between the two men who held each other in such disdain was awkward. Trump was much more conciliatory than anyone expected, even asking Obama for people he would recommend as hires. Obama personally urged Trump not to hire Michael Flynn as his national security adviser. Obama had fired Flynn when he was head of the military's intelligence branch, and he was strongly against bringing him into the White House to fill such an important position. Trump did not take Obama's advice, hiring Flynn but then firing him less than a month after he started. Trump kept trying to bring their discussion back to how he and Obama both were able to draw the kinds of huge crowds that Hillary Clinton could not. ("He knows absolutely nothing," Obama privately said to a visitor about Trump directly after the meeting.)

Trump brought along his son-in-law, Jared Kushner, and Hope Hicks, who was his press secretary during the campaign. Psaki, now playing the role of the seasoned White House veteran, sat down with Hicks to walk her through the workings of the press office, as Perino and Fratto had done for Psaki years before.

"This all must be overwhelming. Let us know how we can be helpful," Psaki said to Hicks.

"I'm just so proud of Mr. Trump," Hicks replied fawningly. She had only one pressing question for Psaki: "How do you ensure that President Obama can see and edit every statement?"

After a moment, Psaki, who was dumbstruck by the question, replied, "He doesn't see and edit every statement." There is no way any president has time to read the dozens of statements the press office puts out daily, some of which are pro forma, acknowledging national holidays and bill signings.

"Oh, that's very different, because Mr. Trump approves and edits *everything* that goes out," Hicks said. Trump is obsessed with how he is perceived, and while he publicly slams reporters, he really loves the media. But there is no way he could see everything. They would have a lot to learn. During the visit, Kushner asked questions of Obama's aides, insinuating that he thought the White House staff were going to stay—"Yeah, no," they told him.

"We were still in shock; we were forcing ourselves to be as welcoming and classy as we could be, even though people on President Obama's staff had serious personal and emotional problems with Trump," Psaki said. "And here we were saying, 'Come on in, can we get you a drink?' It was emotionally exhausting and unnatural. It felt dishonest, but it was also important, and it came from the top."

According to Rhodes, on their last foreign trip after the election, Obama told him backstage before a press conference with German chancellor Angela Merkel, "Maybe this is what people want. I've got the economy set up well for him. No facts. No consequences. They can just have a cartoon." When people ask him for advice on how to deal with Trump, Obama tells them, "Find some high ground, and hunker down."

Publicly, Obama made it clear right after Trump's election that he was going to follow the Bush family's lead. "President Bush could not have been more gracious to me when I came in. And my intention is to, certainly for the next two months, just finish my job," he said at a press conference two weeks after Trump's victory. "I want to be respectful of the office and give the president-elect an opportunity to put forward his platform and his arguments without somebody popping off in every instance." He added, to laughter from the crowd, "What I do know is, is that I have to take Michelle on vacation."

Privately, the story has been slightly more complicated than that.

THE *TITANIC*

In the hours and days after an election, world leaders clamor to talk with the new president. Great Britain, historically the most important U.S. ally, usually gets the first call. But it was so chaotic during his first days in office that somehow Trump managed to talk with nine world leaders before talking to then–British prime minister Theresa May. Egyptian president Abdel Fattah el-Sisi was able to get a call through to Trump's transition headquarters in Trump Tower shortly after he won the election. "I love the Bangles!" Trump reportedly told him. "You know that song 'Walk Like an Egyptian'?" Meanwhile, the British ambassador to the United States scrambled to get the president on the phone with the prime minister, who eventually went to bed for the night.

Inside the White House, chaos reigned. Working on the Obama-Trump transition was "like parachuting onto the deck of the *Titanic* after it hit the iceberg," said a former career national security staffer who served during both the Obama and Trump administrations. Many of the career staffers whose job it was to maintain continuity at the National Security Council during presidential transitions curtailed their assignments after the election and returned to their home agencies. They did not want to stay on and work in the Trump White House.

The transition staffer thought it was "bad form" to leave an NSC assignment early because, he insisted, the job is far more important than who is in office at any particular time. But he could understand their frustration. "I spent a good portion of my time during the new administration changing materials written by political newcomers who began everything with 'After the failed eight years of the last administration . . .'" The West Wing seemed to be on a permanent war footing more typical during a campaign than a presidency.

"IT MAKES MY BLOOD BOIL"

Trump has disparaged all the former living presidents and has not said much about the dead ones. The only president he seems to truly admire is the nineteenth-century populist Andrew Jackson. He has a portrait of the slave-owning general who fought Native Americans hanging prominently in the Oval Office. Unlike most presidents, who are too busy with policy to make decorating decisions, Trump picked out wallpaper and rugs for the West Wing and the Oval Office. He enjoyed moving Winston Churchill's bust back to the Oval, after Obama had it moved to a hallway outside the Treaty Room on the second floor of the residence. Everything Obama had done, from letting the rug in the West Wing corridors get dingy to moving that bust, was anathema to Trump.

Trump enjoys giving tours of the White House, which is the country's closest thing to Buckingham Palace. During the walk-throughs, he reportedly points to where Bill Clinton conducted an affair with Monica Lewinsky and shows guests the private dining room off the Oval Office, which he says was badly cared for

Michelle Obama wraps her arms around George W. Bush during the 2016 dedication ceremony of the Smithsonian National Museum of African American History and Culture. "They have become *best* friends," said a person close to the Bush's.

President Barack Obama speaks to his staff in the Oval Office the morning after the 2016 election. "So that happened," was his stunned reaction after Donald Trump won the presidency.

President Barack Obama and President-elect Donald Trump shake hands after their meeting in the Oval Office on November 10, 2016. They have not spoken since Trump's inauguration, despite one failed attempt.

First Lady Michelle Obama meets with Melania Trump for tea in the Yellow Oval Room of the residence on November 10, 2016. Recalling the day the Obamas moved out of the White House, their social secretary Deesha Dyer said, "Everything was basically reset, like we were never there."

"That was some weird shit," George W. Bush grumbled after Trump delivered the bleakest inaugural address in American history.

Michelle Obama would "never forgive" Trump for his chief role as a leader of the so-called birther conspiracy that she said put her family's safety at risk.

A few days after leaving the White House, the Obamas spent more than a week on Virgin CEO Richard Branson's private Necker Island in the British Virgin Islands. When the former first lady got off the plane, she declared, "We're free!"

"His friendship has been one of the great gifts of my life," Bill Clinton said after George H. W. Bush's death. Here Clinton, who jokes that he is the "black sheep" of the Bush family, stands between a statue of Bush 41 and Bush 43 in 2017.

Michelle Obama and Laura Bush have worked together as former first ladies. Bush is the only former first lady who has any relationship with Melania Trump.

Melania Trump joined the Obamas, the Bushes, and the Clintons at Barbara Bush's funeral in April 2018. Donald Trump was not invited, and he told me that he understood why. "I ran against his [George H. W. Bush's] son and that wasn't exactly, I would say, positive toward the relationship with the father . . . or the mother."

After his death, George H. W. Bush's official portrait was draped in black fabric, and white roses were placed on a table beneath it, in keeping with a long-held White House tradition.

The Trumps met with the Bushes on December 4, 2018, while they were in Washington for George H. W. Bush's state funeral. It was the only time George W. Bush and Donald Trump had ever spoken in person. They chatted for just twenty-three minutes.

The Trumps attend George H. W. Bush's funeral at the Washington National Cathedral on December 5, 2018. "The Bushes were grateful Trump came," said a senior aide to George W. Bush. "They didn't want it to be like McCain's funeral where the funeral was not about John McCain. It was about Donald Trump."

President Trump sat awkwardly next to the former presidents and first ladies. Three months after Bush's funeral, Trump told me his relationship with "the father" was "excellent" until he ran for the Republican nomination.

Even as he tries to distance himself from the men who came before him, Donald Trump relishes being counted among them. He even has his shirt sleeves monogrammed "45," his position in the presidential lineup.

and even had a hole in the wall when he moved in. He tells them Obama would spend much of the day watching basketball there. Obama's aides say there was no hole in the wall, and Obama obviously did not spend his days watching basketball. Trump has since gotten a larger flat-screen television to replace the one Obama used. A senior diplomat who has met with Trump several times said he has a "reptilian brain" and judges a person almost entirely by his or her appearance: "Straight out of central casting," he often says of his aides, including Vice President Mike Pence, who, according to Trump, looks just how a vice president should look. Cabinet members privately lament Trump's refusal to embrace what is an endearing trait in any politician: a willingness to be self-deprecating.

The Trumps have had only a handful of interactions with George W. and Laura Bush, President Trump had a ten-minute phone call with Jimmy Carter, and he has had no interaction with any of the others. But they have stuck to tradition by relying on former residence staffers to help keep the private floors of the White House running smoothly. Former chief usher Gary Walters, who worked at the White House from 1986 to 2007, is in touch with the Trumps' chief usher, Timothy Harleth, who worked at the Trump International Hotel in Washington and whom the Trumps chose for the most important position on the residence staff. The Trumps brought a maid who worked in their homes in Bedminster, New Jersey, and Trump Tower. As has always been the case with the residence staff, people will not quit based on who is currently occupying the White House, even if they disagree with him. "They're just so happy to have a good job!" a current staffer told me. "Somehow you learn to separate the politics from the house."

Like the former presidents—who are often frustratingly restrained in their public views of Trump—the one hundred maids, butlers, chefs, and florists who make the White House run every day try to stick to a strict code of not criticizing the sitting president. Their jobs depend on it (presidents and first ladies expect the staff to stay quiet), and they also sympathize with the enormous pressure that all presidents face. They see members of the first family as three-dimensional people in a way that few get to witness. Trump mostly treats the residence staff well, according to several recently retired staffers, even offering to slip them hundreds of dollars in cash as tips for jobs well done, only to be told every time that they cannot accept tips because they are residence employees. Brian Rock, the head engineer of the White House from 1988 to 2017, and Joel Jensen, who purchased food for the family and worked in the White House for more than thirty years, between 1986 and 2018, describe the Trumps as easy to work for. Rock said then-eleven-year-old Barron Trump, like any boy his age, wanted to see how things worked behind the scenes and got a tour of the White House chill room (where the air conditioners that cool the enormous house during blisteringly hot Washington summers are kept).

Jenny Botero was the head of the housekeeping department at the White House from 2007 until 2018 and worked for the Bushes, the Obamas, and the Trumps. Instead of the chaos that many decry—what with the early-morning Twitter storms and Trump's alleged past infidelity—she said there is relative domestic tranquility in the private living quarters on the second and third floors. "It was interesting to see how his grandchildren interacted with him. They adore him," Botero told me. "I'd see them sitting on his lap in the Family Dining Room on the second floor. He was very gracious and very genuine when I worked there. There was this disconnect: I'd ask myself, *What's wrong? Why is he saying that on Twitter? That's not who he is behind closed doors.* I think he wants people to think he's a tough guy." It is a WWE match on the world stage, with the president playing a role he cannot, and will not, step away from.

I asked Trump if he has trouble sleeping, like other presidents have, given the enormous gravity of the job. Clinton often slept less than five hours a night, a habit he formed when a college professor at Georgetown said that great men often need less sleep than mere mortals. "No," Trump said, shaking his head and waving his arms toward the office where his staff sits, called the outer Oval. "You walked through, we have a very calm White House. They try and build it up. A month ago I was with six or seven executives and we're in a room where there was a television and it was very calm and we were negotiating some important thing for the country. It was on the news—*Donald Trump is up in his residence walking back and forth, screaming.* They actually said, 'That's terrible. You're here.' And it was so calm. It's fake news, it's all fake news, it's really terrible. . . . We have a very calm and very good White House."

Trump's bluster is an act, according to residence staffers. "*No one expected Trump to win!*" Botero said, adding that the president can be surprisingly kind. "Sometimes I'd walk up to the fence on Pennsylvania Avenue after going out for lunch and I'd look at the protesters and think, *Oh, boy, do they have that all wrong.*" But there are differences between the private world of this White House and the way things were when the Obamas, the Bushes, and the Clintons lived there. Engineer Brian Rock said he had a strange experience the night of Trump's inauguration. Rock was in charge of the room temperature in the residence. On Inauguration Night 2017, he was getting calls from the chief usher saying that the president was hot. Two minutes later he would get a call saying that the first lady was cold. "I asked him, 'Who are we catering to here?' Because 99.9 percent of the time we cater to the first lady. Only then did we realize: They sleep in separate bedrooms." Not only do they sleep in separate bedrooms, they reportedly sleep on separate floors: Trump sleeps in the master bedroom on the second floor and Melania stays in a two-room suite on the third floor that was occupied by Michelle Obama's mother, Marian Robinson, when they lived in the White House.

One recently retired staffer told me that she is in a book club where only three of the twenty club members know that she worked in the White House when Trump was in office. If she told them, "there would be too many questions," she said. Whenever anyone asks her where she worked, she tells them that she worked for the federal government. If they want more details, she tells them that she worked for the Department of Defense. "People never know how to follow up on that!" she said, laughing.

But one longtime current residence staffer, who does not always agree with President Trump's policies, lamented to me privately, "There are days when I think, *Why am I making this person's life easier?* . . . It makes my blood boil."

TRUMP KNOWS BEST

Whether the Presidents Club is strengthened or unravels once Trump joins their ranks remains to be seen. One thing is clear, Trump is not worried about it. When he was asked to grade his presidency, he gave himself an A-plus. When a Disney World production crew went to the White House to record the president's voice so that he could be added to their animatronic Hall of Presidents, Trump was thrilled at the thought of himself onstage with Abraham Lincoln and FDR. He clearly considers himself one of the greats, which is why he agreed to talk with me in the first place—so he could explain how much better he is at being president than the other living men who've had the job.

There are weighty issues that vex every president: energy and the environment, health care, human rights and civil liberties, the economy, abortion, nuclear proliferation, and drugs among them. But there is usually more agreement across party lines and administrations on foreign policy. Because Donald Trump has no government experience and has refused to learn from the people who came before him, some of his cabinet members have felt compelled to reach out to the men and women who served in other administrations. They believe they could learn from their predecessors.

Secretary of State Mike Pompeo called former secretary of state Hillary Clinton—about whom Donald Trump led chants of "Lock her up!" at his rallies—because he was hungry for advice from Clinton, who had logged almost a million miles as secretary of state. Tony Blinken, who was deputy national security adviser and deputy secretary of state under President Obama, told me he spoke with then–secretary of defense Jim Mattis in February 2017. Mattis called Blinken and asked for his advice on how to deal with North Korea and its nuclear arsenal. Michèle Flournoy, who was undersecretary of defense during the Obama administration, was in touch with H. R. McMaster when he was Trump's national security adviser. Bill Clinton's former chief of staff Leon Panetta told me that he kept in touch with John Kelly when Kelly was Trump's chief of staff; they had worked together before. These calls were always ad hoc and obviously not run through Trump.

"Every once in a while he calls me for advice," Panetta said about Kelly, with whom he is close. "The normal relationship of trust between a chief of staff and a president of the United States is not the case with this president. John was in many ways just trying to keep traffic moving in the White House." Panetta, who was also Obama's CIA director and defense secretary, said he is often asked about differences between Clinton and Obama. "Both are very bright, very capable, and willing to listen," he told me.

"When they made decisions, they made those decisions based on what was really in the best interest of the country. Trump so often engages in chaos as a way to deal with people. Most presidents struggle to do the opposite and provide stability; this president loves chaos. He creates a lot of trauma for the country as a result."

It is impossible to imagine Trump going to Obama or Bush to ask for guidance during an international crisis. He has said that Obama "depleted" the military and he has called Bush's invasion of Iraq the worst decision ever made by any president. "They had bad information, they had very bad intelligence, they said there were weapons of mass destruction, and there weren't, and they should have been able to know better than they did. They had none, zero, they had nothing even close." Trump thinks he knows better.

XI

AND THEN THERE WERE FOUR

*Those who travel the high road of humility in
Washington, D.C., are not bothered by heavy traffic.*

—Former Wyoming senator Alan Simpson

The last former president to see George H. W. Bush before he
passed away on November 30, 2018, was not his son, George W.
Bush, but a man who had little in common with him on paper
aside from a shared job title. Three days before he died, Bush,
ninety-four, welcomed Barack Obama, the newest member of the
Presidents Club, into his Houston home. That day, November 27,
Obama saw the man he called "my buddy 41" for the last time.
Bush had been in and out of hospitals and was still mourning the
death of his beloved wife of seventy-three years, Barbara, who
had died less than eight months earlier. He had good days and
bad days now, but Obama was someone he wanted to see, even
on a particularly bad day.

Obama was the most recent inductee to the world's most elite
fraternity, a group of five men at the time, and he was still less than
two years out of office. He had almost nothing in common with
Bush, who was the patrician patriarch of a sprawling family with
roots in New England and Texas and a decorated World War II
Navy pilot. Bush already had a résumé a mile long before he

became president. Obama was born in Hawaii—his white mother was from Kansas and his black father was from Kenya—and he had served only half a term in the U.S. Senate before he became the country's first African American president. The two men were separated by generations and political parties, but they developed a genuine friendship, albeit a much less talked-about one than the father-and-son-like bond between Bush and Bill Clinton. Obama admired Bush, who was among the last of the Greatest Generation, and kept in touch with him. "Obama's a gentleman," the Bushes' son Neil told me, recalling Obama's call to check in on his father during one stay in the ICU. "He looked up enough to my dad to show empathy and concern when Dad was suffering." Three photos on the wall of Neil's office are of Obama. "Dad worked hard to acknowledge the call, even though he couldn't really talk."

As with any meeting between two former presidents (with the obvious exception of Bush 41 and Bush 43, who saw each other often), this one had been in the works for months. Bush's chief of staff, Jean Becker, was in touch with Obama's chief of staff, Anita Decker Breckenridge, to make a plan. Obama was going to be in Bush's hometown of Houston as the keynote speaker at the twenty-fifth-anniversary celebration of the Baker Institute, named after Bush's secretary of state and best friend, James Baker III. Bush told Becker that he would not be able to attend the event because of his health, although, he told her, he really wanted to see Obama. "I hope he stops by," he said.

In October, when Bush returned from his annual summer stay at the family compound in Kennebunkport, Becker and Breckenridge began coordinating in earnest. While they are healthy, former presidents keep daunting schedules crammed with speeches, events, and looming book deadlines. The chiefs of staff to the former presidents speak regularly, sometimes with morbid questions, as was the case that previous winter when Clinton's chief of staff gave Becker a call to get funeral-planning advice. The meeting between Bush and Obama was one that neither former president wanted to miss, knowing that it might be their last opportunity to see each other. Becker, who had been Bush's chief of staff since 1994 and was practically a member of the Bush family, told me that she had a nagging feeling she could not shake: "I've never said this to anyone, but I remember quietly thinking to myself, *I'm not sure President Bush will be here.*"

When Obama arrived that November at the Bushes' home in Houston's upscale Tanglewood community, Bush was having one of his bad days. He had Parkinson's disease and used a wheelchair or a motorized scooter, and he was not feeling well. His wife's death had shaken him; she had always said she hoped she would pass away before he did, because she could not imagine living without him. Now he was forced to live without her and it was taking a heavy toll. The day after Barbara Bush's funeral, he was hospitalized because of an infection that spread to his blood. When asked if he really was up for a visit from Obama, Bush could not be swayed: he replied, "No, no, I feel good." But Becker knew better.

As she ushered Obama into Bush's living room, she whispered to him, "If it were anybody else but you, we would have canceled this visit." Neil Bush and Pulitzer Prize–winning historian Jon Meacham joined the two former presidents. Bush was sitting in his wheelchair in the middle of the three men, "smiling ear to ear" as he sat quietly listening to the discussion, even though he was not able to participate in it much himself. Neil, who is the Bushes' fourth child, told me that Obama specifically told Bush how much he admired his handling of foreign policy. After about forty minutes, Obama asked if he could spend just five minutes alone with Bush. Everyone left the room to give them privacy for what would be their last moments together.

When Obama was president, Bush returned to the White House several times, including two visits to the Oval Office and the unveiling of the official White House portraits of his son and daughter-in-law, in May 2012. The two men had grown fond of each other. Obama's young staffers were in awe of Bush, who represented a different era in American politics, which, to be sure, was not always kind but was not as relentlessly partisan as the politics of today. Before he needed a wheelchair, Bush walked up and down the hallways of the West Wing that he knew so well, and teased Obama's aides, many of whom were in their twenties and thirties and were little kids when he was president: "Have you ever gone skydiving? Well, what are you waiting for?" He exuded graciousness and old-world manners, and because of his large, close family, he seemed to convey the message that politics is something that is a *part* of one's life, but it should not *define* one's life.

His kindness extended to private interactions with staff. Before Bush visited the White House for a July 2013 event honoring the winner of the 5,000th Daily Point of Light Award, part of the nonprofit encouraging volunteerism that Bush created and continued long after he left office, he called the Obamas' social secretary, Deesha Dyer, to thank her and her staff for their work in preparing for his visit. During their call, he told her how excited he was to see members of the residence staff who had taken care of his family when they lived in the White House. It was quintessential Bush.

"Given the humility that's defined your life, I suspect it's harder for you to see something that's clear to everybody else around you, and that's how bright a light *you* shine," Obama said at the event, in the White House's regal East Room, as Bush sat smiling in his wheelchair. "We are surely a kinder and gentler nation because of you."

In 2014, the Obamas had gone to Houston for a fund-raiser, and Bush wanted to surprise them on the tarmac when Air Force One landed at George Bush Intercontinental Airport. The Bushes considered the visit a generous gesture on their part, since Obama was very unpopular in Texas. Obama saw it differently. "We thought President Bush would like to be seen as being healthy, since they had both been through health challenges, and so we invited them on the tarmac," said Obama aide Bobby Schmuck, who helped coordinate the meeting. "Bush wanted it to be a surprise for Obama, but of course I had to tell him ahead of time. Obama still acted surprised when he walked down the steps and saw Bush." Bush, in his wheelchair and wearing the colorful socks he was known for, talked with the Obamas for ten minutes on the tarmac. Afterward, the former president who had left office more than twenty years earlier wanted to chat with members of the media who were traveling with the Obamas. He knew veterans like Doug Mills, a *New York Times* photographer who has been covering the White House since 1983. The reporters and photographers were floored, not because Bush was so warm—they expected nothing less—but because they had not expected to see him. It was a small, short visit between a former Republican president and a sitting Democratic president thirty-seven years his junior, but it carried the broader message that the presidency is much bigger than the individual who possesses it. And that message can be conveyed on any stage, even on a nondescript airport tarmac.

Years later, and three days after their final private visit, Bush, the last president to have served in combat during wartime, passed away. That evening, after Obama said his private goodbyes to a Republican predecessor he so greatly admired, he praised Bush and his former chief of staff and secretary of state, James Baker III, at the black-tie gala at the Baker Institute. He said the two men "deserve enormous credit for managing the end of the Cold War in a way that could have gone sideways."

George W. Bush called his father the night he died. "Dad, I love you, and you've been a wonderful father," he said. His father replied simply, "I love you, too." Bush was not at his father's bedside that night, but they had said their goodbyes so many times before. Bush was not only the son of a former president and a former first lady; he was also only the second president to be sworn in with both parents there to witness the moment (Ulysses S. Grant's parents were alive but they did not both attend his inauguration)—the other time was in 1961, when Joseph and Rose Kennedy looked on as their son John was sworn in. And he is the only former president to leave office with both parents still alive. He certainly knew how lucky he was. In 2013, the younger Bush had asked friends for ideas for a eulogy as his dad was fighting off a terrible case of bronchitis. But Bush pulled through again and again. After he was released, he issued a statement through his office telling people to "put the harps back in the closet."

It was not only family members who were touched by George and Barbara Bush. They were adored by the residence staff who served them in the White House and beloved by the Secret Service detail who followed them to Houston and Kennebunkport during the years after they left Washington, D.C. Brimming with empathy, Bush, when he found out that one of his agents had a two-year-old son being treated for leukemia, shaved his head at eighty-nine years old in solidarity. His agents, who referred to Bush by his code name, Timberwolf, were honorary pallbearers during some of the events celebrating him after his death. At the end of a week of events, his Secret Service detail tweeted, "Timberwolf's Detail concluded at 0600 hours on December 7,

2018 with no incidents to report at the George Bush Presidential Library—College Station, Texas. God speed Former President George H. W. Bush—you will be missed by all of us."

That decency was something that resonated with Obama, who said that Bush left behind a "legacy of service that may never be matched, even though he'd want all of us to try." His life, Obama wrote in a statement after Bush's death, was a "testament to the qualities that make this country great. Service to others. Commitment to leaving behind something better. Sacrifice in the name of lifting this country closer to its founding ideals." Obama has called Bush "one of the most underrated presidents" and echoed what Bush's son Jeb once said: "How great is this country that it could elect a man as fine as our dad to be its president?"

Chase Untermeyer, a longtime aide to the elder Bush, lived in Texas and traveled with Bush's casket to Washington, D.C., for his state funeral. He marveled at how the Bushes were able to put aside grudges. Barbara Bush, who was less willing to forgive than her husband, accompanied him to the Republican presidential debate at the University of Houston days after their son Jeb dropped out of the 2016 Republican primary. The Bushes were devastated by his loss. It had been a brutal fight. Jeb, Bush's second son and the former governor of Florida, was the GOP front-runner early in the race and a frequent recipient of Trump's mockery. One of Trump's favorite nicknames for his rival was "low-energy Jeb." Trump even ridiculed him for asking his mother to campaign for him: "Just watched Jeb's ad where he desperately needed mommy to help him," he tweeted. "Jeb—mom cannot help you with ISIS, the Chinese or with Putin." Trump's insults did not go unnoticed by Bush 41. At one campaign stop in New Hampshire during the 2016 presidential race, Jeb joked that his father was "throwing shoes at the TV when his son gets attacked and insulted by our favorite candidate."

Jeb called his mother when he decided the time had come to leave the race. "I just want to let you know I'm heading home," he told her. All she could say was "I love you." Untermeyer was impressed that they attended the debate in Houston. "Why go there and be in the same room with Trump?" he said. "They went because they knew it was a big deal for Houston and for the University of Houston. The easiest thing for people in their nineties is to stay home!" It was about more than politics; it was about supporting their home state and, at the time, at least, the Republican Party. Bush "did not live in the past," Untermeyer said.

So much about the party was changing. The elder Bushes were indeed baffled by Donald Trump and his brand of populism and name-calling. At night, as the election dragged on, George watched the evening news while Barbara, who still had a proudly placed JEB! campaign sticker on her walker, put on her headphones, listened to a book on tape, and stitched, too annoyed to watch it. Neil Bush told me that when he talked to his mother about his fears before the election, she sighed and said, "It's in God's hands."

The elder Bush's dislike of Trump ran deeper than Trump assumes. Bush was particularly disturbed when Trump, who received four student deferments from military service between 1964 and 1968, famously attacked John McCain at a Christian conservative gathering during the campaign. "I like people who weren't captured," Trump said referring to the Arizona senator's five and a half years as a prisoner of the North Vietnamese when, as a Navy pilot during the Vietnam War, he was captured, held prisoner, and tortured at the infamous "Hanoi Hilton." "He's not a war hero. He was a war hero because he was captured," Trump said at the event in Iowa during the Republican primary.

"I can't understand how somebody could say that and still be taken seriously," Bush said, particularly upset because of his own history serving in World War II. An aide said of the election, "It's keeping him young." This was a painful time for Bush, who did not recognize his own Republican Party. "I'm getting old," he told friends, "at just the right time."

Remarkably, Bush, the standard-bearer of the Republican Party, voted for Hillary Clinton in 2016. It was the first time he had ever voted for a Democrat for president. Barbara Bush wrote in their son Jeb's name on the last day of early voting. "I could not vote for Trump or Clinton," she wrote in her diary. George W. Bush and his wife, Laura, left the space for president blank on their ballots. According to *USA Today* Washington bureau chief Susan Page, who wrote a book about Barbara Bush, the former first lady even kept a red-white-and-blue Trump countdown clock in her bedroom that marked how much time—down to the second—remained in his first term.

At the Baker Institute that night, Trump's name did not come up directly during the conversation, but the contrast between his take-no-prisoners leadership style and Bush's genteel leadership was clear. "He's Voldemort," Jon Meacham said, comparing Trump to the villain in the Harry Potter series whose name is not to be mentioned. "I won't say his name."

"THIS IS SO UNCALLED FOR"

Once Donald Trump was elected president, those kinds of honest responses were harder and harder to come by from the five men who once occupied the Oval Office. They were each shocked, in their own way, by his victory, but they each held fast to the unwritten rule that former presidents should not criticize the sitting president. Republican matriarch Barbara Bush made the boldest statement of all when she decided not to include Trump on the guest list when she planned her funeral. In February 2018, she made an astonishing admission when asked whether she was a Republican anymore: "probably" not, she said, blaming her health trouble on the "angst" caused by Trump during the campaign. "I have heard that she was nasty to me, but she should be," Trump said in response. "Look what I did to her sons." Neil Bush said his mother was "a fiercely loyal mother and wife and anybody who *ever* attacked her husband or her kids would get on her wrong side. Forever." She had spent seven decades living with someone whose life's work was to "serve others with humility through lifting others up and not motivating people through negative bullying tactics," Neil said.

Three months after George Bush's funeral, Trump, who had told me how close he was with Bill Clinton, also said that his relationship with "the father" was "excellent" until he ran for the Republican nomination. "It was a little rough when I was running against his son. His son's a nice person—Jeb—but I ran against his son and that wasn't exactly, I would say, positive toward the relationship with the father, or the mother." He continued, "I actually raised money for him [George H. W. Bush]. I remember I had a fundraiser for him, I was with [boxing promoter] Don King."

Trump had been pointedly left off the guest list for John McCain's funeral, but he was invited to George H. W. Bush's funeral, because Bush wanted him to be there. Also, it would have been quite another thing for Bush, a former president, not to invite the sitting president. And it made sense to invite Trump, given how much Trump had dominated media coverage of McCain's funeral. "The Bushes were grateful Trump came," said an aide to George W. Bush who asked to speak anonymously because his boss insists on a low-key post-presidency. "They didn't want it to be like McCain's funeral, where the funeral was not about John McCain; it was about Donald Trump." If Bush, a former president, had banned the sitting president from his own funeral

(funeral planning for former presidents is done years in advance), it would have been an unprecedented statement. And Bush, a rule follower and institutionalist, was not about to do it. Trump was glad to be invited and seemed genuinely moved by it. "I know that he took it very personally the way it worked out for his son," Trump told me when I asked about his relationship with Bush senior. "He loved his sons, he loved his family, he was a good father, a good husband. I think he took it very hard, but they did ask me to go and I went out of respect. I thought it was a beautiful funeral, actually." It may have been a rare moment of camaraderie between Trump and his successors, even though the former presidents and first ladies were noticeably tense around Trump.

There had been so much bad blood. The summer before Bush passed away, Trump inexplicably made fun of his Points of Light initiative. "What the hell is that? Has anyone ever figured that one out?" he asked the crowd at a political rally in Montana. Bush's friends and allies were shocked. "This is so uncalled for. Going after a 94-year-old former President's promotion of volunteerism," Ari Fleischer, who worked for both George H. W. Bush and George W. Bush, wrote on Twitter. But during the events surrounding Bush's funeral, Donald and Melania Trump were subdued and respectful. They paid their respects to Bush as he was lying in state in the Capitol Rotunda for two days before his state funeral. It must have felt good to not be at war with the club, even for a moment.

For Republicans and Democrats alike, Bush's passing marked the end of an era. Most people walked stoically by Bush's casket, but one person, who grew up in the world of the Presidents Club, broke down in tears. "I loved Papa Bush so much, he was just wonderful," Lynda Bird Johnson Robb, the eldest daughter of President Lyndon Johnson and his wife, Lady Bird, told me. "I thought of all the history he had seen, all the changes, how fortunate he had been to see his son inaugurated as president. What an honor. I was honoring a president and honoring a friend." The Johnsons and the Bushes were from different political parties, but both hailed from Texas and shared a long history. Johnson was friends with Bush's father, Prescott, when he was a Connecticut senator. "When [George H. W.] Bush was elected to Congress, my father had him come for a one-on-one visit at the White House," Robb recalled. "It was pretty unusual for a sitting president to ask a freshman congressman from the other party to come for a visit, but it was because of his friendship with Bush's father." As president, Bush quoted fellow Texan LBJ often. One of the most colorful phrases had to do with the importance of loyalty. Someone who was disloyal "could paint his ass white and run with the antelope." And in politics, loyalty is everything.

It was an incredibly different time, and that is partly what made the Johnsons' daughter so emotional. As she walked by Bush's casket, she kept thinking of a famous William Shakespeare quote from *Julius Caesar*: "The evil that men do lives after them; the good is oft interred with their bones." Bush needed to be remembered for all the good he had done and not the mistakes he had made in office. In 1969, Bush, a Republican congressman at the time, left the inaugural celebration for Johnson's Republican successor, Richard Nixon, to say goodbye to the Johnsons at Andrews Air Force Base, outside Washington. "He's my president, and he's leaving town," Bush said. "And I don't want him to leave without my being out here and paying my respects to him." It was an act of kindness that Lady Bird Johnson and her daughter always remembered. "That touched us very much," Robb recalled. "You remember when people are good to you, at times when it's not to curry favor or get any public recognition." It was an ultimate act of loyalty.

Shortly after Bush moved into the White House, in 1989, he invited Robb and her husband over for dinner and a movie. The Bushes showed her her old bedroom and asked her what it had been like living there in the 1960s. Barbara Bush summed up the families' bipartisan friendship in a 1998 letter to Lady Bird: "All Bushes love the Johnsons." Robb cried when she recounted how Laura Bush, a native Texan and University of Texas alumna, did the "Hook 'em Horns" sign at the end of Lady Bird Johnson's 2007 funeral as the UT band played the school spirit song, "The Eyes of Texas." She said the relationship between her parents and her father's successors did not end with the Bushes—that it extended to President Carter, who would check in on her mother as she was aging. "There's a lot of goodness out there," she said. The bonds between these presidential families are unshakable. Bill Clinton came to treasure his relationship with Bush 41. "I just loved him," he wrote in a *Washington Post* op-ed after his death.

On December 5, 2018, Bush was given a grand state funeral at Washington's National Cathedral. Everyone there had their own special memory of Bush and his basic decency and kindness. Al Gore recalled getting an unexpected call after he gave his concession speech following the Supreme Court's ruling that he had lost the 2000 presidential election to Bush's son. "I've lost a few times myself," Bush told him, "and I know how you feel." It could have been an awkward conversation, but instead it was a moving display of Bush's empathy. "I was in the Secret Service car going back to the vice president's residence and it was President George H. W. Bush calling me on the telephone, and he was overcome with emotion and he said the kindest things. It was really a touching call."

Bush's funeral was the first state funeral in Washington since former president Gerald Ford passed away in 2006, and all five living presidents attended. Funerals and library openings are the major public events that bring them together. Since 1991, there have been at least six such gatherings, including Bush's funeral. When Obama learned of Bush's death, he told George W. Bush that he would of course attend the funeral but that Michelle would be on her book tour in Europe and would be unable to make it. The former first lady then decided to cancel her stops in Paris and Berlin. "It's important to me to join the Bush family in celebrating President George H. W. Bush's exemplary life," she said.

"THE GREAT I AM"

Seating arrangements at Bush's funeral followed a long-held tradition dating back to the middle of the nineteenth century, when President William Henry Harrison died of pneumonia a month after taking office. The presidential party is seated in the front pew, followed by heads of state, who are arranged alphabetically according to the names of their countries. The strict protocol can make for some awkward moments. Presidential children are seated next to one another. At Bush's funeral, this meant that first daughters Ivanka Trump and Chelsea Clinton were seatmates. The two had been New York society friends who ran in the same social circles, but that was before Trump ran for president and made his Democratic rival, Hillary Clinton, the primary object of his scorn. Now their friendship was over. Chelsea had criticized Ivanka in an interview seven months earlier when, after being asked about Ivanka's having to do her father's bidding, she said, "She's an adult. She can make the choices for herself." One former Clinton aide, who asked to speak anonymously because of how vindictive both the Clintons and the Trumps can be, said, "I know it was protocol, but I bet they [the Bushes] were having some fun with it!" Chelsea, this person told me, plans to run for office herself one day, and she was banking "on being first lady" if her mother had won. This onetime close friend of Bill Clinton's said the Bush people "would take a bullet for each other. That is not the case for the people who worked for Clinton." There was always a feeling, with Clinton, that loyalty worked only one way.

While the focus was on Bush's life and legacy, there was an inescapable awkwardness in the front pew. The man who was being honored had lived by his mother, Dorothy Walker Bush's, admonition to be humble and always to beware of "the Great I Am." Donald Trump, however, is known for his braggadocio. He is all about the Great I Am. The Trumps arrived at the last minute and the president threw off his overcoat and handed it to a military escort. He shook hands with Barack and Michelle Obama but did not extend a hand to the Clintons. It was the first time Trump had seen the Obamas and the Clintons since his inauguration, and he had attacked them mercilessly since. He sat in the seat next to the aisle in the first row, and Melania sat snugly next to Barack Obama, whom she had famously called illegitimate at the height of her husband's birther blitz. Next were Michelle Obama, who had just called Trump out in her memoir; Bill Clinton, whom Trump called a "predator" and "one of the great women abusers of all time"; Hillary Clinton, whom Trump made a sport of ridiculing; and the Carters, whom he has also criticized.

Before his father's funeral began, George W. Bush, who is now the patriarch of the family, walked across the aisle and shook hands with the Trumps and the other former presidents and first ladies. During the ceremony, Trump seemed uncomfortable and did not recite the Apostles' Creed along with the others in his pew. Trump sat closest to Bush's flag-draped coffin, and at times he folded his arms and pursed his lips. Bush's biographer Jon Meacham delivered the first eulogy and, like the three that followed, it lionized a man who stood in stark contrast to Trump. "His life code was: Tell the truth. Don't blame people. Be strong. Do your best. Try hard. Forgive. Stay the course," Meacham said. "And that was, and is, the most American of creeds."

Trump must have felt awkward knowing that the men and women he sat a few feet away from felt a shared sense of disbelief that he was now one of them. He was not supposed to have been elected president, but there he was. And he would make them pay for looking down on him. A week before Bush's funeral, Trump had retweeted a photograph that included photoshopped images of Obama and Hillary and Bill Clinton behind bars, with the caption "Now that Russia collusion is a proven lie, when do the trials for treason begin?" One high-ranking diplomat who attended the funeral recalled watching Trump walk in at the last moment and leave early so that he could avoid talking to anyone. "He probably thought no one would want to talk to him," the diplomat said. "He seems desperate for compliments, and he wasn't going to be getting any there."

Former Republican Wyoming senator Alan Simpson, one of Bush 41's closest friends, delivered a stirring, warm, and occasionally funny eulogy, in which he pointed out how poisonous Washington can be. "Those who travel the high road of humility in Washington, D.C., are not bothered by heavy traffic," he said, to laughter. Simpson had begun preparing the remarks at the Bush family's request in 2012, during one of Bush's many health scares. He cried when he wrote them, which is why, he said, he did not break down when he actually delivered them. Reflecting on the funeral, he told me, "The Bushes are filled with grace and honor and manners and charity. Who would have invited Trump other than the Bushes? They think, *Why pick scabs?*"

Bush, Simpson said, did not have enemies; he had adversaries. It was a sharp contrast to Trump, who revels in his seemingly ever-growing enemies list. One prominent Republican television personality said, "Forty-three and Obama took their cues from forty-one, who had developed a very good relationship with Bill Clinton. It all goes back to the Bushes' respect for the presidency. They're gracious, they're not hateful, they're very forgiving. They put politics in a different box than maybe some people might today."

Bush's decency extended beyond how he treated other politicians. About a dozen former residence staff attended his funeral; the Bush family made sure they were given prime seats. White House usher Chris Emery sat two rows in front of Obama's secretary of defense, Leon Panetta, and across the aisle from Bush's secretary of state and best friend, James Baker III. One residence staffer who worked in the housekeeping department recalled a time when Bush invited him to sit in the Family Dining Room, on the second floor. "He told me to have a seat at the table and we sat there and talked," the staffer said, shaking his head. "Sitting at the table with the president, having a conversation. None of the rest of them would have done a thing like that." After the funeral, the staffers went for beers at the famous D.C. restaurant Old Ebbitt Grill, a block from the White House, and reminisced about the man they loved.

Bush's body was flown back to Texas, where he was buried at his presidential library in College Station, next to his wife and their daughter Robin. Looking back at his old friend's funeral and Donald Trump sitting there in the front row, Simpson said, "If anybody came off top of the line, it was the Bushes, in accepting this man who savaged them."

GETTING OFF THE STAGE

In free governments the rulers are the servants, and the people their superiors and sovereigns. For the former therefore to return among the latter was not to degrade but to promote them.

—Benjamin Franklin

F. Scott Fitzgerald famously wrote that "there are no second acts in American lives," but that is not the case for the former presidents, who have huge platforms long after they leave the White House. Though Jimmy Carter's White House years were plagued with problems and regret, including the failed rescue mission during the Iran hostage crisis, Carter has redefined the post-presidency. Through his tenacious compassion, he and his wife have helped eradicate disease and given hope to millions of people around the world. George H. W. Bush projected warmth and empathy in his years out of office. Clinton's post-presidency has been complicated by scandal and by his wife's political ambitions, but his philanthropic work to end HIV/AIDS, among scores of other projects, has been redeeming.

Post-presidential years are a time for atonement. Leaving behind unfinished business can be haunting and eventually debilitating. When Lyndon Johnson left the White House, in January 1969, he was an exhausted man who seemed well beyond his sixty years. "I want to miss it. I want it to hurt good," he said. Vietnam was consuming his presidency, and on March 31, 1968, he had made a surprise announcement—not even his closest aides knew about it—that he would not be seeking reelection. He could not find a way out of Vietnam, and he thought he would die from the stress if he stayed. Once, around the time of his announcement, White House electrician Traphes Bryant walked into the room just as Johnson was railing about the war to his aides. "They [critics of the Vietnam War] shot me down. The only difference between the Kennedy assassination and mine is that I am still alive and feeling it," he yelled. His daughter Luci Baines Johnson told LBJ biographer Robert Dallek, "My daddy committed political suicide for that war. And since politics was all he had, it was like committing actual suicide." At his ranch in Stonewall, Texas, Johnson suffered from major heart problems and fell into a deep depression. His approach to his brief time as a former president—he lived only four years beyond his time in the White House—and to life in general can be summed up by a favorite needlepoint pillow that he kept at the ranch: THIS IS MY RANCH AND I DO AS I DAMN WELL PLEASE.

Johnson started smoking again the minute he got on the plane from Washington home to Texas, and he abandoned any attempt to limit his consumption of his favorite Cutty Sark whisky. He grew out his white hair and had long, unkempt sideburns that made him look more like some of the people protesting the Vietnam War than a former president. Still, Richard Nixon recognized the importance of keeping his predecessor informed, and he dispatched a plane with briefing papers for Johnson. The attention lifted Johnson's spirits, but he still missed being the most powerful man in the world. Retirement did not suit him well. He was sure he could beat Nixon if he ran in 1968, but he had launched a secret study in 1967 on his life expectancy, and the results were devastating. "My daddy was only sixty-two when he died," he said, "and I figured that with my history of heart trouble I'd never live through another four years. The American people had enough of Presidents dying in office." The trauma of John F. Kennedy's assassination was fresh in his mind. It was predicted that Johnson would die at sixty-four—which he did.

The political careers of George H. W. Bush's two sons allowed him to remain engaged in politics for years after he left office, so in many ways "getting off the stage" was easier for him than it was for the Clintons and the Carters. He would always have a reason to be involved, even on the periphery. On July 8, four months before the 1992 election, Bush wrote in his diary, "I have this marvelous feeling that no matter what lies over the horizon, it will be good, I think I'll win—I'm convinced I'll win. But this little creeping thought comes to mind—if I don't win, I'll be a very happy guy. I'll be opening the beans and franks Sunday nights, I'll be washing the dishes with Bar. I'll be going to bed early every once in a while; do something to help someone else; hold my grandchildren in my arms; look for shellfish; take them fishing . . . we'll have no press corps, no following, no frantic statements, and we'll look back together and say these were interesting times."

For George W. Bush, redemption has been continuing his work to fight HIV/AIDS in Africa. Though he says he does not regret the wars he launched in Iraq and Afghanistan, his portraits of wounded veterans belie a sense of guilt, or at least a preoccupation with the human toll those wars have taken. "I've studied every one of their stories," he said of the veterans featured in his book *Portraits of Courage*. "I know each person I painted, I was thinking about their backgrounds, their service, their injuries, and their recovery. So there's a lot of compassion and a lot of energy in each one of these paintings."

Obama is still defining his legacy, beyond becoming the first

African American president, a historic feat in and of itself. Looking at what he was not able to accomplish in his two terms might provide clues into what he will do now that he is out of office. "I think he regrets that when we had a Democratic majority in Congress in the first term that we didn't take fuller advantage of that on guns and immigration," Chris Lu, who held several jobs in the Obama administration, including deputy secretary of labor, told me. Obama was focused on the economy and health care, Lu said, in part because his chief of staff, Rahm Emanuel, had worked in the Clinton White House and saw Bill Clinton get bogged down in social battles that led to the Democrats losing the House in 1994. But, said Lu, "The most emotional I've ever seen him is post–Sandy Hook Elementary School," referring to the devastating shooting in Newtown, Connecticut, where a twenty-year-old opened fire with a military-style assault rifle, killing twenty first graders and six adults. Obama called it "one of the worst days of my presidency," a tragedy that brought tears to the eyes of normally stone-faced Secret Service agents. "He always thought the fever would break," Lu said, "and we could get something done in the second term."

TRUMP AND THE CLUB

When I asked President Trump where he thinks he'll build his presidential library, he used our interview to distinguish himself from his predecessors—and to take a swipe at them. "That's a very interesting question. I have thought about it very little. I'm more thinking about all of the things that we're doing, which are a lot," he continued, jutting his chin out proudly. "I don't know if you saw the little press conference we just gave, but we're straightening out the Middle East, North Korea, Venezuela. I was left *a lot*, I was left a lot of problems that could have been solved a long time ago. I'm much more focused on that." He paused, because of course the thought had crossed his mind. "I have given it a little thought, and New York seems to be the most natural place, but Florida is another one.

"I know location, I guess, like nobody," said the former real estate developer. "We'll pick somewhere very appropriate."

All the former presidents are unsure how to handle Trump, who, in his own words, is a "different kind of president," unconcerned with tradition and unhindered by established norms of behavior. One source who asked not to be named because of the sensitivity of the matter said that even at a private dinner in Dallas with just fifteen close friends, George W. still would not talk about Trump. Even in that setting, he was genuinely passionate on this point: "I'm not going to say anything I don't think is appropriate for a former president to say. I thought it was extremely important not to have to worry about Clinton badmouthing me." Bush's former press secretary Ari Fleischer put it well when he said, "There is a nice nonpartisan loftiness you hope exists among the ex-presidents—they don't take potshots at their successors. Isn't it nice to have one island of people who behave?"

The intractable problem, of course, is that Trump does not apologize for taking a flamethrower to the Presidents Club. It seems like a waste not to use the intellect and experience of these so-called formers. Senate majority leader Mike Mansfield told John F. Kennedy he had an idea for how to best use former presidents: put them on a kind of consultative council where they could advise the sitting president. It is an interesting thought, though it would complicate life for the sitting president. Former president Harry Truman said he was happy to retreat into a semi-private life. "I've had it in mind ever since I got my—promotion." As citizens, former presidents can provide useful confidential perspective that is not clouded by politics.

At their core, these are human relationships that lend them-selves to empathy, understanding, and appreciation for what they each have been through. They have each had to make serious decisions that have affected an untold number of lives. They know what it is like to have regrets and to have made mistakes. They have the shared experience of running the country and representing the United States of America around the world. None of that seems to concern Donald Trump, who may seem gregarious and larger than life but in reality is a loner.

Trump does not seem to care that he will be an outcast from the Presidents Club. When I asked him if he thought he would fit in, he replied with a knowing smile, "I don't think I fit very well." A part of me was expecting him to lament how things have gone, and maybe even admit that sitting at the Resolute desk in the Oval Office has given him a new sense of appreciation—maybe even empathy—for the men who have sat there before him. But when I asked him if that was the case, he shook his head and said, without hesitation, "No, no."

ACKNOWLEDGMENTS

This book is about a bygone era when the people at the very top of the political food chain formed genuine friendships with one another, even after bitterly duking it out for the presidency. It is about a time when presidents were humbled by the job, which seems like a quaint notion today. And it is about the sanctity of the American presidency and how those who have served as president use their power and influence long after they have left office. None of these men are perfect, but they are all bound by shared respect for the institution of the presidency. My literary agent, Howard Yoon, and my editor, Gail Winston, helped me focus and they guided me in important ways, especially when it came to tuning out the never-ending noise of today's politics. They are total pros, and they both deserve my unending gratitude.

I was lucky to get to sit down with Donald Trump in the Oval Office to ask him where he sees himself in relation to the men who came before him, and I have Sarah Huckabee Sanders to thank for setting up that interview. I made a delightful pilgrimage to Maranatha Baptist Church, in the small town of Plains, Georgia, to hear Jimmy Carter deliver a stirring Bible lesson and to visit with the Carters in their home, all thanks to Carter's longtime confidant and White House communications director Gerald Rafshoon, whom I now call a good friend. I'd also like to thank the many current aides to Barack Obama and George W. Bush who asked to speak with me anonymously because their bosses prefer it that way. I am grateful to the people who spoke with me on the record: Dick Cheney, Laura Bush, Barbara Bush, George H. W. Bush, Leon Panetta, Jean Becker, Don Evans, David Ferriero, Mack McLarty, Jen Psaki, Rich Bagger, Stephen Rochon, Bob Scanlan, Jill Stuckey, Tony Blinken, Phil Wise, Deanna Congileo, Kate Bedingfield, Clay Johnson, Ben LaBolt, Russell Riley, Luis Miranda, Jim McGrath, Eugene Kang, Deesha Dyer, Josh Earnest, Chris Lu, Alan Simpson, Ben Rhodes, Jackie Norris, Anita McBride, Russell Riley, Susie Tompkins Buell, Melanne Verveer, Bobby Schmuck, Mike O'Neil, Lynda Bird Johnson Robb, Luci Baines Johnson, Reggie Love, Ian Bassin, Terry Adamson, Martha Kumar, Susan Porter Rose, Steven Hochman, Chase Untermeyer, Natalie Gonnella-Platts, Jim McGrath, Jenny Botero, Brian Rock, Joel Jensen, and Ari Fleischer.

My husband, Brooke, is my guiding light, and our three children are my pride and joy. I'd also like to thank Gail Ross and Jody Hotchkiss for always being in my corner, and Alicia Tan, Kate D'Esmond, and Tina Andreadis at HarperCollins for expertly shepherding the book through to its publication. Researching and writing can be lonely, and there were times when I needed the support of my strong group of friends, whom I feel lucky to know, including Maura Merlis; my sister, Kelly; Erica Werner; Carol Lee; Christina Warner; Annie Kate Pons; and Carolina Saizar Renart. My parents, Christopher and Valerie Andersen, are among my very favorite people, and they deserve special thanks for always being there. I hope to be half the parent to our children that they have been to me and my sister.

SOURCES AND NOTES

NOTES ON REPORTING

My research for *Team of Five* took me from a candid conversation with President Donald Trump in the Oval Office to a visit with Jimmy and Rosalynn Carter in their modest living room in Plains, Georgia. I interviewed more than a hundred presidential aides, family members, White House residence staff, and former first ladies and vice presidents. When aides asked to talk on background because of the confidential nature of some of these conversations, I respected their wishes. This is an especially sensitive story that is unfolding every day in unexpected ways. Accounts of life as a former president were supplemented by extensive research from archival materials, including oral histories from presidential libraries; memoirs penned by former presidents and first ladies, residence staffers, and political aides; and biographies. I especially want to thank the Miller Center at the University of Virginia for the incredible work they do documenting what really happens inside the West Wing.

PROLOGUE: "I'M A DIFFERENT KIND OF PRESIDENT"

Donald Trump, interview with the author, March 27, 2019. Published sources include James Fallows, "Donald Trump's Telling Change to the Oval Office," *The Atlantic*, August 25, 2017, and Nancy Gibbs and Michael Duffy, *The Presidents Club: Inside the*

World's Most Exclusive Fraternity (New York: Simon & Schuster, 2012). Chandelis Duster and Kevin Liptak, "Bill Clinton: Impeachment Shouldn't Stop Trump from Working with Democrats," CNN, November 14, 2019.

I. THE PEACEFUL TRANSFER OF POWER

Interview subjects include Laura Bush, Jimmy and Rosalynn Carter, Christine Limerick, Stephen Rochon, George Hannie, Gerald Rafshoon, Don Evans, and Nelson Pierce. Published sources include Lady Bird Johnson, *A White House Diary* (New York: Holt, Rinehart & Winston, 1970); Kate Andersen Brower, *The Residence: Inside the Private World of the White House* (New York: HarperCollins, 2015); Kenneth T. Walsh, *Air Force One: A History of the Presidents and Their Planes* (New York: Hyperion, 2003); Presidential Transition Act of 1963, Pub. L. No. 88–277 (1964); Nancy Gibbs and Michael Duffy, *The Presidents Club: Inside the World's Most Exclusive Fraternity* (New York: Simon & Schuster, 2012); Letitia Baldrige, *A Lady, First: My Life in the Kennedy White House and the American Embassies of Paris and Rome* (New York: Viking, 2001); Ryan Lizza, "Waiting for Obama," *Politico Magazine*, November 26, 2019; George H. W. Bush, *All the Best, George Bush: My Life in Letters and Other Writings* (New York: Touchstone, 1999); Bill Clinton, "Bill Clinton: George H. W. Bush's Oval Office Note to Me Revealed the Heart of Who He Was," *Washington Post*, December 1, 2018; Jon Meacham, *Destiny and Power: The American Odyssey of George Herbert Walker Bush* (New York: Random House, 2015); Barbara Bush, *Barbara Bush: A Memoir* (New York: Scribner, 1994); Laura Bush, *Spoken from the Heart* (New York: Simon & Schuster, 2010); Kevin Liptak, "Exclusive: Read the Inauguration Day Letter Obama Left for Trump," CNN, September 5, 2017; Dan Balz, "Obama, Ex-Presidents Gather to Dedicate George W. Bush Library," *Washington Post*, April 25, 2013; Tim Alberta, *American Carnage: On the Front Lines of the Republican Civil War and the Rise of President Trump* (New York: Harper, 2019); Lou Cannon, *President Reagan: The Role of a Lifetime* (New York: Simon & Schuster, 1991).

II. THE UNWRITTEN RULES OF THE CLUB

Author drew on conversations with Jimmy Carter, Donald Trump, Dick Cheney, Alan Simpson, Nelson Pierce, Justin Cooper, Chase Untermeyer, Leon Panetta, Melanne Verveer, Jean Becker, Katie Hill, Eugene Kang, Luis Miranda, Bobby Schmuck, Ed Nixon, Lonnie Bunch, Pete Seat, and Jenny Botero. Published sources include Harry S. Truman, *Memoirs*, vol. 2, *Years of Trial and Hope* (New York: Doubleday, 1956); Andrew Glass, "Adams-Jefferson Correspondence Resumes, May 27, 1813," *Politico*, May 26, 2017; Alexander Hamilton, James Madison, and John Jay, *The Federalist Papers* (1788; reprint, Signet, 2003); George H. W. Bush, *All the Best, George Bush: My Life in Letters and Other Writings* (New York: Touchstone, 1999); Associated Press, "Hurricane Relief Effort Led by Ex-US Presidents Raises $41M," AP News, January 24, 2018; George W. Bush, *41: A Portrait of My Father* (New York: Crown, 2014); Kent Garber, "Teddy Roosevelt, on the Bull Moose Party Ticket, Battles Incumbent William Howard Taft," *U.S. News and World Report*, January 17, 2008; Mark K. Updegrove, *Second Acts: Presidential Lives and Legacies After the White House* (Guilford, CT: Lyons Press, 2006); Barack Obama, Remarks on Earthquake Relief Efforts in Haiti, January 15, 2010, White House; Bill Clinton, *My Life* (New York: Knopf, 2004);

Jimmy Carter, *Faith: A Journey for All* (New York: Simon & Schuster, 2018); Bob Greene, *Fraternity: A Journey in Search of Five Presidents* (New York: Crown, 2004); Michelle Obama, *Becoming* (New York: Crown, 2018); Betsy Klein, "Chelsea Clinton Defends Fellow First Kid Barron Trump," CNN, August 23, 2017; Barack Obama, *The Audacity of Hope: Thoughts on Reclaiming the American Dream* (New York: Crown, 2006); Richard Reeves, "Hail to the Chief—in Public, That Is," *New York Times*, March 20, 2009; John Heilemann and Mark Halperin, *Game Change: Obama and the Clintons, McCain and Palin, and the Race of a Lifetime* (New York: HarperCollins, 2010); George W. Bush, Remarks at the Dedication Ceremony for the George W. Bush Presidential Library and Museum, April 25, 2013, Dallas; Barack Obama, "Weekly Address: Strengthening Our Economy by Passing Bipartisan Immigration Reform," July 13, 2013; Barack Obama, Remarks at a Campaign Rally, September 7, 2012, Portsmouth, NH; Barack Obama, Remarks on Presenting the Presidential Medal of Freedom, November 20, 2013, White House; Barack Obama, interview with John Dickerson, *Face the Nation*, CBS News, July 24, 2016; Barack Obama, Remarks at Georgetown University, June 25, 2013, Washington, D.C.; Mark K. Updegrove, "An Interview with George W. Bush (Transcript)," *Texas Monthly*, October 26, 2010; Nancy Gibbs and Michael Duffy, *The Presidents Club: Inside the World's Most Exclusive Fraternity* (New York: Simon & Schuster, 2012); Kate Andersen Brower, *First Women: The Grace and Power of America's Modern First Ladies* (New York: HarperCollins, 2016); Bob Woodward, *Shadow: Five Presidents and the Legacy of Watergate* (New York: Simon & Schuster, 1999); Dan Balz, "Obama, Ex-Presidents Gather to Dedicate George W. Bush Library," *Washington Post*, April 25, 2013.

in Search of Five Presidents (New York: Crown, 2004); Andrew Kaczynski, "The Assault Weapon Ban Would Have Never Passed If It Wasn't For Ronald Reagan" Buzzfeed, December 19, 2012; Presidential Transition Act of 1963, Pub. L. No. 88–277 (1964); Mark Landler, "Michelle and George: The Embrace Seen Around the World," *New York Times*, September 25, 2016; Michelle Obama, *Becoming* (New York: Crown, 2018); Tim Alberta, *American Carnage: On the Front Lines of the Republican Civil War and the Rise of President Trump* (New York: Harper, 2019); David A. Fahrenthold, Tom Hamburger, and Rosalind S. Helderman, "The Inside Story of How the Clintons Built a $2 Billion Global Empire," *Washington Post*, June 2, 2015; Todd S. Purdum, "The Comeback Id," *Vanity Fair*, June 4, 2008; Peter Baker, "The Mellowing of William Jefferson Clinton," *New York Times Magazine*, May 26, 2009; Richard Reeves, "Hail to the Chief—in Public, That Is," *New York Times*, March 20, 2009; Amy Chozick, "When Clinton Joined Obama Administration, Friction Was Over Staff, Not Email," *New York Times*, March 5, 2015; "The Story Behind Clinton's Trip to North Korea," CNN, August 5, 2009; George W. Bush, "PEPFAR Saves Millions of Lives in Africa. Keep It Fully Funded," *Washington Post*, April 7, 2017; Kevin Sullivan and Rosalind S. Helderman, "How the Clintons' Haiti Development Plans Succeed—and Disappoint," *Washington Post*, March 20, 2015; Mark K. Updegrove, "An Interview with George W. Bush (Transcript)," *Texas Monthly*, October 26, 2010; Nancy Gibbs and Michael Duffy, *The Presidents Club: Inside the World's Most Exclusive Fraternity* (New York: Simon & Schuster, 2012); John Heilemann and Mark Halperin, *Game Change: Obama and the Clintons, McCain and Palin, and the Race of a Lifetime* (New York: HarperCollins, 2010); Gerald R. Ford, *A Time to Heal: The Autobiography of Gerald R. Ford* (New York: Harper & Row, 1979); Tamara Keith, "5 Things You Should Know About Hil-

2015); Taylor Branch, *The Clinton Tapes: Wrestling History with the President* (New York: Simon & Schuster, 2009); David Eisenhower with Julie Nixon Eisenhower, *Going Home to Glory: A Memoir of Life with Dwight D. Eisenhower, 1961–1969* (New York: Simon & Schuster, 2010); Ryan Lizza, "Waiting for Obama," *Politico Magazine*, November 26, 2019; "Clinton's Confession, the Transcript," *Newsweek*, August 11, 2000; Sandra Sobieraj Westfall and Sam Gillette, "Michelle Obama's Not Allowed to Drive Herself, Can't People-Watch at Cafés: 'We Still Live in a Bubble,'" *People*, November 15, 2018; Jeff Zeleny, "For a High-Tech President, a Hard-Fought E-Victory," *New York Times*, January 22, 2009; Yesha Callahan, "Michelle Obama Talks Post-White House, Relationships, and Living a Healthy Life at Essence Festival," *Essence*, July 7, 2019; "CNBC Meets: President Bill Clinton, Part One," CNBC, March 26, 2013; Hayley Garrison Phillips, "President Obama Officiated at a Wedding in D.C. This Past Weekend," *Washingtonian*, January 23, 2019; Ben Rhodes, *The World as It Is: A Memoir of the Obama White House* (New York: Random House, 2018); "Bush Reveals Contents of His Pockets: No Wallet or Keys," *USA Today*, November 2, 2005; Bob Greene, *Fraternity: A Journey in Search of Five Presidents* (New York: Crown, 2004); Katherine Skiba, "Obama's Post-Presidential Life Beginning to Take Shape," *Chicago Tribune*, January 16, 2017; George W. Bush, *41: A Portrait of My Father* (New York: Crown, 2014); "Bush's Final Approval Rating: 22 Percent," CBS News, January 16, 2009; Dana Calvo, "Bush Challenges Gore to Publicly Condemn Clinton for Past Behavior," *Los Angeles Times*, August 12, 2000; Kevin Robillard, "Bush: 'History Will Judge,'" *Politico*, April 22, 2013; Ret. Sgt. Mike Elliott, Golden Knights Parachute Team, recalling skydiving with George H. W. Bush in interview with Dana Bash, CNN, December 1, 2018; Scott Stump, "George H. W. Bush Takes a Skydive: That's One Way to

E. Sanger, *The Inheritance: The World Obama Confronts and the Challenges to American Power* (New York: Random House, 2009); Judy Kurtz, "Obama: 'I'm Actually Surprised by How Much Money I Got,'" *Hill*, July 17, 2018; Bill Clinton, *My Life* (New York: Knopf, 2004); Raymond Hernandez, "Clintons Accused of a Failure to Disclose Gifts' True Value," *New York Times*, February 13, 2002; Peter Grier, "George Bush 'Decision Points'—How Many Books Will He Sell?," *Christian Science Monitor*, November 9, 2010; Jonathan Alter, "Bush Nostalgia Is Overrated, but His Book of Paintings Is Not," *New York Times*, April 17, 2017; Presidential Transition Act of 1963, Pub. L. No. 88–277 (1964); Daniel Halper, *Clinton, Inc.: The Audacious Rebuilding of a Political Machine* (New York: HarperCollins, 2014); Sam Dangremond, "How Much Money Can Ex-Presidents Pull In?," *Town & Country*, March 23, 2017; David A. Fahrenthold, Tom Hamburger, and Rosalind S. Helderman, "The Inside Story of How the Clintons Built a $2 Billion Global Empire," *Washington Post*, June 2, 2015; Todd S. Purdum, "The Comeback Id," *Vanity Fair*, June 4, 2008; Peter Baker, "The Mellowing of William Jefferson Clinton," *New York Times Magazine*, May 26, 2009; Dan Alexander and Chase Peterson-Withorn, "How Trump Is Trying—and Failing—to Get Rich Off His Presidency," *Forbes*, October 2, 2018; George H. W. Bush, *All the Best, George Bush: My Life in Letters and Other Writings* (New York: Touchstone, 1999); Thomas B. Edsall, "Clintons Take Away $190,000 in Gifts," *Washington Post*, January 21, 2001; Taylor Branch, *The Clinton Tapes: Wrestling History with the President* (New York: Simon & Schuster, 2009); Bob Greene, *Fraternity: A Journey in Search of Five Presidents* (New York: Crown, 2004); Adam Liptak, "How Far Can Trump Go in Issuing Pardons?," *New York Times*, May 31, 2018; Husna Haq, "George W. Bush Charges Vets Group $100,00 for Speech. Too Much?," *Christian Science Monitor*, July 9, 2015; Roberto Suro,

"The Inauguration: Bowing Out; Citizen Bush Goes Home and Says He Is Satisfied," *New York Times*, January 21, 1993; Bill Clinton, *My Life* (New York: Knopf, 2004); Weston Kosova, "Backstage at the Finale," *Newsweek*, February 25, 2001; Kevin Sullivan and Mary Jordan, "The Un-Celebrity President," *Washington Post*, August 17, 2018; Maureen Dowd, "When Hillary and Donald Were Friends," *New York Times*, November 2, 2016; Peter Baker, "Trump Pardons Scooter Libby in a Case That Mirrors His Own," *New York Times*, April 13, 2018; Andy Sullivan, Emily Stephenson, and Steve Holland, "Trump Says Won't Divest from His Business While President," Reuters, January 11, 2017; David A. Fahrenthold and Robert O'Harrow Jr., "Trump: A True Story," *Washington Post*, August 10, 2016.

VI. REDEMPTION

Information in this chapter was based in part on conversations with Jimmy and Rosalynn Carter, Gerald Rafshoon, Zbigniew Brzezinski, Mack McLarty, Walter Mondale, Leisa Easom, Betty Monkman, Jill Stuckey, Roland Mesnier, Steven Hochman, and Terry Adamson. Published sources include Mark K. Updegrove, *Second Acts: Presidential Lives and Legacies After the White House* (Guilford, CT: Lyons Press, 2006); Kate Andersen Brower, *The Residence: Inside the Private World of the White House* (New York: HarperCollins, 2015); Rosalynn Carter, *First Lady from Plains* (Boston: Houghton Mifflin, 1984); Michael Gold, "Bill Clinton and Jeffrey Epstein: How Are They Connected?," *New York Times*, July 9, 2019; William E. Schmidt, "President Praises Carter at Library," *New York Times*, October 2, 1986; Kate Andersen Brower, *First Women: The Grace and Power of America's Modern First Ladies* (New York: HarperCollins, 2016); Gwen Ifill, "The 1992 Campaign: The Democrats; Clinton Assails

G.O.P. Attacks Aimed at Wife," *New York Times*, August 20, 1992; Nancy Gibbs and Michael Duffy, *The Presidents Club: Inside the World's Most Exclusive Fraternity* (New York: Simon & Schuster, 2012); Jimmy Carter, *A Full Life: Reflections at Ninety* (New York: Simon & Schuster, 2015); Jimmy Carter, *White House Diary* (New York: Farrar, Straus & Giroux, 2010); George H. W. Bush, *All the Best, George Bush: My Life in Letters and Other Writings* (New York: Touchstone, 1999); Jimmy Carter, *Beyond the White House: Waging Peace, Fighting Disease, Building Hope* (New York: Simon & Schuster, 2007); Stephen Collinson, "Jimmy Carter's Rewarding Post-Presidency," CNN, August 20, 2015; Hamilton Jordan, *Crisis: The Last Year of the Carter Presidency* (New York: G. P. Putnam's Sons, 1982); George Stephanopoulos, *All Too Human: A Political Education* (New York: Little, Brown, 1999); Charlotte Curtis, "Carter: 20 Months Later," *New York Times*, August 17, 1982; Mark Leibovich, "When Former Presidents Assail the Chief," *New York Times*, May 22, 2007; Kevin Sullivan and Mary Jordan, "The Un-Celebrity President," *Washington Post*, August 17, 2018; Bob Greene, *Fraternity: A Journey in Search of Five Presidents* (New York: Crown, 2004); Douglas Brinkley, "Clintons and Carters Don't Mix," *New York Times*, August 28, 1996; "Roger Clinton Now Target of Pardon Probe," CNN, February 23, 2001; Nicholas Johnston and Kate Andersen Brower, "Obama Tax Deal 'Is a Good Bill,' Former President Clinton Says," Bloomberg, December 12, 2010; Kevin Sack and Sheri Fink, "Rwanda Aid Shows Reach and Limits of Clinton Foundation," *New York Times*, October 18, 2015; Michael Shear, "The Surprise Trip to the Briefing Room," *New York Times*, December 10, 2010; Elise Labott, "The Story Behind Carter's North Korean Trip," CNN, August 25, 2010; Todd S. Purdum, "The Comeback Id," *Vanity Fair*, June 4, 2008; Peter Baker, "The Mellowing of William Jefferson Clinton," *New York Times Magazine*, May 26, 2009.

VII. AMERICA'S PYRAMIDS AND THE WEIGHT OF LEGACY

Interviews include Donald Trump, Jimmy Carter, Russell Riley, David Ferriero, Mack McLarty, Don Evans, Leisa Easom, Jill Stuckey, Steven Hochman, and Terry Adamson. Published sources include Mark K. Updegrove, *Second Acts: Presidential Lives and Legacies After the White House* (Guilford, CT: Lyons Press, 2006); Bob Clark, "In Defense of Presidential Libraries," *Public Historian* 40, no. 2 (May 2018); Jennifer Schuessler, "The Obama Presidential Library That Isn't," *New York Times*, February 20, 2019; Jeanne Marie Laskas, "To Obama: With Love, and Hate, and Desperation," *New York Times*, January 17, 2017; Kate Andersen Brower, *First Women: The Grace and Power of America's Modern First Ladies* (New York: HarperCollins, 2016); Peter Baker, "For Bush, a Day to Bask in Texas Sun," *New York Times*, April 25, 2013; Nancy Gibbs and Michael Duffy, *The Presidents Club: Inside the World's Most Exclusive Fraternity* (New York: Simon & Schuster, 2012); Karl Evers-Hillstrom, "Shining a Light on Presidential Libraries—the Unrenowned Pay-to-Play Scandal," Opensecrets.org, March 13, 2019; Donna Shalala, interview, Presidential Oral History Project, Bill Clinton Presidency, Miller Center, University of Virginia, May 15, 2007; Lisa Lerer, "No One Wants to Campaign with Bill Clinton Anymore," *New York Times*, November 2, 2018; Kate Andersen Brower, *The Residence: Inside the Private World of the White House* (New York: HarperCollins, 2015); Eun Kyung Kim, "President Bill Clinton on Monica Lewinsky, #MeToo and Whether His Apology Was Enough," *Today*, NBC, June 4, 2018; David Marchese, "Robert A. Caro on the Means and Ends of Power," *New York Times*, April 1, 2019; Jonah Engel Bromwich and Matt Stevens, "George H. W. Bush Apologizes After Women Accuse Him of Grabbing Them," *New York Times*, October 27, 2017; Ronald Reagan, *An American Life: The Autobiography* (New York: Simon & Schuster, 1990).

VIII. THE FIRST LADIES CIRCLE

Interview subjects include Barbara Bush, Rosalynn Carter, Laura Bush, Deesha Dyer, Jean Becker, Neil Bush, Anita McBride, Gustavo Paredes, Liz Allen, Susie Tompkins Buell, Jim McGrath, Ann Compton, Don Evans, Russell Riley, Christine Limerick, and Paul Costello. Published sources include "ABC News: Michelle Obama 'Stopped Even Trying to Smile' at Trump Inauguration," CNN, November 12, 2018; Kate Andersen Brower, *First Women: The Grace and Power of America's Modern First Ladies* (New York: HarperCollins, 2016); Hillary Rodham Clinton, *Living History* (New York: Scribner, 2003); Hilary Weaver, "Laura Bush, Michelle Obama, and the Soft Power of Outspoken First Ladies," *Vanity Fair*, June 20, 2018; Mark K. Updegrove, *Second Acts: Presidential Lives and Legacies After the White House* (Guilford, CT: Lyons Press, 2006); Sandra Sobieraj Westfall, "After 67 Years of Marriage, What Do Jimmy and Rosalynn Carter Mean by 'ILYTG'?," *People*, October 8, 2014; Laura Bush, *Spoken from the Heart* (New York: Simon & Schuster, 2010); Yesha Callahan, "Michelle Obama Talks Post-White House, Relationships, and Living a Healthy Life at Essence Festival," *Essence*, July 7, 2019; Jessica Kwong, "Melania Trump Follows Her Husband's Least Favorite Person on Twitter: Barack Obama," *Newsweek*, February 6, 2018; Chris Cillizza, "Michelle Obama Just Compared Donald Trump to a 'Divorced Dad,'" CNN, April 16, 2019; David Nakamura, "President Trump Traveled 250 Yards to Greet George W. Bush. He Used a Stretch Limo and an Eight-Vehicle Motorcade to Make the Trip," *Washington Post*, December 5, 2018; Jim Frederick, "Q & A with Chelsea Clinton," *Time*, September 26, 2012; Barack Obama, Remarks at a Campaign Rally for Democratic Presidential Nominee Hillary Rodham Clinton, October 14, 2016, Cleveland; Hillary Clinton, *It Takes a Village*

(New York: Simon & Schuster, 1996); Dan Merica, "The Clintons Launch Paid Speaking Tour with Plenty of Ire for Trump," CNN, November 28, 2018; Carrie Dann, "Hillary Clinton's Popularity Has Fluctuated During Decades in Public Eye," NBC News, April 13, 2015; Lauren Hubbard, "A Brief History of George W. Bush and Michelle Obama's Friendship," *Town & Country*, December 5, 2018; Nancy Gibbs and Michael Duffy, *The Presidents Club: Inside the World's Most Exclusive Fraternity* (New York: Simon & Schuster, 2012); Kate Bennett, "Melania Trump Hosts Laura Bush for White House Visit," CNN, December 4, 2018; Susan Page, *The Matriarch: Barbara Bush and the Making of an American Dynasty* (New York: Twelve, 2019); Rosalynn Carter, statement on President Trump's border policy, sent to the author by Carter press secretary Deanna Congileo, June 18, 2018; Bob Woodward, *Shadow: Five Presidents and the Legacy of Watergate* (New York: Simon & Schuster, 1999); Michael Rubinkam, "Hillary Clinton Says She's 'Ready to Come Out of the Woods,'" Associated Press, March 18, 2017; Christina Zhao, "Michelle Obama Explains Viral Candy Sharing Moments with George W. Bush," *Newsweek*, December 18, 2018; George Stephanopoulos, *All Too Human: A Political Education* (New York: Little, Brown, 1999); Devan Cole, "Hillary Clinton: 'We Are Living Through a Full-Fledged Crisis in Our Democracy,'" CNN, March 3, 2019; Mark Landler, "Michelle and George: The Embrace Seen Around the World," *New York Times*, September 25, 2016; Jon Meacham, *Destiny and Power: The American Odyssey of George Herbert Walker Bush* (New York: Random House, 2015); Michelle Obama, *Becoming* (New York: Crown, 2018); "Michelle Obama Cancels Part of Book Tour to Attend George H. W. Bush's Funeral," *Today*, NBC, December 2, 2018; Donnie Radcliffe, "Queen Nancy," *Washington Post*, September 8, 1981; "Michelle Obama Opens Up About Family and Finding Her Voice," *Today*, NBC, Novem-

with Steve Inskeep, *Morning Edition*, NPR, December 15, 2016; Barack Obama, Remarks on the Unveiling of the Official Portraits of Former President George W. Bush and First Lady Laura Bush, May 31, 2012, White House; Christi Parsons, "In the Face of Trump's Attacks, Obama and Other Ex-Presidents Remain Silent," *Los Angeles Times*, March 29, 2018; John Wagner, "Trump Denies Report That He Considered Restricting Obama's Intelligence Briefings," *Washington Post*, August 21, 2018; Barack Obama and Bill Clinton, Remarks at a Campaign Event November 4, 2012, Concord, New Hampshire; Doris Kearns Goodwin, "Barack Obama and Doris Kearns Goodwin: The Ultimate Exit Interview," *Vanity Fair*, September 21, 2016; Fareed Zakaria, "Inside Obama's World: The President Talks to *Time* About the Changing Nature of American Power," *Time*, January 19, 2012; Barack Obama, Remarks to Texas A&M University Marine Corps Cadets, October 16, 2009, College Station, TX; Aidan Quigley, "Former Presidents Walk Fine Line in Trump's America," *Politico*, May 9, 2017; Sandra Sobieraj Westfall, "What Does Barack Obama Really Think of Donald Trump? 'He's Nothing But a Bullsh——ter,'" *People*, May 17, 2017; George H. W. Bush, *All the Best, George Bush: My Life in Letters and Other Writings* (New York: Touchstone, 1999); Ronald Reagan, *An American Life: The Autobiography* (New York: Simon & Schuster, 1990); Michelle Obama, *Becoming* (New York: Crown, 2018); Simon Carswell, "Irish Embassy Arranged Trump-Kenny Call Through Associates of Rudy Giuliani," *Irish Times*, November 11, 2016; Christina Caron, "Obama's Letter to President Trump on Inauguration Day," *New York Times*, September 3, 2017; Jonathan Allen and Amie Parnes, *Shattered: Inside Hillary Clinton's Doomed Campaign* (New York: Random House, 2017); Jeremy Diamond, "Trump Pushes Back at Michelle Obama," CNN, November 10, 2018; Kate Andersen Brower, "Former White House Residence Staff Appalled by Donald Trump's

Writing George H. W. Bush's Eulogy—So He Wouldn't Cry While Giving It," *Washington Post*, December 4, 2018; Ryan Lizza, "Waiting for Obama," *Politico Magazine*, November 26, 2019; Richard Reeves, "Hail to the Chief—in Public, That Is," *New York Times*, March 20, 2009; Kate Bennett, *Free Melania: The Unauthorized Biography* (New York: Flatiron Books, 2019);Laura Ratliff, "President George H. W. Bush's Beautiful Last Moments and Words to His Son," *Today*, NBC, December 2, 2018; Decca Aitkenhead, "Chelsea Clinton: 'I've Had Vitriol Flung at Me for as Long as I Can Remember,'" *Guardian*, May 26, 2018; Mark K. Updegrove, *Second Acts: Presidential Lives and Legacies After the White House* (Guilford, CT: Lyons Press, 2006); Maureen Dowd, "When Hillary and Donald Were Friends," *New York Times*, November 2, 2016; Michael Lewis, *The Fifth Risk* (New York: W. W. Norton, 2018); Jonathan Capehart, "Pat Nixon Predicted Donald Trump's Rise—29 Years Ago," *Washington Post*, March 15, 2016; Richard Reeves, *President Nixon: Alone in the White House* (New York: Simon & Schuster, 2001); James Hohmann, "The Daily 202: Reagan White House Viewed Trump and His 'Large Ego' Warily," *Washington Post*, June 22, 2016; Nancy Gibbs and Michael Duffy, *The Presidents Club: Inside the World's Most Exclusive Fraternity* (New York: Simon & Schuster, 2012); George W. Bush, *Decision Points* (New York: Crown, 2010); Kate Andersen Brower, "Former White House Residence Staff Appalled by Donald Trump's 'Real Dump' Comment," *Time*, August 2, 2017; Ben Rhodes, *The World as It Is: A Memoir of the Obama White House* (New York: Random House, 2018); Jonathan Martin and Matt Flegenheimer, "Bush at 91: Irritated and Invigorated by '16 Race," *New York Times*, October 24, 2015; George H. W. Bush, *All the Best, George Bush: My Life in Letters and Other Writings* (New York: Touchstone, 1999); Jimmy Carter, *Beyond the White House: Waging Peace, Fighting*

Disease, Building Hope (New York: Simon & Schuster, 2007); Bill Clinton, "George H. W. Bush's Oval Office Note to Me Revealed the Heart of Who He Was," *Washington Post*, December 1, 2018; Associated Press, "Bush's State Funeral Follows Generations of Tradition," AP News, December 4, 2018; Dianna Wray, "President Obama and James Baker Celebrate No Indictments at the Baker Institute's 25th Anniversary Gala," *Houstonia*, November 28, 2018; Cliff Sims, *Team of Vipers: My 500 Extraordinary Days in the Trump White House* (New York: Thomas Dunne Books, 2019); Robert M. Gates, *From the Shadows: The Ultimate Insider's Story of Five Presidents and How They Won the Cold War* (New York: Simon & Schuster, 1996); Mark Leibovich, "When Former Presidents Assail the Chief," *New York Times*, May 22, 2007; "Bush: 'Politics Does Not Have to Be Mean,'" CNN, December 1, 2018; Alexander Burns, "Obama Quietly Gives Advice to 2020 Democrats, but No Endorsement," *New York Times*, February 18, 2019; Mark K. Updegrove, *The Last Republicans: Inside the Extraordinary Relationship Between George H. W. Bush and George W. Bush* (New York: Harper, 2017); Dade Hayes, "George W. Bush Kicks Off A&E Upfront with History Plug and Trump Subtweets," *Deadline*, March 27, 2019; Peter Baker, "The Mellowing of William Jefferson Clinton," *New York Times Magazine*, May 26, 2009.

XI. AND THEN THERE WERE FOUR

Interview subjects include Donald Trump, Dick Cheney, Jean Becker, Neil Bush, Alan Simpson, Deesha Dyer, Bobby Schmuck, Lynda Bird Johnson Robb, Laura Bush, Barbara Bush, and Jim McGrath. Published sources include Marie B. Hecht, *Beyond the Presidency: The Residues of Power* (New York: Macmillan, 1976); Tim Naftali, "How Obama's Note to Trump Defied History,"

CNN, September 5, 2017; Karen Tumulty, "Alan Simpson Cried While Writing George H. W. Bush's Eulogy—So He Wouldn't Cry While Giving It," *Washington Post*, December 4, 2018; Laura Ratliff, "President George H. W. Bush's Beautiful Last Moments and Words to His Son," *Today*, NBC, December 2, 2018; Decca Aitkenhead, "Chelsea Clinton: 'I've Had Vitriol Flung at Me for as Long as I Can Remember,'" *Guardian*, May 26, 2018; Mark K. Updegrove, *Second Acts: Presidential Lives and Legacies After the White House* (Guilford, CT: Lyons Press, 2006); William Cummings, "After Phone Call About China, White House Says Trump 'Always Liked' Jimmy Carter," *USA Today*, April 16, 2019; Adam Nagourney, "George Bush, Who Steered Nation in Tumultuous Times, Is Dead at 94," *New York Times*, November 30, 2018; Nancy Gibbs and Michael Duffy, *The Presidents Club: Inside the World's Most Exclusive Fraternity* (New York: Simon & Schuster, 2012); George H. W. Bush, *All the Best, George Bush: My Life in Letters and Other Writings* (New York: Touchstone, 1999); George W. Bush, *41: A Portrait of My Father* (New York: Crown, 2014); Bill Clinton, "Bill Clinton: George H. W. Bush's Oval Office Note to Me Revealed the Heart of Who He Was," *Washington Post*, December 1, 2018; Associated Press, "Bush's State Funeral Follows Generations of Tradition," AP News, December 4, 2018; Dianna Wray, "President Obama and James Baker Celebrate No Indictments at the Baker Institute's 25th Anniversary Gala," *Houstonia*, November 28, 2018; "Bush: 'Politics Does Not Have to Be Mean,'" CNN, December 1, 2018; Susan Page, *The Matriarch: Barbara Bush and the Making of an American Dynasty* (New York: Twelve, 2019); Chris Mills Rodrigo, "Jimmy Carter Says Trump Called Him to Discuss China," *Hill*, April 14, 2019; Mark K. Updegrove, *The Last Republicans: Inside the Extraordinary Relationship Between George H. W. Bush and George W. Bush*

(New York: Harper, 2017); Caitlin Oprysko, "Trump Hits Back at Barbara Bush: 'She Was Nasty to Me, but She Should Be,'" *Politico*, April 5, 2019.

EPILOGUE: GETTING OFF THE STAGE

This chapter includes interviews with Donald Trump, Chris Emery, Luci Baines Johnson, and Chris Lu. Published sources include Marie B. Hecht, *Beyond the Presidency: The Residues of Power* (New York: Macmillan, 1976); George W. Bush, interview with Kathie Lee Gifford and Jenna Bush Hager, *Today*, NBC, February 27, 2017; George H. W. Bush, *All the Best, George Bush: My Life in Letters and Other Writings* (New York: Touchstone, 1999); Mark K. Updegrove, *Second Acts: Presidential Lives and Legacies After the White House* (Guilford, CT: Lyons Press, 2006); Kate Andersen Brower, *The Residence: Inside the Private World of the White House* (New York: HarperCollins, 2015); Chris Emery, *White House Usher: Stories from the Inside* (self-pub., booklocker.com, 2017); Leo Janos, "The Last Days of the President," *The Atlantic*, July 1973.

PHOTO INSERT SOURCES AND CREDITS

Insert one: George H. W. Bush Presidential Library and Museum; photo courtesy Richard Nixon Foundation; photo by Eric Draper, courtesy of the George W. Bush Presidential Library and Museum; photo by Eric Draper, courtesy of the George W. Bush Presidential Library and Museum; AP Images/Gerald Herbert, Pool; AFP/Getty Images; courtesy George H. W. Bush Presidential Library and Museum for both skydiving photographs; courtesy The Carter Center; Saul Loeb/Getty Images; photo by Eric

Draper, courtesy of the George W. Bush Presidential Library and Museum; Mandel Ngan/AFP/Getty Images; Official White House photograph by Pete Souza; Official White House photograph by Pete Souza.

Insert two: AP Images/Pablo Martinez Monsivais; White House photograph/Alamy Stock photograph; AP Images/Pablo Martinez Monsivais; Official White House photograph by Chuck Kennedy; Joe Raedle/Getty Images; AFP/Getty Images; Jack Brockway/ Getty Images; George W. Bush Presidential Center; George W. Bush Presidential Center; Handout/Getty Images; Official White House photograph by Keegan Barber; Official White House photograph by Shealah Craighead; Official White House photograph by Andrea Hanks; Pool/Getty Images; Doug Mills/the New York Times/Redux.

BIBLIOGRAPHY

Alberta, Tim. *American Carnage: On the Front Lines of the Republican Civil War and the Rise of President Trump.* New York: Harper, 2019.

Allen, Jonathan, and Amie Parnes. *Shattered: Inside Hillary Clinton's Doomed Campaign.* New York: Random House, 2017.

Baldrige, Letitia. *A Lady, First: My Life in the Kennedy White House and the American Embassies of Paris and Rome.* New York: Viking, 2001.

Bernstein, Carl. *A Woman in Charge: The Life of Hillary Rodham Clinton.* New York: Knopf, 2007.

Biden, Joe. *Promises to Keep: On Life and Politics.* New York: Random House, 2007.

Branch, Taylor. *The Clinton Tapes: Wrestling History with the President.* New York: Simon & Schuster, 2009.

Brower, Kate Andersen. *First Women: The Grace and Power of America's Modern First Ladies.* New York: HarperCollins, 2016.

———. *The Residence: Inside the Private World of the White House.* New York: HarperCollins, 2015.

Bush, Barbara. *Barbara Bush: A Memoir.* New York: Scribner, 1994.

Bush, George H. W. *All the Best, George Bush: My Life in Letters and Other Writings.* New York: Touchstone, 1999.

Bush, George W. *Decision Points.* New York: Crown, 2010.

———. *41: A Portrait of My Father.* New York: Crown, 2014.

Bush, Laura. *Spoken from the Heart.* New York: Simon & Schuster, 2010.

Cannon, Lou. *President Reagan: The Role of a Lifetime.* New York: Simon & Schuster, 1991.

Carter, Jimmy. *Beyond the White House: Waging Peace, Fighting Disease, Building Hope.* New York: Simon & Schuster, 2007.

———. *Faith: A Journey for All.* New York: Simon & Schuster, 2018.

———. *A Full Life: Reflections at Ninety.* New York: Simon & Schuster, 2015.

———. *An Hour Before Daylight: Memories of a Rural Boyhood.* New York: Simon & Schuster, 2001.

———. *White House Diary.* New York: Farrar, Straus & Giroux, 2010.

Cheney, Dick. *In My Time*. New York: Simon & Schuster, 2011.

Clinton, Bill. *My Life*. New York: Knopf, 2004.

Clinton, Hillary Rodham. *It Takes a Village*. New York: Simon & Schuster, 1996.

———. *Living History*. New York: Scribner, 2004.

DeFrank, Thomas M. *Write It When I'm Gone: Remarkable Off-the-Record Conversations with Gerald R. Ford*. New York: G. P. Putnam's Sons, 2007.

Eisenhower, David, with Julie Nixon Eisenhower. *Going Home to Glory: A Memoir of Life with Dwight D. Eisenhower, 1961–1969*. New York: Simon & Schuster, 2010.

Emery, Chris. *White House Usher: Stories from the Inside*. Self-pub., booklocker.com, 2017.

Ford, Gerald R. *A Time to Heal: The Autobiography of Gerald R. Ford*. New York: Harper & Row, 1979.

Gates, Robert M. *From the Shadows: The Ultimate Insider's Story of Five Presidents and How They Won the Cold War*. New York: Simon & Schuster, 1996.

Gibbs, Nancy, and Michael Duffy. *The Presidents Club: Inside the World's Most Exclusive Fraternity*. New York: Simon & Schuster, 2012.

Greene, Bob. *Fraternity: A Journey in Search of Five Presidents*. New York: Crown, 2004.

Halper, Daniel. *Clinton, Inc.: The Audacious Rebuilding of a Political Machine*. New York: HarperCollins, 2014.

Hamilton, Alexander, James Madison, and John Jay. *The Federalist Papers*. 1788. Reprint, Signet, 2003.

Hecht, Marie B. *Beyond the Presidency: The Residues of Power*. New York: Macmillan, 1976.

Heilemann, John, and Mark Halperin. *Game Change: Obama and the Clintons, McCain and Palin, and the Race of a Lifetime*. New York: HarperCollins, 2010.

Hoover, Herbert. *The Ordeal of Woodrow Wilson*. New York: McGraw-Hill, 1958. Reprinted with new introduction by Mark Hatfield. Washington, D.C.: Woodrow Wilson Center Press, 1992.

Johnson, Lady Bird. *A White House Diary*. New York: Holt, Rinehart & Winston, 1970.

Jordan, Hamilton. *Crisis: The Last Year of the Carter Presidency*. New York: G. P. Putnam's Sons, 1982.

Lewis, Michael. *The Fifth Risk*. New York: W. W. Norton, 2018.

Meacham, Jon. *Destiny and Power: The American Odyssey of George Herbert Walker Bush*. New York: Random House, 2015.

Obama, Barack. *The Audacity of Hope: Thoughts on Reclaiming the American Dream.* New York: Crown, 2006.

Obama, Michelle. *Becoming.* New York: Crown, 2018.

Page, Susan. *The Matriarch: Barbara Bush and the Making of an American Dynasty.* New York: Twelve, 2019.

Pence, Charlotte. *Where You Go: Life Lessons from My Father.* New York: Center Street, 2018.

Perino, Dana. *And the Good News Is . . .* New York: Twelve, 2015.

Reagan, Ronald. *An American Life: The Autobiography.* New York: Simon & Schuster, 1990.

Reeves, Richard. *President Nixon: Alone in the White House.* New York: Simon & Schuster, 2001.

Rhodes, Ben. *The World as It Is: A Memoir of the Obama White House.* New York: Random House, 2018.

Sanger, David E. *The Inheritance: The World Obama Confronts and the Challenges to American Power.* New York: Random House, 2009.

Sims, Cliff. *Team of Vipers: My 500 Extraordinary Days in the Trump White House.* New York: Thomas Dunne Books, 2019.

Stephanopoulos, George. *All Too Human: A Political Education.* New York: Little, Brown, 1999.

Truman, Harry S. *Memoirs.* Vol. 2, *Years of Trial and Hope.* New York: Doubleday, 1956.

Updegrove, Mark K. *The Last Republicans: Inside the Extraordinary Relationship Between George H. W. Bush and George W. Bush.* New York: Harper, 2017.

———. *Second Acts: Presidential Lives and Legacies After the White House.* Guilford, CT: Lyons Press, 2006.

Walsh, Kenneth T. *Air Force One: A History of the Presidents and Their Planes.* New York: Hyperion, 2003.

Wilson, Woodrow. *George Washington.* New York: Harper & Brothers, 1897. Digital reprint, Littoral Books, 2017. Kindle.

Woodward, Bob. *Shadow: Five Presidents and the Legacy of Watergate.* New York: Simon & Schuster, 1999.

INDEX

NOTE: Bush 41 is George H. W. Bush; Bush 43 is George W. Bush. All references to presidents in subentries use last name only; first ladies are identified by first and last name.

ABOUT THE AUTHOR

KATE ANDERSEN BROWER is the author of the #1 *New York Times* bestseller *The Residence, First Women*—also a *New York Times* bestseller—and *First in Line*. She is a CNN contributor who covered the Obama White House for Bloomberg News and is a former CBS News staffer and Fox News producer. Her writing has appeared in the *New York Times*, *Vanity Fair*, and the *Washington Post*. She lives outside Washington, D.C., with her husband and their three young children.